In a Green Shade

Books by Allen Lacy

In a Green Shade: Writings from Homeground
The Inviting Garden: Gardening for the Senses, Mind, and Spirit
Gardening with Groundcovers and Vines
The Gardener's Eye and Other Essays
The Garden in Autumn
The Glory of Roses
Farther Afield: A Gardener's Excursions
Home Ground: A Gardener's Miscellany
Miguel de Unamuno: The Rhetoric of Existence

Edited by Allen Lacy

The American Gardener: A Sampler
Gardening for Love: The Market Bulletins, by Elizabeth Lawrence
A Rock Garden in the South, by Elizabeth Lawrence
　　　Nancy Goodwin, Principal Editor

Translated and Edited by Allen Lacy
　　　(with Martin Nozick and Anthony Kerrigan)

The Private World, by Miguel de Unamuno
Peace in War, by Miguel de Unamuno

In a Green Shade
WRITINGS FROM HOMEGROUND

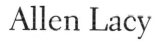

Allen Lacy

Drawings by
Martha Blake-Adams

Houghton Mifflin Company
Boston • New York 2000

For information about permission to reproduce selections from this book, write to Permissions, Houghton Mifflin Company, 215 Park Avenue South, New York, New York, 10003.

Library of Congress Cataloging-in-Publication Data
Lacy, Allen, date.
    In a green shade : writings from Homeground / Allen Lacy ; drawings
    by Martha Blake-Adams
            p. cm.
    Includes bibliographical references (p.).
    ISBN 0-618-00378-9
    1. Gardening. I. Title.

    SB 455.3 .L34 2000
    635.9—DC21   99-086379

Design: *Dianne Schaefer/Books By Design*
Typesetting: *Carol Keller, Dianne Schaefer/Books By Design*

Printed in the United States of America
QUM 10 9 8 7 6 5 4 3 2 1

For Martha Blake-Adams

Contents

VI Peeves, Complaints, and Observations 237

Preface

IN JUNE 1992 I stopped writing about gardening for the *New York Times*. I had been a columnist there for seven years, and at the *Wall Street Journal* for the preceding five. Twelve years of columns seemed enough — and members of my family let pass few chances to comment on the strange pursuit they called gardening at the computer.

Soon after I gave up my column in the *Times*, my younger son, Michael, a magazine art director, began mumbling that he and I should publish a gardening newsletter together. I resisted, but he persisted, entreating me to consider the wonders of desktop publishing and the miracles of software programs with strange names not in any known language. Finally, on Christmas Eve, he nudged me again. This time I said yes. On New Year's Eve Michael dropped by to show me the design dummy for what he calls *Allen Lacy's Homeground* and what I just call *Homeground*. ("Dad," he said, "it's working for Martha Stewart." I pointed out the obvious to him, but he prevailed anyway.)

The newsletter comes out quarterly and runs to sixteen pages an issue. It's now approaching its eighth year. I had new things to worry about, such as the costs of paper, advertising, and postage. We started off with no subscribers, and then we got a few, and a few more every month. We have had a satisfying renewal rate, but Martha Stewart need not fear our competition.

Working with Michael has been sometimes a joy for me and sometimes something else. I imagine he'd say the same if asked. For both of us it has been that great rare thing, a father and a son with different but complementary skills, working at something that we find mutually satisfying. We have had some indispensable help too. Michael's mother and my wife, Hella, has been constantly supportive, although she feared at first that Michael and I might stop speaking to each other over some minor point. Michael's wife, Christine, kept watch over subscriptions and bill-paying. Martha Blake-Adams, who has been Hella's and my most faithful friend since the 1950s, has contributed wonderful line drawings for every issue. I wish it were possible here to provide more than a small sample of her delightful and varied work. One subscriber, Catherine Brown, who edits a medical journal, volunteered to proofread after noticing that I wasn't very good at it.

The subtitle of this book speaks of "writings" from *Homeground*, not essays. An essay strikes me as something that shouldn't change much, once published. Writings, somehow, sound more fluid. I have allowed myself to change my mind about this or that plant, also to correct past judgments on the basis of later experience. I have sometimes combined two or more pieces touching on the same topic and have shortened pieces that seemed verbose.

Some features of *Homeground* are not represented here, including articles about that great joy of gardening, visiting other people's gardens that are better than one's own. But perhaps another time, another book . . .

    —Allen Lacy
    August 1999

❧ *In a Green Shade*

❧ Introduction: A Private Eden

FOR ALMOST THIRTY YEARS NOW my wife, Hella, and I have been making a garden on a patch of sandy land near the coast of southern New Jersey, at about 39° north latitude and 74° west longitude. The garden is not finished—no garden ever is—but every year it is closer to what we had in mind in the beginning.

The garden is our retreat from the world, but paradoxically we find in it the reflection of the world in the largest possible sense. In this plot of earth just 100 by 155 feet we find private refreshment for body, soul, and mind, but it also leads out of itself into a much wider world.

Although our house, built around 1812, was originally a farmhouse on a dusty country lane, it now sits on the busiest road in town. Traffic never stops day or night. When we moved in, the front yard was open to the street. We could see the people in every passing car, and they could see us. The first order of business in making the garden we wanted was to get some visual privacy, enclosing ourselves within a barrier that marked the boundary between the public

The house in 1972

world of the street and the personal and intimate world of the household. Municipal laws prohibit high fences or walls as such barriers,
so we settled on another, somewhat slower solution. We decided to
make our garden inside a thicket, to plant the edges of our property
with a hedgerow of woody plants that would in time grow dense and
tall. Eventually they did. Bayberries, junipers, red-twig dogwoods,
hollies, and many other kinds of shrubs and small trees closed us in
and shut the world out.

Behind its encircling hedge the garden is now the sanctuary we
hoped for. Half of the old front lawn is now a cottage garden, in constant bloom from the first snowdrops of January to the last rose of
November. The other half, just this side of the large colony of yellow groove bamboo, is a woodland garden, where bloom peaks in
midspring, just before the shade from the bamboo, some hackber-
ries, and a walnut tree moves in. On the south side of the house and
part of the west, there are decks on three levels, partly sunny, partly
shaded by pergolas. Beyond the deck there's a tiny back lawn half-
shaded by an old swamp maple, a greenhouse (new since 1997), a
shady perennial border, and then more of the trees and shrubs that
encircle and enclose us.

Here in this private and set-apart space we have made a garden
for all the senses. It invites us to come outside, ready to brush our
fingers across the velvety leaves of peppermint geranium and then
breathe deeply of their fresh and bracing scent. It invites us to walk
barefoot on the grass at dawn in summer, to listen to the songs of
birds that share our garden with us, to see the way late summer light
turns cannas into stained glass at sundown, to sip nectar from honeysuckle, and to know that it's good to be alive on this earth.

We are content here, in this private refuge where little can
intrude. For a time at least, we can forget about what's in the newspapers, much of it bad. We know that the world is unsafe, but we are
secure in our haven of sweet fragrance and bright color. Even the
traffic out in the street seems farther away, its din somewhat muffled
by our protective hedge.

Our feelings of being at home in a garden are in keeping with
the most ancient traditions. The Garden of Eden, after all, was a
protected paradise. In many languages the word for a garden means

The house today

a place that is enclosed, a secluded asylum of safety and quiet. The very best gardens, some have held, are secret ones whose very existence cannot be suspected from the outside, as ours cannot.

But our garden, like all gardens, is much more than a retreat. It is also a place where we encounter the world. Gardening engages the mind in an unending quest for knowledge, for it would take many lifetimes to know and understand everything that is found in even one small garden like ours. Just learning the names of all the plants that grow here, their botanical names and their common names, if any, is a formidable task, but it goes farther when we begin to consider relationships—how, for example, strawberries, plums, potentillas, and many other plants of beauty or utility are all in the Rose family. Such knowledge leads us momentarily away from the sheer pleasures of the garden into an appreciation of the work of the many botanists who have brought scientific order to our understanding of the plant kingdom.

If we become curious about how it is that we grow two hollies, *Ilex cornuta* and *I. opaca*, the first native to East Asia and the second to our own nearby American woodlands, we are led into questions about tectonic plates and the drifting apart of continents. North

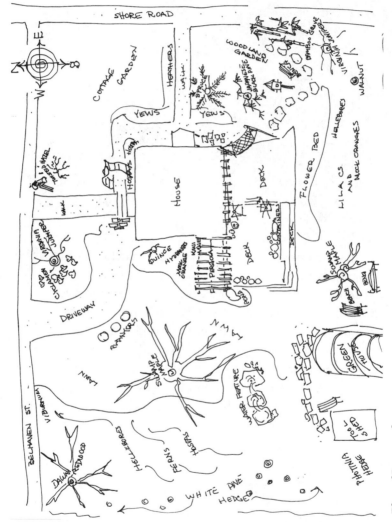

Plan of Lacy garden

America and East Asia now sit halfway across the world from each other, but they were once part of the same landmass, where the common ancestor of our two hollies thrived before the further evolution of the genus. Here what we know about our garden intersects with both geology and biology. It's no surprise, for gardening intersects with everything.

Every plant has its history, and to know that history brings us out of the seclusion of the garden into the world of other human beings. Our garden would be impoverished without its host of plants from many other places on our planet, courtesy of a great company of plant explorers. Early Spanish missionaries to South America brought back nasturtiums from Argentina and four o'clocks from Peru. For begonias and fuchsias we must be grateful to Father Charles Plumier (for whom the genus *Plumeria* is named), who discovered the first species of both genera on islands in the Caribbean. Alexander von Humboldt and Aimé Bonpland gave us the scarlet sage from Mexico and the Victoria water lily from Bolivia (which we don't grow, as it's vast). To John and William Bartram, the eighteenth-century Philadelphia Quaker botanists, we are indebted for rescuing *Franklinia alatamaha*, on the very eve of its extinction in the wilds of Georgia. In several seasons our own garden owes much to the English explorer/collector Robert Fortune and to his four trips to China and Japan in the middle of the nineteenth century. In January winter jasmine brightens our landscape and our spirits with its shower of bright yellow. April brings us the graceful arching sprays of pink and white bleeding heart and its delicate little locket-like flowers. In September the elegant blossoms of Japanese anemones refresh our little cottage garden where the front lawn used to be. Robert Fortune introduced into Western gardens all three of these treasures and others besides.

We are indebted, and the debts keep accumulating, for plant explorers are still at work although they travel now by jet planes and measure their journeys in days, not months or even years.

Hella and I are not hermits, nor do we consider ourselves selfish in our desire for privacy. We don't think we owe anything to strangers hurtling by at excessive speeds, but we are always delighted when someone calls through the hedgerow and asks to see the garden. We've made some good friends that way because of a common interest in plants.

We have made our own mark on both house and the land it sits on. My second-story study was once two cramped bedrooms. In the summer we virtually live on three conjoined decks that were not here when we moved in. French doors now open out from our living room onto the last deck that was built, and on warm days and nights we can fling them open and listen to Bach or Mendelssohn.

When we arrived over a quarter of a century ago, there were only a few woody plants on the property—two Virginia junipers that I admire immensely (one of them crowned with a trumpet vine that is a magnet for hummingbirds in high summer), two black cherry trees (despicable for their abundant crop of messy fruits), and an ancient swamp maple out back that is lovely in autumn, although voracious in appetite for moisture and nutrients. Today, after years of gradual accumulation, there is a great diversity of trees and shrubs. I have some favorites. I would not want to be without the twisted hazel whose branches are so lovely in winter, when they seem to be trying to embrace the air, and I would not easily forgo the dawn redwood, now fifty feet tall, that was thought to be extinct until its discovery in a remote region of China after World War II. In some of the writings that follow, I will have more to say about these and other woody plants. Not surprisingly, however, I will have much more to say about herbaceous ones: small gardens place more limits on our choice of shrubs and trees than they do on annuals and perennials.

Our mortgage is now paid off, but we do not consider ourselves owners of the land we occupy. We believe instead that we are its stewards, and we know that most gardeners hold this same belief. It grows naturally out of constant acts of caretaking.

When this old house passes into the hands of its next owners, they may make changes I would never endorse. The cottage garden out front may revert to a typical suburban lawn. But thousands of daffodils and other parts of our legacy will remain. One of these will surely be the green shade—as in Andrew Marvell's "The Garden"— that comes from the trees we once planted here.

I Spring

❦ Closely Watched Quince

IN VERY LATE WINTER, on the cusp of spring, when the pale gray, slightly gnarled branches of the quince tree just outside the casement windows of my study are bare of leaves, I have a fine view down into my back garden. On a bright and sunny morning a red-twig dogwood and the sparkling evergreen leaves of a native holly catch my eye. Occasionally there is the flash of a red far richer than that of the bare branches of the dogwood, when a male cardinal perches high in the quince tree, surveying the world and sometimes seeming to gaze through the window to take my measure.

In late February buds begin to show on the tips of every twig of the quince tree, foretelling the end of winter and the approach of another season of growth. The buds gradually change from gray to pale, pale green, swelling slowly but inexorably, promising that spring is on its way. My quince is slow to leaf out; thus before it begins to unfold its leaves of soft gray-green, I still have an unimpeded view of the garden. I can glimpse the first daffodils—the diminutive pale yellow trumpets of *Narcissus obvallaris*, the Tenby daffodil—as they greet one of those dawns that bring the assurance that spring is not just something we dream about in winter. I watch a distant colony of pulmonarias come into their delicate flowering of pink and blue. I take note of primulas gathering force, of hellebores at their height of bloom, of the unfurling croziers of many different species of ferns.

By the first of May, however, when the study windows are finally flung open to the warm spring breeze, my view of the garden is blocked. The quince tree, which was planted some twenty years ago, now stretches upward toward the eaves of the house, blocking all view of the garden when in leaf. I do not care, for to my mind a quince tree is one of the finest things in all creation. Its flowers are beautiful, but quietly so. They do not force themselves on the attention, as do the double flowering cherry trees that are so oddly favored by many of my neighbors. A quince flowers sparingly, presenting its large, goblet-shaped blossoms of the palest pink together with its fresh new leaves. It lacks the insistence—pushiness, even—

of crab apples, like the 'Van Esaltine' crab just outside another window of my study, which so covers itself with flowers that no twig and no leaf can be seen until petal-fall, when the ground beneath the tree becomes a pool of deep rose.

A quince tree, moreover, is not a creature of a single season. In late May its fruits (more reminiscent of pears than of apples) begin to appear. Many drop off early, but the rest are pregnant with summer, swelling until their gravity and heft cause the branches they occupy to bend earthward. Light green when small, they turn pale gold by midsummer, but the color comes from a thick coating of down that rubs off when harvest time arrives. The lightest touch removes the down, bringing the surprise discovery that the fruits of my quince are smooth, waxen, and as gleaming a green as jade.

The quince tree outside my window links my garden with history, legend, and literature. Mrs. Grieve's *A Modern Herbal* (1931) points out that this native of Persia and Anatolia has been in cultivation since remote antiquity. The golden apples that Paris gave to Aphrodite, thus starting the Trojan War, were probably not apples at all, but quinces. In Greek and Roman times well into the Middle Ages the quince was a symbol of conjugal love. Plutarch reports that the great Athenian lawgiver Solon urged that brides should ensure their future happiness in marriage by nibbling on quinces before retiring to their bridal chambers. Roman mythology associated the quince with Venus, the goddess of fertility and love. In Christian iconography the quince was symbolic of immortal virtue and also of the Resurrection, because new trees could sprout from cuttings left in the ground over winter. In several of Giovanni Bellini's paintings of the Madonna and Child, the Infant Christ is shown with a quince in his hand.

Quinces were also believed to have medicinal virtues, especially in curing digestive ailments, and they made fine preserves and jellies that added flavor to roasted meats. The seventeenth-century English herbalist John Gerard wrote in his *Herball* (1633) that quinces "strengthen the stomacke, stay vomiting, and also the bloody flux, are good for those that spit up blood or that vomit blood, and for women also that have too great plenty of their monthly courses." Gerard also passes on the classical tradition associating the quince with fertility and marital love: "The woman with childe, which eateth many quinces during the time of her breeding, shall bring forth wise children, and of good understanding."

For those who want to have quinces at the dining table as well as in the garden, Gerard even gives us a recipe for quince marmalade, according to which we should pare the fruits, cut them into pieces, and boil them with equal amounts of water and sugar until they are soft, then strain and boil again until "they be stiff," and then finish the marmalade off with a bit of rose water.

❧ A Woodland Garden in Spring

MORE AND MORE spring-blooming perennials have crept into my garden, for the simple reason that my garden has gradually become shadier and shadier, as I have pointed out already. Small saplings of sourwood, sassafras, and other favorites have in time become substantial trees that cast shade far and wide. About half of the almost entirely sunny garden I started with about thirty years ago—essentially a suburban open lawn more akin to a meadow than a forest—has evolved toward being a woodland garden.

Many of the perennials of spring are woodland creatures whose life cycle demands that they break dormancy early, when the deciduous trees above them are still bare of leaves. They must spurt quickly into growth, flower to attract their pollinators, and produce seed before the canopy of leaves high above closes in for the remainder of the growing season. Some of them lapse quickly into summer dormancy.

I have some favorite woodland plants. High on the list are two natives of eastern North America that hobnob together wonderfully well. Celandine poppy (*Stylophorum diphyllum*) bears burnished, glossy, deep yellow blossoms set off by soft, finger-lobed leaves of glowing pale green. Its downy buds, like those of many other plants in the Poppy family, hang downward almost until their segments explode to release the crinkled petals. The silvery seedpods that follow the several weeks of bloom are themselves handsome and distinctive. Virginia bluebell (*Mertensia virginica*) is marvelous on its own, transcendentally lovely if there are celandine poppies nearby. In rich, moist soil it will self-sow and colonize almost endlessly. The buds are on the pinkish side, the flowers mainly pale blue, but in a large stand there will generally be occasional flowers of pink or cream. The season of the bluebell is brief, for immediately after flowering it lapses into dormancy, but it is surprisingly tough when in active growth and flower. I have seen it hold its own in a Delaware garden against a tide of dwarf green-and-gold running bamboo that had already galloped over everything else within reach. Virginia bluebell's exaggerated period of dormancy calls for planting something else to take over the scene while it is in hibernation. Gardeners who are afraid of bamboo—a reasonable fear—can substitute hostas, which are handsome in a woodland setting.

Another native woodland plant is bloodroot (*Sanguinaria canadensis*); like celandines, it is in the Poppy family. The double cultivar, 'Multiplex' or 'Plena', is worth looking for, but the much more common single-flowered form is ingratiating for its little, upward-facing cups of the purest white. Bloodroot, which takes its name from the yellowish-red sap of its rootstock (used by American native tribes as an ingredient in war paint), is undoubtedly the most ephemeral of all spring ephemerals, staying in bloom only five or six days.

Continuing with this catalog of native American perennials, merry bells or bellworts (*Uvularia grandiflora*, *U. perfoliata*) are cheerful little creatures of forest fringes. They burst up swiftly in late spring, as quick and lusty of growth as asparagus, their buds already showing the ashy yellow of their odd little pendant flowers. They combine nicely with American barrenwort, *Vancouveria hexandra*, which much resembles its close kin from both Europe and eastern Asia, the epimediums. Low and traveling by stolons, with a fine crop of tiny white flowers in very late spring, this native of the Pacific Northwest sports ferny foliage that persists into winter, and it dotes on dry shade.

The real sweethearts of the spring woodland garden can only be the several species of *Phlox* and their multitudinous hybrid progeny, which more often than not are of disputed parentage. *P. divaricata*, called wild sweet william for no fathomable reason (and the same common name is confusingly also applied to *P. maculata*, a summer bloomer), occurs in blue, white, and mauve forms. It is the earliest species to bloom, at least in my garden, where it makes its appearance at the outset of the daffodil season. Somewhat later is *Phlox stolonifera*, which has several superb cultivars, all spreading low-growers, to about six inches. 'Blue Ridge' is pale blue; 'Bruce's White' is, unsurprisingly, white; and 'Pink Ridge' is just what you might imagine. *Phlox pilosa*, one of the very latest of the spring phloxes, is also stoloniferous and spreading. Its flowers are a delicate shade of pink. About the ancestry of 'Chattahoochee' there is so much dispute and so many rival hypotheses that I shall not venture an opinion. Suffice it to say that it is a lovely blue with a contrasting bold red eye and that it prolongs the season of woodland phlox to the verge of summer.

Thus far, the perennials described as ideally suited for woodland gardens before their shade deepens into summer are all natives of North America, but with columbines and solomon's seals we have a choice. Do we want to stick strictly to the home team, or are the impulses of our hearts catholic and cosmopolitan? Both of these genera evolved from common ancestors that grew before the great landmasses began to drift apart, and their continuing evolution produced new species peculiar to other parts of the world as well as our own. If we are ideologically of a nativist bent, our columbines will be species like our eastern columbine, *Aquilegia canadensis*, native from Nova Scotia to Texas, and *A. chrysantha*, native from Texas westward to California. We will not be growing the European species *A. vulgaris*, and we will not be growing the fan columbine, *A. flabellata* 'Nana' from Japan. Hybrids are also out; there's just no telling what might be in their ancestry. Our solomon's seals will be restricted to *Polygonatum biflorum* and the closely related *P. pubescens*, both from eastern North America. We will not be growing the European and Asian species, *P. odoratum*.

I am not in the slightest degree a horticultural isolationist. I love the eastern columbine for its birdlike flowers of pale scarlet and light lemon and for its habit of seeding itself into spots where it always seems to find a companion that sets it off. It combines well with the coppery new growth of barberry or with the frothy mass of the pure white flowers of *Deutzia gracilis* 'Nikko'. But I do not see why I should deprive myself of the superb Japanese fan columbine, either. In both milk white and steely blue, its flowers introduce and extend the columbine season, blooming several weeks before any of the American species get going. And as for solomon's seal, I do not choose to let loose on my small garden *P. biflorum*, a beast that can reach seven feet high and quickly spread very far. I much prefer the more demure species *P. odoratum*, in its lovely form 'Variegatum'. The leaves along its gracefully arching stems are margined in soft white. The white flowers that hang below the stems in pairs (occasionally trios) are sweetly fragrant, especially as evening approaches. This solomon's seal lends foliar interest to a woodland planting from spring to late fall. It virtually demands to be planted with a swirl of maidenhair ferns around it, a combination that marries delicacy to quiet, graceful dignity. It also combines splendidly with the romping European lesser celandrine (*Ranunculus ficaria*), whose best form is the cultivar 'Brazen Hussy', with chocolate-colored foliage and starry golden flowers that gleam as if varnished.

❧ The Best Flowering Cherry

I HAVE AN ACTIVE DISLIKE for the widely planted Japanese ornamental double-flowered pink cherry 'Kwanzan', but I will not say why. Instead, I will simply quote Vita Sackville-West, who called it, somewhat incorrectly, "that wickedly vulgar Kansan, so strong and crude that it will spread like measles in an infectious rash."

I prefer to sing the praises of *Prunus* × *incamp* 'Okame'. I received this flowering cherry many years ago as a small rooted cutting in one of J. C. Raulston's distributions from the arboretum he directed at North Carolina State University, which is now named in memory of this remarkable plantsman.

Our tree has now grown about twenty-five feet tall, with three main trunks and a fairly compact spread. It is beautiful in every season, even in winter, for its trunks are an agreeable shade of coppery red and its twigs form a delicate tracery against the sky, moving gracefully in the merest hint of a breeze. Its summer foliage is richly green and glossy, turning to bright apricot in the fall. The tree has a beautiful silhouette, in leaf or out.

But its season of glory is spring. Its deep pink flowers are small, but abundant, and the bloom is prolonged beyond that of any other flowering fruit tree in the neighborhood, for two reasons. First, the plant is sterile, and thus does not cease blooming once it has been pollinated, for it puts no energy into formation of fruit. Second, its buds appear in pairs that open a week or more apart. The flowers have a faint almond scent, and branches can be forced for indoor bloom as early as Valentine's Day.

'Okame' is a hybrid between two Asian species, the Fuji cherry (*Prunus incisa*) and the Taiwan cherry (*P. campanulata*). It was bred in England by Collingwood Ingram, who was so associated with cherry trees that his nickname was "Cherry." Ingram hybridized many species, and in 1948 published *Ornamental Cherries*, the standard reference on them. He also worked with rhododendrons, kniphofias, gladiolas, and hydrangeas over a long career. He lived to be 100. I'm glad of that, for my life would be poorer without his gift of 'Okame'.

✿ The Little Tulips

WHENEVER I PLANT TULIPS in the fall, anticipating their April splendor in the year to come, I tip my hat in gratitude to Ogier Ghiselin de Busbecq and to the year 1562, when he returned to Vienna from Constantinople, where he had been Emperor Ferdinand's ambassador to Suleiman the Magnificent. De Busbecq brought with him three plants destined to transform European gardens in the spring. Two—lilac and mock orange—were woody plants of transcendent fragrance. His other gift was the tulip, in several species.

The introduction of new plants often causes a stir but the excitement that tulips brought to European gardening was extraordinary.

The English herbalist John Parkinson praised them in the highest terms in *Paradisi in Sole: Paradisus Terrestris* (1629):

> Next unto the Lillies, and before the Narcissi or Daffodils, the discourse of Tulipas deserveth his place. . . . There are not onely divers kindes of Tulipas, but sundry diversities of colours in them, found out in these later dayes by many the searchers of natures varieties, which have not formerly been observed: our age being more delighted in the search, curiosity, and rarities of these pleasant delights, then any age I thinke before.

Shortly after Parkinson's herbal appeared, the strange phenomenon of tulipomania broke out in Holland. Whole fortunes were made in transactions involving as little as a single bulb; when the speculative bubble burst, whole fortunes were lost. Then the Dutch got down to more sensible transactions with tulips, growing great numbers of them commercially and selling them to the rest of the world. They gave us the modern tulip, hybridizing it to increase the height of its stems, the size of its flowers, and their immense range of wonderful colors.

I would not want to endure a spring without hybrid tulips in my garden, but that said, I must also confess to a greater affection for the less flamboyant botanical or species tulips that have evolved in nature instead of being gussied up by humankind.

There are roughly a hundred species in the genus *Tulipa*. Not all are available through commercial sources, but some twenty-five, mostly native to Asia Minor and Central Asia with a tiny handful indigenous to the Mediterranean basin, are fairly easy to obtain in the United States.

After over a decade of trying out a couple of additional species per year, I have some favorites. One is *Tulipa clusiana*, the lady tulip. Its slender buds are red with white feathering on the margins of each petal, giving them the look of peppermint sticks. The flowers open into wide white cups with dark, purplish-black throats. This absolute charmer will naturalize if it's happy and has the dry summer conditions it prefers. I still recall seeing in the early 1970s a hillside meadow with many thousands of *T. clusiana* in the Root Glen

in Clinton, New York, all descendants of a few seeds that Grace
Root collected in Iran right after World War I.

I am also partial to T. *dasystemon* (syn. *T. tarda*), which is distinctly different from any other tulip. Its leaves fan out in a circle,
almost prostrate. Very late-flowering (mid-May for me), it bears clusters of as many as six large, star-shaped, yellow and white flowers on
four-inch stems. Also low and multiflowered, but much earlier to
bloom, T. *urumiensis* sports yellow flowers suffused with bronzy and
green overtones.

Fragrance in tulips is a rare commodity, the major exception to
this rule being the golden-flowered T. *sylvestris*, whose spicy scent is
often likened to that of sweet violets. This April-flowering species, if
indeed it is truly a species, is not known in the wild. For centuries it
has grown as a virtual weed in orchards and vineyards northward
from Italy to Holland, Germany, and even Sweden. Its vigorously
stoloniferous habit accounts for its rapid increase in places that
suit it.

Strange rather than beautiful is the best description of T. *acumi-
nata*, whose status as a species is dubious since no native habitat is
known for it. Its color varies, but most commonly its slender, twisted
petals are red and yellow. This plant is sometimes called the Chinese tulip, a puzzling adjective on strictly geographical grounds, but
possibly deriving from someone thinking that the long, narrow
petals resemble a mandarin's fingernails.

I have an odd affection for T. *turkestanica*, which itself is so odd
that springtime visitors who spot it and ask what it is look at me in
disbelief when I say tulip. Its tiny grayish flowers, which remain
closed on overcast days, are produced in bunches of six or more.

Botanical tulips stay the course, in comparison with their hybrid cousins. All the species mentioned here return reliably every
year, and some of them self-seed, popping up in unexpected places
with each new spring.

The standard advice about bulbs is to order them early (so the
catalogs urge) and plant them early (so the books say). But procrastinators can take heart. One year it was Christmas Eve (a warm day)
before I planted two hundred new daffodil bulbs and another fifty
bulbs of T. *clusiana*. They bloomed just fine when spring came.

❧ A Perfect Narcissus?

"MORE, MORE, MORE" is my gardening motto. If growing a single kind of daylily is one of life's good things, then growing thirty, forty, or even a hundred of them is one of life's even better things. While a garden with three hosta cultivars is on the right track, a garden where one hundred fifty can be seen has almost arrived at perfection, provided that room can be found one day, and soon, to cram in another sixty or so. (I know just such a hosta garden, but it can never be mine, for I have competing passions to satisfy, being more or less in love to the point of utter foolishness with asters, astrantias, carexes, epimediums, peonies, pulmonarias, rodgersias, and a lot of other things, in addition to daylilies and hostas, and here I've touched only on herbaceous plants, leaving woodies aside, as I wouldn't want to do.)

Daffodil 'Hawera'

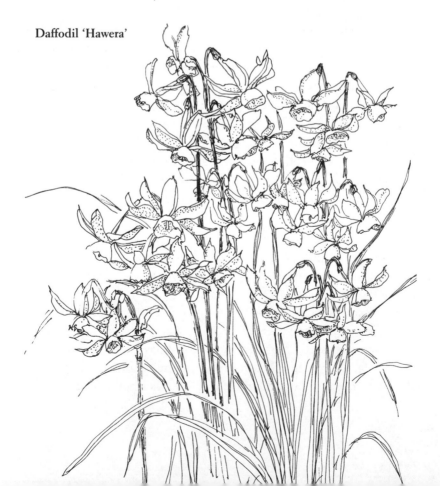

It would therefore be a plu-
perfect nightmare if some Com-
missar of Plant Distribu-
tion should arrive at the
garden gate one day and say,
"You are under pain of death
to grow only one species or cultivar of every genus you favor, in
order to give equal treatment to the genera that you have neglected and discrimi-
nated against so egregiously. One hosta is
your limit, one daylily, one astrantia . . ."

How could I possibly make such
choices? My favorite hosta is 'Sum and
Substance', which stands out in every way, but then
I would never want to be without 'Golden Tiara'
either. Or *Hosta venusta*. Or all the others. Among
daylilies, I have long been most smitten by 'Peach
Fairy', but 'Pardon Me' and at least fifty others
that I know of are indispensable, as are, most
likely, about a thousand I don't know of. Two
hemerocallis that I'd gladly never see again
are *Hemerocallis fulva*, the ugly tawny ditch
lily, and 'Hyperion'. This pale yellow oldie is
still sold and highly touted in some nursery
catalogs that claim no other daylily has ever
surpassed 'Hyperion' although it has been
around for three-quarters of a century, and

Daffodil
'Hawera'

that is why they're offering it. Pure piffle! This claim has no more
truth than the assertion that my father's Model-T Ford is unsur-
passed by the Volvo in my driveway. These nurseries still sell 'Hyperion' simply because it's the only daylily with widespread name-
recognition among the general public.

Choosing just one plant to represent a given genus is akin to
having several children and giving them all away except one. But if I
could grow only one daffodil, the easy choice would be a gem called
'Hawera', after a town in New Zealand. 'Hawera' has every virtue I

can think of. It's a late bloomer, coming pretty much at the rag end of the daffodil season. It stands only ten inches high, bearing small flowers, five or six to a stalk, with swept-back petals surrounding the flaring cup at the center. The blossoms, like little pendulous bells, droop slightly. They are the pale, creamy yellow of lemon pudding and smell wonderfully of violets. On first sight, Hella pronounced it the best of all daffodils for bouquets.

That spring when 'Hawera' first bloomed I had only a dozen bulbs. The following fall, I planted two hundred, all over the garden. It's the daffodil I'd want to have if it were my one and only.

❧ Finding Fritillaries

UNTIL FAIRLY RECENTLY, the genus *Fritillaria* was one of the most frustrating to any American gardener touched with the collector's instinct. Its far-flung species span the globe throughout the Northern Hemisphere, numbering more than a hundred kinds, with new ones still turning up to be classified and named. Most North American gardeners, however, had to forget about most species and settle for a mere three—*F. imperialis*, *F. meleagris*, and *F. persica*. Other species were available only through highly specialized bulb companies in England, at prices that ranged from fifteen to fifty dollars each.

There were three consolations. First, it was helpful to remind ourselves that uncommon species of *Fritillaria* are endangered by collection in the wild. The necessity of not being able to grow them, because they were extremely hard to come by, became the virtue of not having contributed to their possible extinction. Second, we could follow the lead of Reginald Farrer, who early in the twentieth century managed to persuade himself that most species were highly undesirable, anyway. In *The English Rock Garden*, he wrote:

> Many of the race are very miffy or mimpish, or both, and the family all round has a bad character. Not to mention—a fact which catalogues

rarely do—that an enormous number of Fritillaries have more or less stinking bells of dingy chocolate and greenish tones, which often appear transfigured by the enthusiasms of those who want to get rid of them as rich purple or amaranthine violet.

Third, we could congratulate ourselves that the species we could easily obtain were splendid plants, fully worthy of the space they occupied in any well-populated springtime garden. We could say that these particular fritillaries were nothing to sniff at, except for that olfactory drawback Farrer brought up. Polite gardeners call it foxy; the more forthright speak of skunks, but no one has described the odor more colorfully than E. A. Bowles. In *My Garden in Spring* (1914) he called it "an awful stink, a mixture of mangy fox, dirty dog-

Fritillaria imperialis

kennel, the small cats' house at the Zoo, and Exeter Railway Station, where for some unknown reason the trains let out their superfluous gas to poison the travelers."

The star of the genus is *Fritillaria imperialis*, the crown imperial, which was introduced to Europe from Turkey around 1570, starting a craze that lasted well into Victorian times. Originally called *Corona imperialis*, it quickly became a favorite subject of botanical artists. In form it is the most arresting and dramatic flowering bulb of high spring. Rising eighteen inches or more above a low flurry of basal leaves on a sturdy stem of the freshest green, it opens its ring of large, brick-red (or sometimes yellow or orange), bell-like, downward-facing flowers below a topknot pineapple of twisted, swirling foliage.

Handsome from a distance, the crown imperial conceals a secret that can only be appreciated up close (where the plant's foxiness is all too apparent). A large drop of clear nectar is suspended at the heart of each flower, in apparent disregard of the law of gravity. The function of nectar is, of course, attracting pollinators, but a bit of old plant lore offers a theological explanation for this particular nectar. According to legend, when Christ came to the Garden of Gethsemane, all the flowers growing there bowed in humility, except for the fritillary, which was too haughty. Then a white flower, it turned red with shame when rebuked for its stubborn pride. It also began to weep and has done so ever since.

Thomas Jefferson's taste for crown imperials was keen. He ordered them repeatedly—in 1807, 1809, 1811, and 1812—from the Philadelphia nurseryman Bernard M'Mahon, author of *The American Gardener's Calendar*, the first truly American book on gardening. From the correspondence between the two men, it isn't clear whether his orders indicated repeated losses of the plants, which have lamentable annual tendencies, or whether Jefferson just couldn't get enough *Fritillaria imperialis* for his gardens at Monticello to satisfy him. On one occasion, he thanked M'Mahon for two special forms of crown imperial, one with a double row of flowers, the other with silver-striped leaves. (The double form is *F. i.* 'Prolifera', a.k.a. 'Crown-on-Crown'. The silver-variegated cultivar is 'Aureovariegata', and there is also 'Aureomarginata', whose upper leaves are edged in white. These sometimes are found in European nursery catalogs. I almost decided to say nothing about them, lest I raise in readers desires impossible of satisfaction.) In 1811 Jefferson described the part of his garden where he grew these bulbs: "I have an extensive flower border in which I am fond of placing *handsome* flowers or *fragrant*; those of mere curiosity I do not aim at, having too many other cares to bestow more than a moderate attention on them."

Another fritillary of some proportions, though less drama and panache than *F. imperialis*, *F. persica* made its way to western gardens at about the same time as the crown imperial, but was misidentified as "Persian lily," *Lilium persicum*. Available today in the form 'Adiyaman', it has a slenderer stalk than the crown imperial, no top-knot, and grayish leaves. Its little hanging bellflowers, of a muted smoky purple, appear in profusion up and down the stem. Crown imperials shout their presence in a garden, but this one is more modest, which perhaps is why the English herbalist John Gerard virtually dismissed it, writing: "We have in our English gardens many scores of floures in beauty far excelling it."

But there's another fritillary, of even greater modesty, that excited Gerard—*Fritillaria meleagris*—which he called "Turkie

Fritillaria meleagris

Floure" and "Ginny-hen Floure," and even tried to pass off as the "checkered daffodil." Under whatever name, Gerard admired it immensely: it is "greatly esteemed for the beautifying of our gardens and the bosoms of the beautiful." (That last phrase has puzzled not a few, considering the foxy odor.)

The guinea-hen flower is odd, but graceful, with little nodding flowers on slender, arching stems accompanied by sparse, grassy foliage. The most common form has softly checkered flowers in shades of pale mauve tending toward gray or even beige. It has accumulated a number of common names, all pretty dour: death bell, dead man's bell, leper's bell, and snake's head among them. "Snake's head" indicates, I suppose, some resemblance between this plant's buds and a snake poised to strike. If it is a snake, *F. meleagris* may be the proverbial snake in the grass, for this species naturalizes easily in meadows and will self-sow, provided the grass is left unmown until its seeds have ripened in mid-June. This plant is curious rather than beautiful, except for the rare form *F. m.* 'Alba', whose drooping translucent flowers of purest white are touched with pale green where they join the stems. They are lovely.

It is good to be able to report that a number of American bulb companies have begun to offer more fritillaria species than they used to. *F. michailovskyi*, from northern Turkey and once vanishingly rare, is now being nursery-propagated in England by the hundreds of thousands, and being sold very reasonably for under ten dollars for twenty-five bulbs. Only six inches high, it bears flaring, bitoned purplish brown and creamy yellow, bell-like flowers, two or three to a stem. It grows happily for me among low ferns in a shady spot, blooming early (with pulmonarias) and then swiftly lapsing into dormancy. I am also growing *F. acmopetala*, which much resembles *F. michailovskyi*, except that it hails from Cyprus and is olive green, white, and pale lilac. Two species native to western North America round out my little collection. A selected form of *F. biflora* named 'Martha Roderick' has flowers that are white inside, brownish purple and white on the outside. The flowers are more open and anemone-like than those of many other species. Finally there is *F. pudica*, whose nodding flowers of bright gold smell of ripe grapes.

✤ *The Pleasures of Pulmonarias*

HORTICULTURAL PASSIONS are peculiar things. A mild interest in this plant or that can suddenly flame into something more nearly describable as an obsession. Thus it has been of late with me and pulmonarias.

Pulmonarias are not new to my garden. I've grown them for years in a shady border in my back garden. I don't remember the names of all the kinds I originally planted. One was called 'Sissinghurst White', as I recall, another was 'Mrs. Moon', and still another was labeled 'Roy Davidson'. But now I don't know which is which, and there were others whose names I never wrote down. Anyway, for reasons I'll get round to eventually, the names of pulmonarias don't really matter a lot in the long run, as they do in the case of, say, daylilies.

Pulmonarias bloom pleasantly in early spring, with flowers that resemble forget-me-nots. Depending on the species or cultivar, the blossoms can be white, pale red, pink, various shades of blue, or blue and pink on the same plant. But I class them with hostas, not only because of their affinity for shade but also because they are primarily foliage plants whose brief season of bloom is a bonus. I would never dream of digging up and discarding all my hostas and replacing them with pulmonarias, but they do have some advantages over hostas. They keep their foliage most of the year, for one thing, and slugs have little appetite for them, for another. Neither, or so I hear, do deer—but butterflies adore them. With grape hyacinths, they are the earliest plants to offer these bright little creatures of the air a sip of nectar.

The common English names for various species of *Pulmonaria* include Jerusalem sage for *Pulmonaria officinalis*, and Bethlehem sage for *P. saccharata*. Collectively they are all known as spotted dogs in some quarters, but the much more usual common name is lungwort. The word is pretty much a literal translation of the Latin name, and both derive from the ancient notion embodied in the medieval Doctrine of Signatures. This doctrine holds, correctly, that many plants have powers to heal disease, but then leaps much farther to assert, incorrectly, that the way a plant looks is a clue to the ailments it might cure. Thus, a plant with heart-shaped leaves may remedy cardiac disease. Pulmonarias, it was fancied, have somewhat lung-shaped leaves, and spotted ones at that in some species, and so must offer medicine for treating diseases of the lung. About their "vertues" John Parkinson wrote, "It is much commended of some, to bee singular good for ulcered lungs, that are full of rotten matter. As also for them that spit blood, being boyled and drunke." There is a great deal of interest today in herbal medicines, but the Doctrine of Signatures no longer has any adherents, and extracts of lungwort have no place nowadays in our pharmacies and medicine cabinets.

Over the past several decades the number of pulmonaria cultivars has gradually increased, with a sharp acceleration in the process very recently. Some of the breeding and selection resulting in new sorts has taken place in Germany, as witnessed by cultivar names like 'Blaues Meer' and 'Frühlinghimmel'. Great Britain has been the source of many others, such as Beth Chatto's 'David Ward', a selection of *P. rubra* with the coral red flowers typical of the species, but also large, straplike leaves of silvery white. Still other cultivars, such as 'Spilled Milk' and 'Victorian Brooch', originated recently in North America.

Pulmonarias, incidentally, are somewhat tricky where summers are hot and muggy. Southern readers accordingly will be interested to know that in a three-year test at the University of Georgia several cultivars received an outstanding rating: *P. angustifolia* 'Mawson's Variety', *P. longifolia* 'Bertram Anderson', *P. longifolia* 'Little Blue', and *P. saccharata* 'Highdown'.

Now, back to that business about the names of pulmonarias not mattering very much. The reason is that some genera of plants (for example, columbines) hybridize among themselves with huge abandon. Pulmonarias self-hybridize easily; the ones I'm growing now bear little resemblance to what I started with. Crosses between cultivars in the same species—like *P. longiflora* 'Little Blue' and *P. l.* ssp. *cevennensis*—are only to be expected, but there's more to say. Hybridization across species lines has also occurred frequently. Many of the new cultivars on the market are in fact the result of interspecific hybridization, whether deliberately done by humans or incidentally as the result of butterflies and bees seeking nectar and oblivious to the botanical distinctions between one pulmonaria and another. And there's another source of sudden novelties in the lung-wort patch. When a pulmonaria is lifted for division, tiny pieces of roots are almost always left behind. These sprout to form new plants, but the trauma that the roots have suffered often induces mutations.

✿ Texas in Bloom

UNTIL I WAS IN MY MID-TWENTIES, when Alaska was admitted to the Union, I was convinced that my native Texas was not just the biggest state in the United States but also the best, in anything that mattered much. I no longer hold that view. I do not believe that my two sons are seriously disadvantaged by having been raised mostly in New Jersey nor my five grandchildren blighted by having been both born and bred here. That said, I must add that every year when spring rolls around again I yearn to be back in the Lone Star State, driving along its main highways and country lanes, feasting my eyes and my soul on the rich tapestry of wildflowers blooming there in explosive and lovely profusion.

After years of fruitless longing, I finally came home briefly late one March, not to my native Dallas but to Corpus Christi, to see my brother John—and to revisit those roadside wildflowers. On our second day together, Johnny and I set out on a 300-mile drive from Corpus to Rockport, Cuero, Goliad, and Beeville and back. We took mostly state highways and backcountry roads, and except for one barren stretch of Interstate 37, there was scarcely a square foot of roadside that was not radiant with colorful wildflowers, just as spectacular as I remembered them from childhood.

Three species dominate the early spring roadscape. Leading the census is the showy evening primrose (*Oenothera speciosa*), which despite its name is open all day and isn't really a primrose. Its delicate pink, intricately veined, four-sepaled, flat-cupped flowers are so pretty that it's easy to understand why so many gardeners have invited it onto their home ground. This invitation is a dreadful mistake that a little attention to its roadside habits might prevent. It is a hideously invasive perennial that spreads by both underground runners and copious production of seeds. This gorgeous evening primrose forms a low carpet of bloom, barely above the surface of the soil.

Indian or Texas paintbrush (*Castilleja indivisa*), the second most common wildflower at this time of year, is much more erect and grows to eighteen inches or more. To the casual glance, the flowers of this plant are soft orange, but a closer look reveals that the true flowers, which are quite small, are white and their apparent "petals" are actually bracts; this physiological fact explains the unusual length of floral display, from early February almost into July.

The flowers I was happiest to see were, as anyone can probably guess, bluebonnets. There are five species in this genus of legumes, all of them equally and legislatively qualified since 1971 to be called the state flower of Texas. The one Johnny and I encountered on our journey was *Lupinus texensis*, the most common and widespread species. This bluebonnet sometimes grows rather sparsely, mixed in with other plants, its deep violet-blue punctuating the brilliant magenta of wine cups or poppy mallows (*Callirhoë involucrata*), the scarlet and gold of gaillardias, the truer blue of blue-eyed grass (*Sisyrinchium sagittiferum*). But its beauty is heartstopping when it grows by itself in huge colonies, forming great sweeps of color over prairies or hills. It did not happen on this trip, but on the blackland prairies north of Dallas I have seen fields of bluebonnets stretching to the far horizon, looking as if heaven itself has fallen to earth. The sight remains indelible in my memory.

Even if Texas didn't have its bluebonnets, showy evening primroses, and Texas paintbrushes, its roadsides in spring would still be a wonder for their diversity of wildflowers—coreopsis, Mexican hat, early sunflowers, ruellias, delphiniums, blackfoot daisies, hesperaloes, and many, many more. Especially handsome in late March, however, are the prickly poppies, several species of *Argemone*. The loveliest of all is the white prickly poppy (*A. albiflora*), which bears an abundant crop of large, pure white flowers with the texture of muslin and a large central boss of bright yellow stamens. Prickly poppies favor lean, well-drained soils, but another handsome white Texas springling grows only in wet and marshy low places. It is *Hymenocallis liriosome*, one of several different plants commonly called spider lily. This hardy species in a mostly tropical or subtropical genus is an arresting sight for the architecture of its flowers—a circular disk at their center superimposed on six very long and narrow, quite starlike petals.

Thanks to its size and the diversity of soils and climates within its borders, Texas has considerably more wildflowers than any other state—an estimated 5,000 species. Nature alone would assure that its roadsides would sport a few wildflowers every spring, but humanity has given Nature an assisting hand. Since 1936, the Texas Department of Transportation has planted the verges of highways with wildflowers. When this policy was initiated, there were no suitable commercial sources of wildflower seeds, as there are today. Wildflowers were established in new locations by mowing them in old locations shortly after seedset, then gathering the resulting hay and spreading it down the road a piece. Today the Department of Transportation sows 60,000 pounds of seed every year along almost 80,000 miles of roadway. Texans can now brag a bit more—their highways are the largest garden in the world!

❧ The Irises I Grow

THE FIRST IN A LONG PARADE of my horticultural passions was the iris—specifically the bearded irises that breeders for over a hundred years have labored long to transform into one of the most spectacular plants of spring. They have enlarged the flowers (almost beyond the capacity of their stems to support), added ruffles and frills, and broadened the color range to include almost every conceivable hue. (Naming this genus after the Greek goddess of the rainbow required no leap of the imagination; I can think of no other in which the entire spectrum is so well represented.)

Long ago, it was the first sight of an iris patch that awakened my love of plants and gardening. The color play was thrilling—many shades of blues, rich purples, shimmering whites, yellows, coppers, and bronzes, more colors than I could give names to. That year I spent a week's entire allowance, twenty-five cents, for a yellow cultivar named 'Happy Days'. I don't grow bearded irises today. The last ones disappeared from my garden about fifteen years ago. It wasn't that the fires of my first passion had gone out. It was a simple matter of not having enough space to accommodate any plant that took up so much room and looked good for fewer than ten days a year. Every May I still drive out of my way to glory in a garden in town composed entirely of bearded irises. It always makes me wish that I reckoned my own garden in acres, not square feet, for then I could devote space to an iris patch in some out-of-the-way corner and enjoy the splendid show of color in late spring.

Other irises did not depart from my garden with the bearded ones. In fact, a veritable parade of irises flower here over a long season. The season gets under way in late winter or earliest spring with the Algerian iris, *Iris unguicularis*, whose little violet-purple flowers have a delectable perfume. It is followed by the yellow flowers of *I. danfordiae* and the blue-violet ones of *I. reticulata*, which smell deliciously of ripe grapes. These bloom in March, and they are followed in April by the native American *I. cristata*, a low, spreading groundcover with flowers ranging from violet to light blue, depending on the kind.

My garden in May would be devoid of irises, thanks to my having banished the bearded ones, except that I grow two forms of *Iris pallida dalmatica* with variegated foliage. These bloom in late April, sometimes slipping over into May. The flowers of both are sweetly scented, and their foliage looks good throughout the growing season. *I. p. d.* 'Aurea-marginata' has leaves of pale green and gold. The gold is semitranslucent, so the plant becomes radiant when backlit in early morning or late afternoon. *I. p. d.* 'Alba-marginata', with leaves of pale green striped with white, is less spectacular in such light, but still a plant that's worth attention.

In very late spring the Siberian irises strut their stuff. They have attractive narrow and pointed foliage that stays in a nice clump and lends a vertical accent to the mixed border. The flowers come mostly in white and a mixture of blues, violets, and purples.

I don't happen to grow any Japanese irises (*Iris ensata*), but I have 'Aichi-no-Kagayaki', a cross between *I. ensata* and *I. pseudacorus*, the European yellow flag. 'Aichi' blooms sparingly in June, with rather flat yellow flowers of good size, but I would grow it for its marvelous chartreuse foliage even if it never bloomed at all. A friend gave me this iris many years ago, and I have shared it with other friends all over the country. Visitors to my garden often ask for a start of it. The color of its foliage, like that of golden creeping Jenny (*Lysimachia nummularia* 'Aurea') and *Liriope muscari* 'PeeDee Ingot', brings a radiant light to any corner of the garden where it is found. The color, moreover, lasts through the whole growing season.

The last iris in the parade, in late June, is the Gladwyn or stinking iris, *I. foetidissima*. Its scientific name and one of its common names warn that the leaves smell bad.

Bearded iris

The flowers are nothing to get excited about either, but the plant pays its rent when late summer arrives and its seedpods open to reveal seeds as red and shiny as holly berries and with no perceptible odor. One of the merits of this iris is its preference for shade.

❧ *Too Many Heucheras?*

IN RECENT YEARS a lot has been happening to heucheras, especially the kind grown for foliage rather than flowers. The history of the increasingly numerous cultivars of this large genus of North American herbaceous perennials is recent enough to track down fairly easily.

Things got started in the mid-1980s, when Allen Bush, the owner of the now-defunct Holbrook Farm and Nursery in Fletcher, North Carolina, imported from England a heuchera with bronzy and slightly ruffled foliage called Palace Purple. Its taxonomic status was uncertain and still is. Some have suggested that it is a selection of the western species, H. micrantha, perhaps of H. micrantha var. diversifolia. Others have postulated that it derives from the southeastern species H. villosa, although the widely distributed H. americana also has its partisans. My own hunch is that Palace Purple is a hybrid involving two or maybe all of these species, perhaps even other species as well, but I'm not willing to bet anything. I do know some things about Palace Purple, however. The absence of single quotation marks around its name indicates that it is a seed-propagated strain, not a true cultivar that is produced vegetatively. It thus varies considerably in the size, form, and especially color of its foliage, its main asset. (Its sprays of tiny white flowers may be charitably described as insignificant.) The plants Holbrook raised from seed were carefully rogued to eliminate those with poor foliage color, but other growers were not so conscientious, and in any case Palace Purple had a tendency to burn in full sun and did not keep its color well in hot weather. Nevertheless, it was quickly recognized as a valuable plant in the landscape, and eventually the Perennial Plant Association recognized it as one of its plants of the year.

Meanwhile, other American horticulturists were taking an interest in heucheras, the species H. americana in particular. Dr. Richard Lighty of the Mt. Cuba Center for the Study of Piedmont Plants in Delaware selected from this species a form that he named 'Garnet', a reddish or russet self with little or no perceptible patterning in its leaves. It has not attracted much attention, but it is entirely worth growing. The contribution of Dr. Don Jacobs of Eco-Gardens in Decatur, Georgia, was H. americana var. heteradinia, a variety with a distinct patterning in its foliage that he collected in woodlands behind his daughter-in-law's family homeplace in Buncome County, North Carolina. He selected for vegetative propagation one particularly handsome plant that he called 'Eco-Magnififolia'. It had blue-green foliage with chocolate venation and half-inch margins of pale green.

At this point Allen Bush reenters the picture with *Heuchera americana* Dale's Strain (again, no single quotation marks). In the mountains of North Carolina, Dale Hendricks, a Pennsylvanian wholesale nurseryman, came across a specimen of this eastern wildflower that was distinctive for a slightly silvery pattern of netting on its leaves. He passed seed on to Allen Bush, who started offering it in the Holbrook catalog.

The most important link in the genealogy of new heucheras took place in the late 1980s at another North Carolina nursery no longer in business, Nancy Goodwin's Montrose Nursery in Hillsborough. Here, Dale's Strain was crossed with Palace Purple to produce yet one more strain, Montrose Ruby, a real stunner. The Montrose catalog described it as having "dark purple leaves, mottled with silver" and not losing its "dark foliage color even in mid-summer." This description does not even begin to do justice to Montrose Ruby and the gorgeously complex beauty of its foliage. The new leaves emerge in mid-May—somewhat pointed, heavily corrugated, and a glowing reddish purple with silvery highlights. The leaves gradually flatten out, enlarge, and assume a form with five lobes, each lobe slightly deckled on the edges. The pattern of venation is highly architectural, like the leading in a rose window—an appropriate metaphor since the areas between the somewhat lead-colored dark veins are fairly translucent and decidedly red-purple. Gradually this coloration fades but traces of it remain into the next year, when the leaf color has veered toward olive. The leaves can reach six or more inches across.

Montrose Ruby was not widely distributed, certainly not in comparison with Palace Purple. Nancy Goodwin's final catalog, in the fall of 1993, mentioned that it was in very short supply, limited orders to one per customer, and priced it at $20 versus $5 for other strains or cultivars.

No matter what else may come down the heuchera highway, Montrose Ruby is a superb plant. It combines extremely well with *Hakonochloa macra* 'Aureola', ferns, and small hostas, such as 'Golden Tiara'. Montrose Ruby also turns out to be a great parent, but for this part of the story the scene switches to the early 1990s in Portland, Oregon, where breeder and commercial plantsman Dan

Heims backcrossed Montrose Ruby with Dale's Strain. One of the progeny became 'Pewter Veil', a highly distinctive cultivar with large, somewhat wavy leaves that have a silvery shimmer and dark, reddish-brown venation. 'Pewter Veil' was quickly patented and then produced vegetatively by tissue culture at Terra Nova Nurseries in Tigard, Oregon. As is well known, tissue culture makes it possible to produce identical plants at a far, far faster clip than is possible by other, older forms of vegetative propagation. The obvious advantage here is that truly superior new plants (such as 'Pewter Veil') can find their way into our gardens much more cheaply and much more quickly than they can by dividing plants or making cuttings. The accompanying disadvantage is that plants may be rushed into production and distribution as cultivars without proven merit or sufficient distinctiveness from others of the kind.

As I write now, in 1999, Terra Nova, which is strictly a wholesale nursery, propagates and sells almost fifty heucheras, some patented, most of them creations of Dan Heims. Many, those with foliage in the silvery or purplish color range, probably have the Montrose Ruby strain in their ancestry, as does 'Pewter Veil'. I could not possibly undertake growing them all for purposes of comparison, but six years ago I could and did, because there were only fifteen or so cultivars. I was fascinated by the Terra Nova catalog. Reading it was a great experience in dramatic prose style of the "it was a dark and stormy night" variety. The plant descriptions spoke of appliques of silver and pewter, of waves crashing into seashores, and so on. Cultivar names were a lot more romantic than, say, Dale's Strain. Besides 'Pewter Veil' I ordered the following list from a mail-order nursery: 'Burgundy Frost', 'Carousel', 'Chocolate Ruffles', 'Chocolate Veil', 'Crimson Cloud', 'Emerald Veil', 'Palace Passion', 'Persian Carpet', 'Purple Petticoats', 'Ring of Fire', and 'Stormy Seas'.

When the order arrived, I took a close look at 'Stormy Seas'. I didn't see a trace of lavender and not much silver. I didn't have any visions of waves of any color crashing ashore, but it was a juvenile plant after all, and really rather nice, as were all the others.

Here is as good a place as any to comment on the word "purple," as it has appeared from Palace Purple onward, not only in descriptions of heuchera strains and cultivars but also in their fancy names. Some heuchera leaves, including those of the Palace Purple that started it all, are genuinely and recognizably purple, but *only on their undersides*. I have yet to see heuchera foliage that comes even close to purple on its upper surface, which is what shows and counts in the garden. Maroon, which my dictionary defines as "reddish-brown to purplish-brown" is much nearer the mark—chestnut, in other words, or maybe the color of warm root beer in the sun.

Why, then, call things purple that aren't in fact anywhere near purple, in the sense of a crayon by that name or a scrap of cloth? One answer is that the word has more appeal than, say, chestnut. People who might be tempted to buy a plant called 'Purple Petticoats' would likely say no thanks to 'Chestnut Petticoats'. After all, purple is often a favorite color of children, and its aura of desirability may linger into adulthood. Besides, gardeners have long been willing to allow hybridizers and nursery people a large measure of poetic license in naming the plants they offer, as well as in choosing color-words to describe them. (Many plants are described as having blue flowers, but few really qualify. Most turn out to be mauve or lavender or lilac or some other hue not within real striking distance of genuine blue.)

I planted my new collection of heucheras together, close to the deck, properly labeled, and I've kept a sharp eye on them ever since. There's no real purple, but that's okay. The patterned foliage of these plants, generally in dark tones, is lovely, although in shade the plants so tend to fade into dimness that they need to be set off by something bright, like the English ivy cultivar 'Buttercup'.

Over time, the labels on these plants have disappeared, and although I have no trouble finding Montrose Ruby and 'Pewter Veil', the others are hard to identify. I have no idea which is 'Stormy Seas' and which is 'Purple Petticoats'. I also have trouble telling some of them apart from some of the volunteer seedlings in the Montrose Ruby strain, which certainly is a fine parent. My guess is that eventually all of these heuchera cultivars will sort themselves out, some will emerge as distinctive, and the also-rans will fade from view.

But when this happens, there will be other contenders for lasting recognition, the heucheras bred by Charles Oliver, who with his wife Martha owns The Primrose Path nursery in Scottdale, Pennsylvania. Oliver has gone to other, more neglected species for some of his work. His cultivar 'Larenim Queen', a hybrid between *H. pubescens* and *H. sanguinea*, which has rather large pink flowers and green leaves marbled lightly with gray, was introduced in the late 1980s, about the same time as Montrose Ruby (which Oliver praises highly). Much more recent introductions are 'Regina', 'Silver Scrolls', and several cultivars in what is called the "Petite series." 'Regina' has dark, silvery leaves and pale pink flowers on thirty-six-inch stems. 'Silver Scrolls', which Oliver, who is much given to understatement, describes as "extraordinary" and "a breakthrough in heuchera breeding," has rounded leaves of "metallic silver marked with a scrollwork of dark veining" and "wands of white flowers in spring."

❧ *Tiarellas — and Heucherellas*

FOAMFLOWERS OR TIARELLAS (the name means little crown, and refers possibly to the shape of the seedpod, unless it refers to the shape of the pistil instead) are not the kind of plant that captures the immediate attention of the beginning gardener. These modest woodland denizens, which like heucheras are native North American plants in the Saxifrage family, have none of the pizzazz and drama of other spring performers, such as bearded irises, trumpet narcissus, and tulips. But they have winning ways, and in time they insinuate themselves into the affections of experienced gardeners who have learned how to appreciate quiet, restrained beauty in plants with nothing of the showoff in their nature. The assessment of *Tiarella cordifolia* by H. Lincoln Foster in *Cuttings from a Rock Garden* (1990) could cover the entire genus. Comparing it to the Little Red Hen, he wrote that it is "serviceable, somewhat retiring, always fittingly but not flamboyantly adorned." He continues, "Given the right situation and a modicum of appreciation, she flourishes, gracing rather elegantly the pleasant, congenial combinations we bring together in our woodland gardens."

Tiarellas are all built to the same general plan, with delicate white to pinkish flowers appearing on spikes that rise about eight inches above the attractive foliage. They are happiest in at least partial shade and are at their loveliest if sited where they can be backlit by early morning sun, which makes their flower spikes fairly sparkle in the crystal air. The blooming season in the middle of spring can last a month, longer if the weather is unseasonably cool. There is considerable natural variation of flower color, foliage, and habit within the species *T. cordifolia*. The leaves can be rounded, heart-shaped (as the species name implies), lobed, or deeply cut. They may be glossy or dull and hairy. Contrasting markings may be absent, present but faint, or pronounced and impossible to overlook. The plants may be stoloniferous and running, in which case they make effective groundcovers, or they may remain contained within tight, mounded clumps.

These differences and their permutations mean that highly observant gardeners who find some combination of characteristics in a foamflower that they especially like may propagate it vegetatively and pass it along to friends. (Right after his remarks about tiarellas resembling the Little Red Hen, Linc Foster tells us that he did just that with "one form I discovered by chance when I stopped to relieve myself along the Massachusetts Turnpike.")

In the closing decade of the twentieth century there has been a flurry of activity regarding tiarellas—with some of the same dramatis personae we have seen with heucheras. Sometimes the activity has been a matter of selecting naturally occurring specimens of *T. cordifolia* and giving them fancy names. Don Jacobs has introduced three such cultivars, all with white flowers. 'Eco Eyed Glossy' has shiny foliage, 'Eco Red Heart' is blotched dark red at the center of its leaves, and 'Eco Running Tapestry' spreads widely by stolons and has conspicuously marked leaves. His 'Eco Blotched Velvet' offers pink flowers and soft, rather furry foliage. Nancy Goodwin also played a role with her offering of *T. cordifolia* 'Montrose Selection', which is not stoloniferous, has unusually dark foliage, and blooms well after every other tiarella has put in its word for the year.

Cultivars originating as selections come into being by serendipity, as interesting variants spotted by sharp-eyed gardeners or nursery people. Deliberation and intent, however, come into the picture in hybridization, as with Charles Oliver and Dan Heims, whom we have met already. Oliver has to his credit cultivars that are hybrids between *T. wherryi* and several forms of *T. cordifolia*. He has successfully crossed one of these hybrids, 'Tiger Stripe', which bears pink flowers atop purple-netted glossy green leaves, with the Pacific Northwest species *T. trifoliata* var. *laciniata* to produce what he calls his trifoliate hybrids. 'Elizabeth Oliver', a running cultivar, has pink flowers and maroon-striped leaves. 'Filigree Lace' has lacy, purple-patterned foliage and white flowers. 'Martha Oliver', also white, has shining, round-lobed leaves that turn an attractive shade of red in the fall. These trifoliate hybrids bear the genes for late blooming of their western parent, extending the period of foamflower bloom well into summer.

Seed-grown *T. cordifolia* had grown in my garden for years, and I thought it merely an okay kind of plant for shade; it was a head-turning encounter with 'Martha Oliver' some years ago in a splendid garden in Overland Park, Kansas, that turned my mild interest in tiarellas into something deeper. Since then, I have grown every foamflower I can lay hold of. They appeal to my plant-collector's soul. There is intellectual beauty in contemplating the small differences among them that make them individual and distinctive, and in the similarities that relate them to one another. Such beauty is the horticultural equivalent of a theme and variations in music. It is a source of delight, enrichment, and refreshment.

I know, however, that my desire to have at least one of every tiarella that has come into the world, through either the workings of nature or the hand of humankind, is doomed. Dan Heims and Terra Nova are now giving tiarellas the same treatment they gave heucheras. In what seems like no time at all they have come forth with some thirteen cultivars, from 'Black Velvet' to 'Skeleton Key'. More will surely follow as thunder follows lightning. A few, no doubt, will stick around for years.

Anyone (if there be such a person) who thinks that it's needful to choose between heucheras and tiarellas has the option of choosing neither yet, in a certain sense, choosing both, for the two genera cross readily with one another to form the bigeneric hybrid genus × *Heucherella*.

The noted French breeder Pierre Louis Victor Lemoine (1823–1911), who hybridized many mock oranges and bred over 600 fuchsia cultivars, also hybridized heucheras with tiarellas, and introduced two of his creations — × *Heucherella alba* (a cross between × *Heuchera brizoides* and *T. wherryi*) and × *Heucherella tiarelloides* (× *H. brizoides* × *T. cordifolia*). Later, England's Alan Bloom repeated the second of Lemoine's crosses to produce 'Bridget Bloom', a deep pink with conspicuous flowers. Since heucherellas are sterile and invest no energy in production of seed, their blooming period is more prolonged than that of either of their parents.

Charles Oliver doesn't seem to think that Monsieur Lemoine and Mr. Bloom exhausted the promise of such bigeneric hybrids. He has given us new heucheras and new tiarellas, but he's also been busy arranging marriages between members of the two genera. Already introduced are 'Pink Frost', 'Snow White', and 'White Blush', all with mounded foliage of fresh green. Cultivars slated for introduction in the near future include one with showy white flowers and purple and silver leaves. Also forthcoming is a series of crosses between *T. wherryi* and *T. unifoliata*, the eastern and western species of foamflower.

❧ Hostamania!

I CONFESS THAT I DON'T KNOW the names of all the hostas in my garden — about half of those that I acquired some years ago, when the garden started to get shadier and shadier and hostas seemed just the item to replace some of the sun-loving perennials that were looking decidedly peaked in the gathering gloom. Not knowing their names was a deliberate policy, adopted for the same reason that Ulysses stopped up the ears of his sailors and lashed himself to the mast of his ship when sailing past the Sirens. I didn't want to become a hostaphile. I had just managed to temper (somewhat) a passion for daylilies that had led to a garden so crammed with hemerocallis that there was a serious threat nothing else could grow there. I knew the obsession was grave — and backed off from it a bit — the day I wrote a check for $50 for a fancy new introduction (a cultivar that immediately vanished into obscurity, despite its price) and stubbed it to the American Red Cross. College tuitions for two sons were looming ahead, and I didn't want it known under my roof that I had paid that much money for just one daylily.

Hostaphilia if anything seemed an even worse spiritual affliction than hemerocallimania. I knew its signs. Joining the American Hosta Society. Being able to switch the topic of any conversation to hostas in under forty-five seconds, whether it had been on nuclear physics, the chances of a third-party president, or the most authentic recipe for gazpacho. Being oblivious to the frozen smiles and glazed expressions of people who had been talking about the latest crisis in some remote corner of the world and then discovered that someone wanted to discourse enthusiastically with them about 'Frances Williams'. Referring to all other perennials as "companion plants." That kind of thing.

I thought that if I got a few hostas and threw away their nametags before I memorized them I would be safe. It worked fairly well . . . for a time. Of course, there were some hostas among my new acquisitions from the Andre Viette Farm and Nursery, the Klehm Nursery, and other promising sources of temptation that I couldn't consign so easily to the Orwellian memory hole. Who could forget something as magnificent as 'Sum and Substance', as big as a couple of washtubs when it gets going, with golden-chartreuse leaves large enough not just to use as dinner plates but even to serve a luau on? Or 'Sun Power', with bright gold leaves as graceful as flags when they move in a breeze? Or 'Golden Tiara', a small mound of elegance that proves a hosta need not be elephantine to be worthy? Or tiny *Hosta venusta*, with its thumbnail-sized leaves and its spikes of tapered blue-violet flowers?

Lashed to the mast, I heard those Sirens sing, but thought I was safe from hosta-lust by knowing the names of just a few. Meanwhile, I admired even the anonymous ones. Except during their winter dormancy, hostas make a grand contribution to any garden. Their flowers aren't as impressive as lilies or roses or irises, but they are inoffensive (even if some people remove the scapes when they appear); and occasionally, as with 'Aphrodite', a double cultivar of *H. plantaginea* whose blossoms look and smell like little gardenias, they are truly appealing. Hostas take even fairly deep shade in their stride, and in New Jersey they don't mind full sun either. They appreciate moist, rich soil, but they are amazingly tolerant of both drought and lean rations. They also possess that same kind of intellectual beauty that I find in tiarellas. Although all are built to the same basic form, variations in leaf size (tiny to immense), foliage color (blue-tinted, shades of yellow and gold, many different greens, and hundreds of kinds and degrees of variegation), flower color, and time of bloom make a garden dominated by hostas much more interesting over a longer season than, say, one dominated by hemerocallis or irises.

I kept hostaphilia at bay for a goodly time, but not forever, and when my fall from good sense and proper balance came, the unexpected tempters were my grown sons, Paul and Michael, who had their own homes and had started families and gardens. One Christmas I gave them both a gift certificate from Holbrook Farm and Nursery, thinking they would pick out a nice selection of perennials to plant the following spring. Both of them chose hostas, period. Nothing else, just hostas. Michael even mentioned that he was thinking of joining the American Hosta Society.

I mentioned my alarm at having hostaphiles among my progeny to a nurseryman friend, no mean hostaphile himself. I won't give his name here, lest he spend the rest of his life hearing from people expressing the same alarm I did, and hoping for a similar result. He asked for Paul and Michael's addresses. In March he sent each of them a large crate of hostas—ones I didn't have: 'Aurora Borealis', 'Gold Standard', 'Lovepat', 'Wide Brim', 'Zounds', and twelve others.

My sons didn't share their windfall with me, even though I mentioned that somehow my nurseryman friend had forgotten to send me any hostas, as he surely had intended. I thought it was pretty ungenerous of them to be such dogs in the manger, not to mention ungrateful serpent's teeth.

"So, let the hosta-war commence," I muttered. A few months later I found myself at Hatfield Gardens in Ohio, which is not a bad place at all for someone who's in a competition to acquire hostas. I bought most of those my sons had been given, and more besides. The owner, Handy Hatfield, removed the soil from their roots and boxed them up for me to bring home on the plane back to

New Jersey. (Another nice thing about hostas is that they can be transplanted almost any time without risk. They don't even wilt.)

The hostas all went right away into my garden. No sharing, although in time, of course . . . The next spring I ordered some more, from the Klehm Nursery in Illinois, including *H. fluctuans* 'Variegata' and 'Solar Flare', both pretty hot tickets among aficionados. I then spent a lot of time with several enticing hosta catalogs. Two plants—'Abba Dabba Do' and 'Elephant Burgers'— tempted me purely for their names, but the year's hosta-buying spree was over.

Almost over. In late April, with Martha Blake-Adams, I visited Green Hill Farm, Bob Solberg's hosta nursery near Chapel Hill, North Carolina, which doesn't sell by mail order. I wandered through two big lath houses, and then I saw it—'Patriot', a sport of 'Francee' with wide white margins on the leaves, and distinctive from forty yards away. It was auctioned in 1992 for over $800 a plant, so it was a virtual steal at only $70. 'Patriot' came home with me that day, also 'Fried Bananas', 'Great Expectations', and 'Sea Octopus', as well as the recently discovered Korean species *H. yingeri*. My sons will get a start of each, plus everything else acquired after the hostilities began. *One of these days . . .*

That day at Green Hill Farm, Martha also picked out a few hostas she fancied, just from the look of them. She said she didn't really need to know their names. She called in mid-July to say she'd been back there and picked out a few more. She knew them by name: 'Antioch', 'Blue Umbrellas', 'Halcyon', and 'Swoosh'.

Hostaphilia is a communicable disease. Its transmission from one human being to another can often be recorded scientifically. Its surest telltale sign is taking care to get their names straight.

❦ A Jillion Trilliums

ON THAT SATURDAY AFTERNOON in early May I was visiting friends in the rolling foothills of the Blue Ridge Mountains near Winchester, Virginia. My host and hostess asked me if I would like to take a little trip to see something remarkable, one of the true wildflower spectacles of North America. A few minutes later we were on our way.

We drove through the hills, ascending by a narrow and curving road to higher and higher altitudes. Soon the pavement gave out, and we continued to climb at a leisured pace enjoying the slanting golden light of a late spring afternoon. The route was circuitous. I remember no landmarks. I could not possibly find my way back again to our destination, nor tell anyone else how to get there—and that's a good thing, too.

The trilliums began as we rounded a bend. On a steep wooded hillside there were thousands of what is arguably North America's most beautiful native flowering perennial, *Trillium grandiflorum*. The farther we drove, the more trilliums there were, until we finally arrived at a place to park, where a trail led down into the depths of the woodlands to a solid carpet of trilliums stretching up and down the mountain as far as the eye could see.

It was a staggering sight. I had seen *Trillium grandiflorum* before, but never more than three or four plants at a time, and they had been uniform in their pristine whiteness and in the size of their flowers. This colony of trilliums demonstrated dramatically the wide genetic variation possible within a single species. Perhaps 90 percent of them were white, but the rest were pinks, from the palest wash of color, a mere hint of pinkness, to the deepest rose imaginable without trespassing into red. There were other variations. Flower sizes ranged from the large and showy ones that give the species its name to so small that *grandiflorum* seemed a misnomer. Some flowers had narrow pointed segments, others broad and rounded ones that overlapped. On a few, the edges of the segments were ruffled.

So many trilliums grew on that hillside that they seemed like weeds. It seemed almost reasonable to fetch a shovel, dig enough plants to fill the trunk of the car, and bring them home to my garden. I knew better. Trilliums might not be poised on the brink of extinction, like whooping cranes, but their numbers are dwindling. Residential developments have destroyed some of their habitats. Wildflower collectors, whether amateurs who collect trilliums in small numbers for their personal pleasure, or professionals who collect them wholesale to sell retail, have decimated trilliums and other wildflowers for well over a century.

I know the rules. The genus *Trillium* is difficult and slow to propagate. No one should contribute to its extermination. If I want *T. grandiflorum* in my garden, the only respectable way of satisfying my desire is to obtain plants that have been nursery-grown from seed. If a plant costs under $7, perhaps even under $10, it's safest to pass it by. It has probably been collected. The same is true if it has reached substantial size.

A hundred years ago, enormous colonies of *Trillium grandiflorum* grew in many places in the eastern United States. Now, this patch of forested mountainside in northern Virginia may be one of the few places left where you can see them as they used to be, carpeting the ground in the golden light of a warm late afternoon in early May.

I came home with a memory of this scene that will be with me to the end of my days.

✤ The Effrontery of Poppies

THE DAWNING OF SUMMER—late May into early June—is a feast of poppies, in a season whose splendor is matched by its brevity.

Depending on which botanical authority you choose to follow, there are somewhere between fifty and one hundred species of poppy, but only four species mainly contribute to the spectacle of color in the earliest summer garden. Two, *Papaver somniferum*, the opium poppy, and *P. rhoeas*, the corn or Flanders poppy, are European annuals. *P. nudicaule*, the Iceland poppy, is a short-lived perennial best treated as an annual. The only truly perennial poppy is *P. orientale*, the Oriental poppy, which did not arrive in the West from Southwest Asia until the early eighteenth century. (Opium is made from the milky latex—Latin "pappus," from which the genus takes its name—of this poppy.)

All poppy flowers are variations on a common theme. Their slightly arched or crooked stems hang down as the petals inside their calyces swell in pregnancy, but then the stems straighten upward as the flowers open in a virtual explosion that hurls the calyx to the earth in four separate pieces. Every poppy flower opens to a wide-blown cup that may be either single or double, depending on the kind.

The embellishments on this basic form are rich and diverse. Poppy blossoms may be fringed, feathered, flounced, or splotched or eyed with contrasting colors, for a high touch of drama. The broad spectrum of color embraces milky white, pale pink, deep rose, glowing scarlet and crimson, smoky mauve, raspberry, a forthright orange that is exceedingly difficult to tame, as well as many shades and hues that have no name. Only true blue is missing. (For blue, one must resort to *Meconopsis betonicifolia*, the Himalayan blue poppy that takes its name from μεκον, the ancient Greek name for poppy; it is virtually impossible to grow in most of North America although my friend Wayne Winterrowd in Vermont has proved the impossibility is not absolute.)

Poppies are sumptuous and extravagant. Their rich colors strike the eye first, but then comes the appreciation of their opulent textures. The look and feel of the petals invites comparison to the sheen of silk and satin, and to the crinkled appearance of crepe or crinoline. The abundant pollen-bearing anthers surrounding the turreted ovary at the center of the flower have a feathery look, something like the antennae of a lunar moth.

The leaves of poppies issue their own invitation to the senses. The bluish green foliage of the opium poppy—which some nervous gardeners prefer to call the lettuce poppy, for its notable succulence, or the bread poppy, for its seeds used in baking—is waxen to the touch. Both the foliage and the buds of Oriental poppies are covered with decidedly bristly hairs.

Among poppies, *Papaver somniferum* has a dark history relieved by points of light, as one of our past presidents might have put it. Although its soporific and narcotic properties gave it a place in the ancient medicine of Assyria, Babylonia, and Egypt, the Greek natural historian Theophrastus also records the uses of its sap mixed with hemlock (the umbellifer, not the conifer) as a potent poison of choice. The morphine derived from it still eases pain today, but the heroin it also yields has been a source of tragedy and crime. In a shameful episode, Great Britain fought the Opium Wars with China from 1839 to 1842 partly to open a Chinese market for the opium produced in India under British jurisdiction.

The Flanders or corn poppy—"corn" meaning not maize but wheat, because of the long association of the plant with European wheat fields—has figured prominently in mythology and literature through several millennia. It was believed to have sprung from the tears shed by Venus after the death of Adonis. Ovid called it a symbol of fertility, probably because of the great number of seeds it produced. (I hear tell that a medieval monk, more gifted with patience than piety, neglected his prayers for several days to count the seeds in a single capsule and came up with 32,000.) Both Ovid and Virgil believed further that it stood for sleep, night, and death, all properties more fittingly attributed to the opium poppy. (This tradition is perhaps reflected in the film version of L. Frank Baum's *The Wizard of Oz*. In the scene in which the Wicked Witch of the West spies Dorothy and her friends in her crystal ball, poppies magically spring up around them, as the witch mutters, "I'll get you, my pretty, and your little dog, too!")

Poppies

Corn poppies also figure, if infrequently, in Christian iconography. They were regarded by some as symbolic of the Passion of Christ. In another tradition, they are emblems of the Eucharist, the wheat fields in which they grow signifying the Body of Christ, the poppies themselves His Blood.

The literary career of poppies fairly blossomed in England. In "Sordello," Robert Browning praised "the Poppy's red effrontery." John Ruskin wrote: "It is an intensely simple, all silk and flame, a scarlet cup, perfect edged all round, seen among the wild grass far away like a burning coal fallen from Heaven's altars." Both Browning and Ruskin seem to have been speaking of *Papaver rhoeas* (or perhaps merely of generic poppies), but earlier English writers carried on a more serious affair with *P. somniferum*, inasmuch as George Crabbe, Samuel Taylor Coleridge, and Thomas De Quincey were all opium addicts.

One Victorian British clergyman, among the many of his collar who combined restrained piety with scientific horticultural interests, devoted himself to the improvement of the annual *Papaver rhoeas*. Discovering in 1880 in his vicarage garden in the village of Shirley a single corn poppy whose red flowers were faintly margined in white, the Reverend William Wilks saved and planted its seeds. The following year, four or five plants out of two hundred had white-edged petals. Wilks began selecting plants first for larger and larger white margins, and later for white centers instead of black. In time, he later reported, he succeeded "in obtaining a group of plants with petals ranging in colour from brilliant red to pure white, with all the intermediate shades of pink plus an extensive selection with margined and suffused petals; all the flowers having yellow or white stamens, anthers, and pollen, and a white centre." Today, more than a century after the sharp-eyed vicar spied just one corn poppy with a difference in his garden and understood its possibilities, his Shirley poppies are still available in seed catalogs.

No legends surround either the annual Iceland poppy, which is notable for its delicacy, grace, and pastel shades, or the perennial Oriental poppy, for both arrived in our gardens after the power of the myth-making imagination had faded.

Of all poppies, the Oriental is the most purely sensuous. Its flowers are the largest in the genus, as much as eight inches across in some cultivars. There are delicate pinks with no eye, such as 'Springtime'. Others, such as 'Bonfire' and 'Helen Elizabeth', have bold black feathery blotches at their centers. 'Carousel', a fairly new cultivar that strikes my fancy, sports enormous blossoms with a white ring surrounding the blackish purple eye, then suffuses to pale red at the rim of the flower. But the true forte of these poppies is the flamboyance and incandescence of the more riotous colors, the deep reds and glowing oranges.

Oriental poppies have their defects. Their season of bloom is brief and is followed by an ugly lapse into dormancy until late summer. But during their short season, they add glory to the garden, and lend themselves to simple but striking arrangements. There's a trick involved, however. Poppies wilt quickly when cut unless their cut ends are seared a second or two with the flame from a gas stove or a butane lighter. Fire seals the latex sap, giving the flowers a longer life, if nothing like immortality.

❦ Those Strange and Striking Cobra Lilies

AMONG FLOWERING PLANTS, the Aroid family or Araceae is one of the strangest. Most of the genera are tropical, including elephant ears, caladiums, and philodendrons, to name only three of many. As this trio suggests, highly ornamental foliage is common in the Araceae, but some members of the family—anthuriums and calla lilies, for example—also offer handsome or striking blossoms. The family is by no means restricted to the tropics: the jack-in-the-pulpit (*Arisaema triphyllum*) is native to our eastern woodlands from Florida to New Brunswick and the eastern skunk cabbage (*Symplocarpus foetidus*) blossoms in earliest spring in wet locations over a similar area.

The behavior of skunk cabbage is a tip-off to the strange and bizarre tendencies of this family. For one thing, it takes both its common name and its species name from the distinctly unpleasant odor its flowers waft into the air to attract its pollinators, mostly beetles and flies. For another, its flowers heat themselves up as much as

Arisaema speciosum

50°F above the temperature of the surrounding atmosphere, enabling them to push their way up through snow and ice to blossom. Although the flowers of some aroids are sweetly perfumed, smells that are unpleasant to our nostrils are found as frequently as not in genera and species that play to their audience of pollinators, including flies that feed and lay their eggs on rotting flesh. The enormous flowers of the Sumatran Titan flower (*Amorphophallus titanum*) emanate waves of the most disgusting odor imaginable—in legend, if not in actuality, causing anyone who catches even a whiff of it to faint.

Obviously, the Sumatran Titan is not a suitable garden plant, although it has been flowered successfully both in England, at Kew Gardens, and in the United States, at the New York Botanical Garden.

For years in England and now in North America, there has been increasing interest among plant collectors in cobra lilies, the genus *Arisaema*, especially species native to the Himalayas, China, and Japan. This genus is somewhat familiar here, given our native jack-in-the-pulpit. By any reckoning, the appearance of this plant when it blooms in midspring is an arresting sight. Beneath a parasol of a single large leaf divided into three leaflets, just one flower rises out of the stem, with a protruding phalliform inflorescence (the jack) emerging out of a cuplike structure that folds over at its top (the pulpit). Jack and pulpit are metaphorical or folk names for only one species of *Arisaema*. The botanical terms, which apply to the flowers of all arisaemas and many other aroids as well, are *spathe* for the pulpit and *spadix* for the jack (which consists of numerous true flowers that are remarkably inconspicuous unless viewed with a hand lens).

One peculiarity of our native jack-in-the-pulpit—and of many other species of *Arisaema*, but not all—is its sexual behavior. We are familiar with plant genera whose blossoms all contain both female and male organs of reproduction (roses), with genera that bear some all-male and some all-female flowers on a single plant (squash), and with genera that segregate the sexes entirely, so that some plants are male and others female (holly). Jack-in-the-pulpit and many other (but not all) species in its genus fit none of these familiar categories,

Arisaema angustatum

for they change their sex. An
individual plant may be male
one year, female the next,
and of neither gender the
next. Its sex in any given
year is determined
by its nutrition
in the previous
growing season.
If poorly nourished,
it will produce only
foliage, not expending
energy to engage in re-
production at all. In effect,
it will have no gender. If its
food reserves are adequate
but not abundantly so, it will
be a male, producing only
pollen. If it has surplus nutri-
tional energy, it will be a female,
having enough metabolic strength to
fruit and produce seeds.

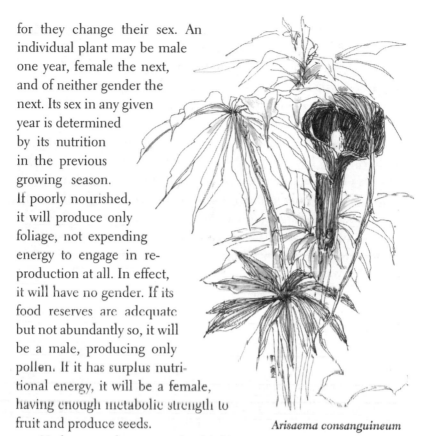

Arisaema consanguineum

Ho hum, gardeners may be thinking
to themselves at this point, all of this may be interesting, if only
barely, as botany, but it has little to do with gardening. It has, however, a great deal to do with gardening today, because *Arisaema triphyllum* has gotten a lot of company recently, in the form of a large
and increasing number of other species collected in East Asia,
imported to our shores, and made available commercially for the
first time. These just happen to be among the most exciting garden
plants I know. Jack's exotic cousins have arrived, and by comparison
they make him look like a very dull fellow, or woman, or neither of
the above.

Before proceeding further, I should emphasize that what is new
with these Asian arisaemas is their availability in the nursery trade,
not their presence in America. Arisaemas are just one of many genera of East Asian plants—many of them Araceae—that Barry Yinger

has introduced to North American horticulture. There are several enthusiastic collectors, such as Nancy Goodwin in North Carolina, who grows A. *amurense*, A. *heterophyllum*, A. *ringens*, and other species. Her original tubers "came from Barry Yinger, the best source of all wonderful arisaemas and gingers," she says, "and I think of him when I see them bloom."

The geographic distribution of species in this genus is uneven. North America has four species, two in the United States and two in Mexico. (These were discovered only recently, and there's a reasonable expectation that further exploration in Mexico may yield additional species.) A larger number of tender species are native to the tropics, but these are of no concern here. The greatest diversity of species is found in Japan, China, and the Himalayas, regions where the genus *Arisaema* has undergone the most extensive evolution.

The interest in *Arisaema* has been lively in the British Isles for some time. One species, A. *candidissimum*, was discovered by George Forrest in Yunnan, China, prior to 1914. It differs from most other arisaemas in several respects. First, it is not a woodlands plant; it is native to dry, rocky hillsides. Second, its spathe lacks the hood that calls cobras to mind. Its open form gives it something of the look of a calla lily—and a lovely one at that. The spathe is vertically striped, brownish-green and greenish-white on the exterior, pale pink and white on the interior. Its wide, waxy foliage is extremely handsome. It also is uncharacteristic of its genus in having sweetly perfumed blossoms. Its popularity in England is evidenced by its having received from the Royal Horticultural Society an Award of Merit in 1924 and a First Class Certificate in 1970.

Another species long popular among British gardeners is A. *sikokianum* from Japan, which earned an Award of Merit in 1938. It has a stubby white spadix, somewhat reminiscent of a mushroom. Its shiny spathe, again unhooded but with two odd appendages that point upward, is striped in white and brownish purple.

As a result of numerous plant-hunting expeditions to East Asia in recent years, the number of species newly available commercially in Great Britain has skyrocketed, as evidenced by the tantalizing lists from several nurseries that among them offer almost fifty species and subspecies.

The vocabulary used to describe arisaemas instructs us properly not to expect roses when we see one. Such words as *sinister, reptilian, bizarre, unearthly,* and even *demonic* occur over and over. So do words like *breathtaking, dramatic, awe-inspiring,* and *utterly beautiful.* A common comment is that these plants look as if they had evolved on some other planet. Their colors—*chocolate brown, pale green and ochre, brownish-purple, straw,* and so on—are somber and muted.

There's good news for American gardeners lusting to give arisaemas a try on their own home grounds. Some of our nurserymen have also mounted their own expeditions to East Asia or joined up with British plant hunters. (I should say "seed hunters," because few plantsmen today would collect plants in the wild—and anyone who did would scarcely admit it.)

The result of these expeditions, as well as extensive trading of seeds among the growing international ranks of aficionados of cobra lilies, is that American gardeners have convenient commercial access to some of the most fascinating plants on earth. In 1999, two nurseries, Heronswood in Washington State and Plant Delights in North Carolina, offered over twenty-five species between them, with more surely to come.

I caught my first glimpse of a collection of these new cobra lilies at Plant Delights in May 1998, but they didn't register at first: two other collections absorbed all my attention—first, a large assortment of East Asian species of *Asarum* or wild ginger brought to America by Barry Yinger; and second, several species and hybrids of our native *Sarracenia* or pitcher plants. When I stumbled on all the arisaemas, time was short. I had to be in Wilmington a few hours later. I couldn't take notes about individual species, just try to take in some of the features of the whole group—their decidedly odd colorations for one thing, but even more their strange variations in form. They all bore a family resemblance to our own jack-in-the-pulpit, but they looked as if they had been on psychedelic drugs while reading *Alice in Wonderland*. In some, the spathe went wandering, turning into a whiplike appendage that dangled to the ground, often to a considerable distance, occasionally with odd twistings and sharp turns along the way. In others, the spadix underwent similar maneuvers. The jack of our native wildflower is a fairly sober fellow, standing erect as a preacher on Sunday, but some of its Asian counterparts lolled and leaned, rather drunkenly, toward the earth. (These oddities may be bridges for the benefit of insect pollinators.) In one clump, four or five inflorescences of what I think was A. *ringens* faced one another, irresistibly reminiscent of a committee of cobras coming to a decision about whether to strike or not.

The species of these plants thus far collected and brought to our shores come from diverse habitats and altitudes and thus vary in both winter-hardiness and the equally important matter of summer-hardiness. Some Himalayan species from higher altitudes have been problematic in places like the Piedmont of North Carolina, where summers are long and sweltering. Some species may not survive where winters are fierce, particularly without snow cover for insulation. With greater experience, American gardeners may learn which species will do well for them, no matter where they live.

At present, the prices of cobra lilies at both Heronswood and Plant Delights range from $8 to $30, which sounds expensive, until you consider the effort that has gone into procuring them and then propagating them. Most cobra lilies can be propagated fairly easily from seed, provided that you have at least two plants of the species you want to increase—and that one plant has decided to try being a female this year, the other a male. Seeds are harvested after fully ripening; then they must be cleaned, as their pulp contains a germination-inhibiting chemical. Because the pulp is toxic and can cause severe skin irritation, even numbness, it should be put in a sealed plastic bag, mauled a bit, and then shaken out into water. The pulp is repeatedly decanted until only clean seeds are left. Pot the seed right away indoors in any good potting mix, covering them with a thin layer of mix, and then water. The seeds will usually sprout within a week or two, grow for two to four months, and then enter dormancy when the leaves turn yellow. The pots must be kept dry; water only twice a month or so. The process from seed to mature plant takes two to four years, depending on the species. Seed size determines food reserve, and food reserve determines speed of growth. A. *francheticum*, A. *candidissimum*, and A. *taiwanensis* get quite large from seed during their first season, but at the other extreme, A. *elephas*, A. *thunbergii*, and A. *aurashima* send out only roots their first season.

I have not yet done justice to these fascinating and exotic plants and all the excitement they may offer American gardeners of an experimental mind, for I have dealt only with their floral characteristics, not their foliage, which is equally handsome and diverse. Most flowers, of whatever sort, are evanescent; they quickly come and quickly go, once they have played out their role in the continuation of their kind. Foliage is different. Because it carries out the photosynthesis on which the lives of plants depend in the most intimate and crucial way, it generally sticks around all through the growing season. The longer we garden, the more convinced we become of this truth and the more valuable to us become hostas, ferns, ornamental grasses, and other plants with great foliar appeal. Arisaemas are accordingly a fine addition to the palette of plants we use to paint our garden pictures. Furthermore, for those of us who garden where deer abound, the potent calcium oxalates produced by these plants—the same sharp crystalline chemicals that give *Dieffenbachia* its common name of dumb cane—may make cobra lilies more than a match for these beasts.

❧ Empress Trees

IF PUSHED TO NAME the most beautiful flowering tree in my garden, I wouldn't hesitate a nanosecond in coming up with the empress tree (*Paulownia tomentosa*), also called princess tree. I acquired mine about fifteen years ago from the Winterthur Museum and Gardens as a tiny seedling, but it didn't stay tiny long. In its first year, it grew to eight feet, with heart-shaped leaves that were almost thirty inches long from stem to tip. (As the tree matured, the leaves decreased much in size, but they're still bold and arresting.) My tree is now over forty feet high.

A paulownia tree in full flower drenches a garden with blessings. Each individual flower is pure loveliness. Emerging from a substantial, light-tan calyx with a texture like suede, the downy, two-inch flowers are tubular, flaring out into ruffles at their open end. Pale lavender on the outside, they are suffused with golden yellow at their throats. The flowers are borne in upright panicles, thirty or more to each cluster. They delight the nose as well as the eye, for they are deliciously scented with an ambrosial perfume reminiscent of honey, apricots, and vanilla that carries far on the late spring air. The blooming season can be as short as ten days or as long as three weeks, depending on whether it's a warm late spring or a cool one.

Paulownias have other virtues. Their panicles of seed capsules, which look like upended clusters of huge green grapes, are visually appealing all summer. When they finally ripen, turn brown, and release their seeds, they break into two halves, each shaped like a little boat, that children love to float. The seed clusters remain on the tree all winter long, together with the buds for next spring's flowers. In a good breeze or when squirrels chase through the tree, the capsules clatter like castanets. (Another common name for paulownia is rattlebox.) The rapid growth of paulownias must also be counted as a virtue; they are great trees for owners of brand-new houses built on former corn fields.

Some gardeners, especially those in England, have another use for paulownias, choosing to stool them rather than let them grow to full size. In stooling, they are whacked back to the ground in midwinter. When late spring arrives, they will grow rapidly to eight or nine feet, and the enormous leaves of their new growth effectively screen out unwanted views. But, treated in this manner, they fail to bloom.

Paulownias do have faults. In autumn, their leaves blacken and fall off at the slightest touch of frost. They are ugly and slow to decay. The seedpods are messy, too, and they contain prodigious quantities of seeds—2,000 seeds scarcely bigger than a speck of dust in just one pod. Some will germinate, but not a great many, and the seedlings are easy to pull up.

These trees, which the Swedish botanist Karl Thunberg first described for Western botanists after a visit to Japan in the 1770s, are named for Anna Paulowna, a granddaughter of Catherine the Great and the wife of Willem II, who ruled the Netherlands from 1840 to 1849. The paulownia is native to China, where it figures

Paulownia tomentosa

prominently in both legend and culture. Ancient Chinese lore holds that it was an emblem of good luck because of its association with the phoenix, the mythical firebird that is consumed in flames and then comes alive again from the ashes. It was also a hallmark of Chinese literary intellectuals, who believed it symbolized the virtues of gentleness combined with strength, as its soft and pliant wood cures with time to great strength and hardness. The leaves and flowers of the paulownia tree also had a prominent role in traditional Chinese medicine; they were reputed to cure baldness, keep hair from turning gray, reduce swelling and inflammation of the feet, and prevent hallucinations.

Centuries ago the paulownia was introduced from China to Japan, where it found many uses. Its wood was used as beams and posts in temples, in musical instruments, and in ceremonial boxes. It was particularly linked with marriage rituals. By tradition, on the birth of a daughter her father would plant a paulownia tree; when she became engaged, he would harvest the wood to make her a tansu or dowry chest. (This custom abated after World War II, however, when a blight much like that which wiped out chestnuts in America decades earlier attacked paulownias in Japan.)

Paulownia tomentosa grows fast, but unlike most other fast-growing woody plants, such as Russian olive, it is not short-lived. In one of the oldest parts of Philadelphia, between Independence Hall and the Delaware River, there is a paulownia of massive girth that is home to a hive of bees in a cavity in one of its upper branches. I suspect this tree is well over a century old. The Philadelphia Museum of Art has some magnificent and venerable specimens right near those steps where Rocky trained. Longwood Gardens at Kennett Square has a truly magnificent allée of the trees, leading up a hill toward the main conservatory.

The empress tree is thought to have arrived in America by accident because its seedpods were used in the nineteenth century as packing material for porcelains imported from China and Japan by wealthy families in the Mid-Atlantic states. The tree quickly escaped to the wild, naturalizing itself in many parts of the country, especially in lower elevations of the Blue Ridge and Smoky Mountains. (This behavior is *not* a virtue!)

In recent decades paulownias have made the news, including crime reports. In the early 1970s a Japanese lumber broker in search of black walnut trees to import to his country spotted some old-growth paulownia trees in the mountains of Virginia. Thanks to that paulownia blight in Japan and the desire of fathers to revive the old custom of presenting their daughters with dowry chests, demand for the wood was strong—at prices as high as $20,000 for the lumber from a single tree. Not surprisingly, a new occupation developed in this country, that of the paulownia rustler, who would find mature trees, steal in, and remove them from public land or private property without benefit of permission or purchase. In one such incident the Winterthur Museum lost seventeen paulownias in a single night.

In China today paulownias play an important part in agroforestry. The trees are planted in rows, with shade-tolerant food crops interspersed during the summer months, full-sun winter food crops the rest of the year. Lumber from the trees is harvested at intervals of about ten years. In this way empress trees do double service in protecting crops and providing material for construction.

A selected, patented cultivar of another species, *P. elongata*, is now being grown in South Carolina in a speculative venture by the Carolina Pacific Company, which has put out many press releases about the multitudinous uses of the plant. It is said to grow even more rapidly than P. *tomentosa*. Young trees can be harvested for newsprint and other paper, and more mature trees find their way into plywood, veneers, and even lumber for furniture and residential construction. The wood is said to be far superior to that of other fast-growing trees, like poplars. It may be hoped that some of this lumber will be exported to Japan for those dowry chests.

If so, perhaps paulownia rustlers will be driven out of work, and the remaining trees at Winterthur will be safe from their predations.

✺ Pitcher Plants for the Home Garden

MOST CHILDREN MANAGE at least once in their young lives to come home in proud possession of a tiny plastic greenhouse containing a Venus flytrap (*Dionaea muscipula*). It generally dies in a few weeks, after the pleasures of feeding it tiny morsels of hamburger have palled. (A hamburger diet is not recommended for these curious North American plants, which are native only to a tiny section of the coastal Carolinas.) The wonder over this plant, however, is not restricted to the very young. While living in Paris in the 1780s, Thomas Jefferson repeatedly wrote home asking for seeds so that he might show off this vegetative marvel to his horticulturally minded French friends.

Fascination with the Venus flytrap is only a small part of a much larger phenomenon: an interest in carnivorous or insectivorous plants in general. In the United States, Great Britain, Germany, and Australia, numerous societies are devoted to the study and cultivation of what Germans call *fleischfressenden Pflanzen*. The reasons are not at all difficult to comprehend. These plants do not conform to our usual expectations about vegetative life. We are accustomed to the notion that insects eat plants, but the Venus flytrap and others of its kind turn the tables.

Several genera of carnivorous plants are native to the United States, especially the Southeast, with its butterworts (*Pinguicula*), bladderworts (*Utricularia*), sundews (*Drosera*), and pitcher plants (*Sarracenia*), as well as Venus flytraps. All are worth attention, as a fine permanent display at the North Carolina Botanical Garden in Chapel Hill makes abundantly clear. But only one genus—the pitcher plant—is apt to have enough true appeal to most gardeners to make it worth their taking the trouble to meet its special needs. There are eight species, as well as a number of hybrids. All species except *S. purpurea*, whose range extends northward along the East Coast from Florida into Canada, are native to the Southeast and the Gulf states.

The major attraction of these plants throughout their growing season is their colorful pitchers, which in some species lie flat on the ground and in others stand upright. In either case these foliar struc-tures are lined on the inside with downward-pointing hairs that mean the doom of any small insect unfortunate enough to land there; it ends up consumed by the plant's digestive system. The

Sarracenia

pitchers are lidded at the top, and in one species, S. *minor*, the lid folds down into a hood, so that the plant looks like a nest of cobras poised to strike. In some species the pitchers are green, but shades of red, purple, chartreuse, and yellow also occur, sometimes with attractive contrasting venation. But the greatest beauty of sarracenias lies in their flowers in late spring. (The plant seems to show consideration for the insects that pollinate it, since the flowers open before the young pitchers have matured sufficiently to capture prey.) The blossoms are large and as spectacular as any orchid. Each is solitary on its own tall stem and hangs downward. The color range extends from bright yellow to garnet to burgundy to a crimson so dark that it veers toward black.

Pitcher plants are not difficult to grow if conditions are provided for them that match their natural habitats, which are sunny bogs and wet savannahs. The best potting medium is a mixture of three-fourths peat moss and one-fourth coarse sand or perlite. They are happy if grown in plastic pots kept in dishpans, or similar containers filled with water, with small holes drilled two or three inches up the side to control the water level.

Pitcher plants require an unfailing source of moisture, at least six hours of direct sunlight, and good ventilation. Although they manufacture their own fertilizer in the usual way of plants, by photosynthesis, and capture insects to supply the nitrogen generally missing in the soils they inhabit, a little liquid acid fertilizer in a very dilute solution applied every month or so during the growing season is all right.

The final requirement is a period of winter dormancy. Pots may be sunk in the ground outdoors to overwinter, but should never be allowed to dry out entirely.

❧ Beauty in Onions

HUMANITY'S LOVE AFFAIR with the genus *Allium*, which can be traced back at least to ancient Egypt and Babylonia, continues unabated today. Several species enrich our tables—onions (A. *cepa*), leeks (A. *porrum*), garlic (A. *sativum*), shallots (a varietal form of A. *cepa*), and chives (A. *schoenoprasum*).

Among the edible alliums beauty is parceled out unevenly. The aesthetics of onions is subterranean. The ripe and pungent bulbs have a fine globular feel in the hand, and the papery white, brown, or purplish-red tunic that covers them is a treat to the touch. It also makes a satisfying sound as it is removed, like the rustling of taffeta. Garlic plants are gawky, but the bulbs are handsome braided together as a useful kitchen decoration. As for leeks, in their fields near my home they are ravishingly beautiful on sunny mornings in February when frost has covered their strappy, pale blue-gray leaves with tiny glistening crystals.

Chives have no demerits I can think of. The cook's friend in the kitchen, they also adorn the garden. They edge a flower border or herb garden neatly, and their abundant lavender-purple flower clusters in June, usually abuzz with bumblebees, give me the gladsome heart that the hymnals of my boyhood promised the righteous. The cultivar 'Forescate' bears lovely pink flowers.

The most beautiful species are strictly ornamental and display great diversity. The majority bloom as spring is turning to summer, from the middle of May to the middle of June, but late summer into early autumn is the season for a few. Some alliums vault upward, hurling their flower heads to as much as sixty inches. Some lack all aerial ambition, growing barely a foot high, and the rest occupy some intermediate niche of altitude.

In color, the flowers of alliums predominantly fall in the lavender to purple part of the spectrum, but some species bear blue, yellow, white, or rose blossoms.

The flowers of the various species of alliums have a family resemblance. All produce many florets in a cluster at the top of the stem, but the architecture of the floral cluster varies greatly. In some species it is loose and informal, for a nodding effect. Others form almost perfectly rounded flower heads, and still others half-domes, as in the stately *Allium rosenbachianum* 'Album'. This grows to thirty-six inches, blooming in late May, with half-rounded umbels of white flowers whose petals surround a dark green ovary. From a distance it looks something like an unusually burly specimen of Queen

Anne's lace. An equally impressive species, A. *siculum* (which some authorities remove from the genus, classifying it instead as *Nectaroscordum siculum*), bears nodding and downward-facing bells of greenish-white flowers brushed with mauve and olive on forty-inch stems. Each floret in a cluster is carried on a long, arching pedicel, making it look as if some little floral explosion has just gone off. A. *sphaerocephalum* makes a flower cluster shaped something like an egg, or like strawberry popcorn still on its cob. Strangest in its beauty is the spidery-looking rarity, A. *protensum*. The stalks bearing the individual florets are such varied lengths that the blossoms would look like Roman candles bursting at a nighttime celebration, except that the flower heads are borne on short stems, almost at ground level.

The most dramatic allium is unmistakably *Allium giganteum*, with its immense globes of starry purple flowers on fat and rounded stems that can reach anywhere between forty-five and sixty inches tall. Often pictured in nursery catalogs with a child hunkered down beneath it, it makes a bold statement in late May, in either a massed planting of nothing else or an ensemble where it adds a majestic touch to carefully selected companions, such as yellow *Iris pseudacorus* and garnet *Centranthus ruber*. The stunning cultivar 'Globe master' aspires no higher than thirty-six inches and veers away from purple toward pink. Some other species that bloom in late spring soar to considerable altitude, without quite matching their giant cousin. A. *aflatunense*, with rounded heads of flowers intermediate in color between lilac and lavender, tops off just under thirty-six inches.

Among the larger alliums, A. *christophii* or star of Persia is a favorite of many gardeners. Its starry florets, composed of long, narrow, pointed petals that are a metallic shade of amethyst, form a ball-shaped cluster. Since its stems reach only twenty inches, star of Persia nestles together in a fetching way with perennials of moderate stature, such as lady's mantle or sea holly. And this species, like A. *giganteum*, offers a bonus. Once its flowers have faded, it can be cut and dried as long-lasting material for indoor winter bouquets.

The genus *Allium* includes little charmers, as well as bold performers. I could not easily live without A. *karavatiense*, the only fairly common species that would be worth growing for its foliage alone. Its grayish pink flower clusters, about the size and shape of a tennis ball, in late May barely rise above a pair of low, arching, and wide blue-gray leaves. I am also partial to A. *moly*, an early-June bloomer with abundant bright yellow flowers. The bulbs are inexpensive and so can be planted in the large masses or drifts that are their most effective use. Other splendid species that bloom at the same time as A. *moly* and also look best in masses are A. *roseum* and A. *oreophilum*. The first grows to about a foot tall, with loose clusters of pale pink flowers; the second, a dark shade of rose, is the most diminutive of all the ornamental alliums, aspiring no higher than six inches.

The advent of summer heat does not write finis to the procession of garden alliums. One of the most beautiful is A. *caeruleum*, which blooms in my garden in late June. Its azure flower heads top fairly lax stems about eighteen inches tall, making it a fine plant to weave among other things, in a summer tapestry. The latest of the summer alliums, overlapping in bloom with A. *caeruleum*, is A. *scorodoprasum*, commonly called sand leek or rocombole. It bears moderate-sized rounded clusters of lilac-purple flowers on thirty-six-inch stems. But this species, whose bulbs can be used much like garlic, calls for caution. Like the wild onions that infest lawns in late winter, it produces many bulbils together with its flowers, making it a seriously invasive plant. The subspecies A. *s. rotundum* forms no bulbils, and has larger and more intensely colored flower heads. It is wonderful planted in a sinuous curve through a perennial border, where its flower heads seem to float above lower plants.

Autumn has its alliums, too, including A. *stellatum* (violet pink) and A. *kurilense* (reddish pink). But I must put in a special word for A. *senescens* var. *glaucum* and A. *thunbergii* 'Ozawa'. The former grows to about fifteen inches tall, has rather wide blue-green foliage, and round clusters of lavender-pink flowers borne over a prolonged period of bloom lasting from midsummer well into late September. I have seen it used en masse in herbaceous borders, running like a river of gray-tinged pink through other plants, lending the entire border a sense of unity and repose. 'Ozawa' is a much more petite plant, blooming in the fall with pyrotechnic little bursts, somewhat like those of A. *flavum* in the spring.

For my money, however, the best allium of the late garden is *A. tuberosum* or garlic chives. Its glossy wide leaves have a flavor intermediate between garlic and chives. It blooms exuberantly, producing a multitude of lovely little white flowers in September and will often bloom again a month later if it is thoroughly deadheaded. The second crop of flowers can be left standing until early winter, when they dry to a pleasant shade of pale parchment accented with the jet black of the seed at the center of each floret. Like the seedheads of *A. giganteum*, they make good winter arrangements, although they are delicate rather than spectacular. A warning, however, is in order: garlic chives is a successful self-seeder, and potentially invasive. And, oh yes, almost all alliums produce seeds that pose problems when they germinate, as they are impossible to tell from the wild garlic that is one of our worst weeds of spring.

❧ Late Spring's White Tide

MY SMALL GARDEN is almost entirely innocent of deliberate color schemes, for the simple reason that I am a magpie gardener, whose main intent is to collect as many different plants as possible, cramming them into my patch of earth wherever I can find room. Some lovely color combinations nevertheless result, by pure serendipity. A few years ago, annual Texas sage (*Salvia coccinea*) seeded itself in the midst of a clump of boltonia 'Pink Beauty'. The tiny red flowers of the salvia looked like little firecracker explosions going off against the softer color of the boltonia. In another year, also by pure accident, porcelain blue brodiaeas bloomed against the chartreuse backdrop of golden feverfew's early June foliage to stunning effect. Without changing my ways about developing an overall plan for color, I have contrived to make a permanent place in my garden for these two particular combinations.

Another feature of my garden seems to be planned, but isn't. From early May until mid-June it is a sea of sparkling, pristine, omnipresent white. Early spring is by comparison a gaudy season. March and April are rich in the blues of grape hyacinths, Siberian squills, glory of the snow, and Grecian windflowers. These early spring months blare with the yellows of daffodils and the varnished-looking golds of both the lesser and the greater celandines, which botanically are *Ranunculus ficaria* and *Stylophorum diphyllum*. Tulips, most of which have played out by early May, among themselves exhaust the entire spectrum of color, save for true blue. There are lovely whites among this vivid rainbow of color, including one of the earliest magnolias, star magnolia or *Magnolia stellata*, wonderful for its fresh lemony scent and the elegance of a multitude of flowers before the leaves appear. But white, in early spring, is only a grace note, not a major theme.

When summer arrives in earnest, the entire gamut of color will return. But meanwhile, there is the spring climax of May, with its whites, all the more dazzling for the fresh greens of lawns and shrubbery and trees. It begins, in my garden, with the perennial candytuft that spills like white foam from the edge of a herbaceous border into a path. Nearby, some native woodland phlox soon chime in, joined shortly by the first clusters of flowers of the sweet alyssum that seeds itself dependably here and there. White spiraea or bridal wreath next puts in its word, a huge and billowing bush voluptuous with high spring and much visited by bees.

Eastern dogwood begins inauspiciously, but with every day its blossoms get larger and whiter, seeming to float suspended in the air, like white butterflies somehow arrested in their flight. This native species, *Cornus florida*, is in trouble in much of the Northeast, thanks to a combination of blight and stress from drought. I shall no doubt eventually have to replace my two trees with the new hybrid, disease-resistant forms developed at Rutgers University, but for now they are healthy and beautiful. One of these days I mean to plant a mass of white azaleas beneath them, borrowing the idea from the garden of Martha Blake-Adams in North Carolina.

In my garden lilacs bloom with eastern dogwood. The ancient hedge that runs along one side of the property for thirty feet or so is mostly made up of the common, pale purple sort, but intermingled with these are several plants, taller than the rest, with sweetly fragrant clusters of frost-colored florets.

By mid-May the native dogwoods and the lilacs have had their say, but the tide of white has not yet begun to ebb. Shasta daisies hold forth in the sunny herbaceous border, and I finally have enough of them to cut for indoor bouquets without noticeably depleting them outdoors. Next to the deck an immense mock orange covers itself in single white flowers of surpassing sweet fragrance, just as the hardy kiwi vines on the pergola above open their clusters of vanilla-scented creamy blossoms.

Meanwhile, next to the driveway and almost arching over it to form a cool tunnel of green and white, an enormous specimen of double file viburnum (*Viburnum plicatum* f. *tomentosum*) is at its height. Atop its horizontal branches, perched like doves in the double rows that give this large shrub its common name, sit white flower bracts, so abundant that from a distance it looks as if there has been a heavy snowfall.

This viburnum is in bloom for only ten days or so, less if the weather turns hot and stays there, but there is one last act in the drama of the whites of late spring. The Asian dogwood *Cornus kousa*, one of the parents of the new hybrid dogwoods from Rutgers, brings everything to a splendid conclusion. The four bracts surrounding its insignificant-looking true flowers start out in early June small and olive green, but they steadily enlarge, gradually paling into glistening pure white, like those of the native eastern dogwood. Our *Cornus kousa* is planted next to the side street that runs from a nearby junior high school to the busy road in front of our house. It blooms just as the school year ends, in mid-June. Parents who pick up their children from school often stop to admire the tree.

It is now almost twenty-five years old. Some twenty feet tall, it spreads over ten feet wide. If that double file viburnum looks as if snow has fallen on its branches, this Asian dogwood looks as if a raging blizzard is in progress. No other tree brings such a satisfying conclusion to the season of white in our late spring garden.

The most magnificent of all white-flowering woody plants overlaps with *Cornus kousa*. I do not grow it, but our neighbors do, and I pay their *Magnolia grandiflora* a visit every June to admire it. A towering giant reaching upward of seventy feet in the Deep South where it is native, it is a more moderate-sized tree in southern New Jersey, near its northernmost range. (In England it is virtually a clinging vine, grown espaliered on the south side of stone walls for winter protection.) Its stiff, highly varnished, dark evergreen leaves are elegance personified. They clasp huge, pointed, creamy-white buds, with the texture of suede, that unfurl to become immense white chalices. The scent is sharply sweet and bracing, like lemonade on a warm summer afternoon. This gigantic magnolia blooms heavily almost to midsummer, then sporadically until autumn, when the large conelike fruits open to reveal glossy and fleshy scarlet seeds imbued with a powerful and sensuous perfume like bay rum. The whites of spring are the prelude, the white flowers of this magnolia the finale in this symphony of the purest color that gardens can offer.

The white-flowering woody plants in my own garden got there by the accumulation of accidents. Acquired individually, each on its own merit, they simply add up to a late spring blizzard of snowy and frosty tones. But what can be done by accident may also be done by deliberation. Many other good whites might be added. Among woody plants, for example, *Cercis reniformis* 'Texas White', *Chionanthus retusus*, *Deutzia gracilis* 'Nikko', *Halesia tetraptera*, and *Styrax japonicum* 'Carillon' all might join the ensemble, each blooming according to its place in the season from midspring to earliest summer. So might white peonies: the lovely hybrid 'Late Windflower', bred in the 1950s by Professor A. J. Saunders of Hamilton College in Clinton, New York, comes to mind for its small single white flowers that are borne three or more to the stem.

I could also wish for 'Mint Frills', one of the cultivars of *Stewartia pseudocamellia* that Polly Hill grew from seed in her garden on Martha's Vineyard and then introduced. Growing to thirty feet or more at maturity, it flowers exuberantly in mid-June, producing masses of large white flowers with five overlapping, spoonlike petals that have fringed edges and light washes of pale green. But I should have planted it many years ago, as it is very slow to start blooming.

Americans sometimes falsely believe the monochromatic garden was invented by Vita Sackville-West, whose white garden at Sissinghurst Castle has achieved international renown. The truth is that we had white gardens long before the mistress of Sissinghurst ever put spade to its earth; in *Old-Time Gardens* (1901), Alice Morse Earle fondly remembered the white gardens of her childhood in Massachusetts.

Given the small size of most American gardens today, a monochromatic planting, white or any other color, seems wasteful of
opportunities to explore the rest of the spectrum. But there is no reason that part of one season might not be given over to a limited
palette. Late spring and white make unusually amiable companions
for such an experiment with time and color.

❧ Old Roses and English Roses

WHEN PLANTS that have never been in garden centers before suddenly show up there it's a sure sign that something really devoted
gardeners have been keeping their eyes on for a while is about to
percolate out into the general population. I've just seen such a por-
tent in the potted rose section of one of our local garden centers.
There, among the familiar hybrid teas such as 'Mr. Lincoln' and
'Peace', I spotted two newcomers — 'Madame Hardy' and 'Graham
Thomas'.

Between them, in different ways, these roses represent two re
cent trends in the world of roses, both of them departures from the
hybrid teas that have been commercially dominant for most of this
century. One trend is the return to the old shrub roses of nineteenth-century gardens. The other is the successful efforts of David
Austin to breed what he calls, for lack of a better term, "English
roses" — roses that combine the best characteristics of hybrid teas,
such as a long season of bloom and a wide range of flower color,
with the best traits of the old shrub roses, including fragrance and
resistance to disease.

'Madame Hardy' is an old rose, dating back to 1832 and named
for the wife of the Empress Josephine's head gardener at Malmaison, her estate outside Paris. The current interest in it is but one
example of the rediscovery of old roses. The Gallicas and the
Damasks and the Centifolias go back, in some cases, to Bronze Age
Crete. The Bourbons and the Noisettes and some other classes of
rose were hybridized in the nineteenth century, for the most part
in France, as crosses between European species and forms of *Rosa*

chinensis collected in the Orient by western plant explorers at the very end of the eighteenth century.

Around 1870 'La France', the first hybrid tea rose, introduced a change of taste, a preference for high-pointed buds and sleek flowers, rather than the buxom forms that delighted the Empress Josephine and other early-nineteenth-century gardeners. The old roses were shoved aside, but now they are enjoying a resurgence.

Old roses have their presumed faults: a color range that extends mostly from blush to pink to magenta—no great distance—and a season of bloom that ends and begins in June. But is their brief prodigality of bloom a true fault? No one despises the dogwood for not being in perpetual flower. Furthermore, the old-timers often are as handsome in the fall for their red or orange hips as for their flowers in early summer. Many of them possess a heady fragrance that has been inadvertently bred out of most hybrid teas. And old roses like 'Souvenir de la Malmaison', 'Reine des Violettes', and 'Belle de Crécy' are often so free of pests and diseases as to make any gardener with even a streak of laziness conclude that hybrid teas are not worth the effort. (The ailments of the hybrid teas are many—black spot, mildew, mottling—and their prevention and cure require a veritable chemical arsenal, including such substances as carboryl, nicotine sulfate, zineb, and benomyl.)

That 'Graham Thomas' rose spotted at my garden center this past spring is another cup of tea altogether from 'Madame Hardy'. Named for Graham Stuart Thomas, one of the greatest British horticulturists of the twentieth century, it bears luxurious and opulent flowers in a rich yellow (a color virtually unknown in nineteenth-century roses). Its fragrance is heady, and it thrives in both England's cool summers and America's torrid ones. It represents the best efforts of David Austin's breeding program to cross modern hybrid teas back to the sturdy, highly fragrant shrub roses of an earlier time. 'Perdita', 'The Wife of Bath', 'Windrush', 'Mary Rose', 'Gertrude Jekyll'—all of these and many others from Austin display full-blown, voluptuous, and sumptuous flowers reminiscent of the roses painted by Pierre-Joseph Redouté after 1817, but they bloom over a season lasting to late fall in a range of colors embracing soft yellow, glowing apricot-gold, and other tones deriving from hybrid teas and unknown in Redouté's day.

Perhaps the day of the hybrid tea is over: the day of roses with tipsy names like 'Brandy', 'Glenfiddich', 'White Lightning', and 'Whiskey Mac'; celebrity-named roses like 'Judy Garland', 'Cary Grant', 'Princess of Monaco', and 'Dolly Parton'; and Disney namesakes like 'Bambi', 'Jiminy Cricket', 'Hi-Ho', and 'Pinocchio'. Perhaps in a decade all American rose lovers will be growing 'Belle de Crécy' and 'Graham Thomas' instead. But perhaps not. The battle has just begun in the aisles of garden centers. Fashion is fickle, and it may be that some gardeners will not want to give up those high-pointed buds of the teas. Florist shops are almost sure to be holdouts in continuing to offer 'American Beauty' to their customers, even though the rose of that name no longer exists. To a florist, any dark red hybrid tea qualifies as an 'American Beauty'.

❀ Oxalis

CHANCES ARE that you're growing one or more species of *Oxalis* in your garden, whether you want to or not. This geographically widespread genus of herbaceous plants contains over 800 species, some of them notorious weeds that typically reproduce by both seeds and underground tubers or bulbs. They seed prolifically, and because their underground structures remain behind in the earth when they are yanked up from above, they have all the tenacity of nut-grass sedge. Most species, whether weedy or ornamental, are not winter-hardy. Gardeners who live where winters are prolonged and cold may not ever experience the pain of trying to extirpate the species *corymbosa, exilis, latifolia,* and *pes-caprae* (the beautiful but insidious Bermuda buttercup), but they're bound to have struggled with the ubiquitous O. *corniculata,* which is winter-hardy through Zone 5. A perennial with tiny, shamrock-like leaves and small yellow flowers, this weed is a low creeper in full sun. If it is shaded by other plants, it can extend itself to a considerable height to carry on photosynthesis and its reproductive agenda.

Fortunately, there's more to say about oxalis than these complaints about the weedy ones. A few species are highly desirable garden plants, more are easy and handsome house or greenhouse plants, and at least one that evolved in the New World has promise as a food plant that could rival maize or potatoes.

The genus *Oxalis* is cosmopolitan in distribution, with species native to the Americas, South Africa, East Asia, Australia, and New Zealand. Some species are indigenous to the tropics, others to the temperate zones. Linnaeus took the name for the genus from the Greek *oxys*, meaning "sour"; the same Greek word gives us *Oxydendron*, the native American sourwood tree. For anyone who has ever chewed oxalis leaves, the generic name seems inevitable; they contain small amounts of oxalic acid, for a pleasantly sour taste, much like that of sorrel, whose leaves are chemically similar. The effect is pleasant, but to be enjoyed only in moderation, as oxalic acid interferes with the retention of dietary calcium.

Two of our native oxalis are among America's most beautiful wildflowers. One, the violet wood sorrel (*O. violacea*) is common in grassy areas and woodland fringes from the eastern United States westward to North Dakota. The white or violet, half-inch flowers, with the buttercup form characteristic of all oxalis, are borne in clusters in late spring and early summer. Another species, the Oregon wood sorrel (*O. oregana*), may be suitably cultivated in gardens as a groundcover for its attractive foliage and its white or red-and-white candy-striped flowers.

For garden use the hardiest, easiest, and most common oxalis is *O. adenophylla*, a bulbous species from Chile and Argentina that is winter-hardy through Zone 5. In the wild its color is variable, but commercially grown bulbs, which are easily and inexpensively available through most mail-order bulb companies, are generally pink. Another pink-flowered oxalis is uncommonly found commercially, but is one of the staples of old-fashioned gardens in the southern states, where it is commonly passed on from one gardener to another. Its name is sometimes given as *O. crassipes*, but it's more probably—the authorities disagree, as sometimes happens—*O. rubra*. Whatever it is, it's a winsome thing, clump-forming and often used to line sidewalks or flower beds. It can throw up the occasional flower in late winter, then bloom profusely in spring. With the advent of summer heat, it languishes toward dormancy. A good shearing back in July will bring forth fresh new leaves in August and a second crop of flowers in early fall.

Gardeners who appreciate a challenge and want to experiment with unusual species of oxalis could try some of the South African species, such as O. *hirta* (pink flowers, yellow throat), O. *lobata* (bright yellow flowers), and O. *purpurascens* (large, pale purple flowers). These all require special care.

Tropical species of oxalis often turn up, usually sans botanical name, in grocery stores as houseplants. One that I found this way is O. *corymbosa* 'Aureo-Reticulata'. It is notable for pink flowers in spring and fetching foliage netted with gold stripes throughout the year, except during its period of summer dormancy. I also added to my houseplant collections O. *regnellii* 'Atropurpurea', which has pale lilac flowers and handsome, dusky, triangular foliage of gorgeous glowing purple.

Oxalis deppei, commonly called the iron cross plant because of its leaf markings, has a place in our house as well. In Great Britain there is some interest in O. *deppei* (syn. O. *tetraphylla*) as a plant whose leaves give a tang to salads. But remember that oxalic acid is to be consumed only lightly, if at all. The bulbous roots can also be boiled and eaten, although they are said to be not especially tasty. One form of this large-leafed species has gorgeous purple foliage that neatly complements the constant crop of pale pink flowers.

The edibility of this species is inconsiderable in comparison with the Andean species O. *tuberosa*, one of several tuberous plants that have long been an important source of carbohydrates and other nutrients in the part of the world where they evolved. When the first Spaniards reached the Andes, they discovered that under difficult agricultural conditions (steep terrain, often heavy rainfall, and harsh alternations between stifling daytime heat and cold, windy nights), traditional farmers managed to thrive on foods unknown to Europeans. One was the potato, almost in its wild state, with a great degree of the genetic diversity that is so important in protecting staple domesticated food crops from disease and insect predation. Another was a species of nasturtium (*Tropaeolum*). Another, and by no means the least important, was O. *tuberosa* — oca.

The potato and oca were both grown in Europe soon after their discovery in the New World. It took the potato a couple of centuries to catch on as a staple food crop. Like the semidomesticated potato of the Andes and unlike the potatoes familiar to us from grocery stores, oca shows tremendous genetic variation and adaptability to a wide range of soils and growing conditions. Its large crop of tubers may be red, pink, white, or green. Varieties with high amounts of oxalic acid are cooked, to remove the acid. Varieties low in acid are eaten raw.

At one time, oca was occasionally grown in England as an alternative to potatoes, but the potato pushed oca aside. Today, however, there is worldwide scientific interest in the potential of O. *tuberosa* as a staple food crop. Fairly successful efforts are reported in marketing it thus in New Zealand (although it is described there as a yam, to overcome humanity's natural tendency to avoid new foods). Oca has also been freeze-dried and ground into a powder as a reasonable substitute for wheat flour.

Out of all the potentially nutritious plants found on this earth, we feed ourselves on only a handful. It is interesting to think that the oxalis leaves we nibbled as children for their sharp, tangy flavor may have been our introduction to the genus *Oxalis* as an important source of food for people far beyond South America, where oca was first brought into cultivation.

II Summer Annuals
and Perennials

❧ Marigolds

ABOUT MARIGOLDS, there is some confusion. Say their name to most people and they will be sure that they know what you're talking about—the brassy, double-flowered summer annuals with strong-smelling foliage sold by the billions every spring. They bloom all summer and are among the most popular of all garden plants.

The confusion starts with their common name. It derives from their traditional association with the Virgin Mary, but these heat-loving annuals, derived from several species of *Tagetes* native to the Americas, are not the first plants to bear this name; it also refers to the European flowering herb *Calendula officinalis*, which is a different beast altogether. The calendula thrives in cool weather and languishes when the temperature begins to crank up as summer comes on. The marigolds of summer, contrariwise, like it hot. Distinguishing between these two kinds of marigold is especially important for people who like the idea of edible flowers. The herbal literature of an earlier day abounds in recipes for marigold pudding and other tasty repasts, but the marigold used in these recipes is actually a calendula. Trying to cook with the wrong marigold leads to a truly ghastly dining experience. (I have heard chefs on television cooking shows mistake *Tagetes* for *Calendula*, unfortunately.)

Even if there were no ambiguity in the name marigold—even if it applied only to cultivars of *Tagetes*—seed catalogs sometimes further confuse the terminology by dividing marigolds into two categories: African and French. There is nothing either African or French about any marigolds. The so-called African ones tend to produce large flowers on tall plants and are derived from *T. erecta*, a species native to Mexico and Central America. The French ones, with smaller flowers on more compact plants, come from *T. patula*, which has a more restricted range, extending from southern Mexico into parts of Guatemala.

How did Africa and France get into the marigold picture? As Claire Shaver Haughton tells it in *Green Immigrants: The Plants That Transformed America* (1978), in 1520 the Spanish priests who had accompanied the conquistadors to Mexico brought seeds of

Tagetes erecta back to their homeland monasteries, from whence they rapidly spread to other monasteries in North Africa and France. By 1535, when Charles V mounted a military expedition against the Moors of Algeria and Tunis, marigolds had already escaped from monastery gardens into the North African landscape. Charles thought they were indigenous there and brought them back to Europe under the name "African flowers," and the name stuck. As for the supposed French connection, *Tagetes patula* was grown in gardens in Paris for some time before it entered England, and English gardeners and herbalists mistakenly thought that it had originated in France.

Some decades ago, Senator Everett Dirksen and David Burpee of the Burpee Seed Company mounted a campaign to make the marigold our national flower. The effort failed. Congress eventually bestowed that honor on the rose. I am of the opinion that it should have been the yucca but suspect that the marigold might have succeeded in coming to symbolize our nation, had it not been for labeling some marigolds as French and others as African. (The Burpee catalog now speaks of American marigolds instead of French.)

I have never been especially fond of most marigolds, although I used to like them better than I do now. My taste has not changed but marigolds have. When I was a lad, the ones labeled "African" used to be sizable plants. A package of seed would yield an entire row of plants for the cutting garden—plants so tall you almost had to look up at them. Their long stems made them highly suitable for bouquets. Then the hybridizers set to work, diminishing the stature of the marigold, meanwhile increasing the size of its blossoms. The result is grotesquely out of scale. The plants look as if they were made in a factory.

The marigold has some economic uses. A feed meal made from its dried flowers is used by poultry farmers to enhance the color of egg yolks and chicken sold in grocery stores. Shrimp farmers use the same stuff to make uncooked shrimp look brighter. Some tobacco manufacturers add oil of marigold to cigarettes, but I'm not sure why.

I like some marigolds better than others, and I'm keen on several. First, there are several hybrid cultivars of *T. tenuifolia*, the signet marigold from Mexico. These are easily grown from seed in several strains that come true to color, such as Lemon Gem and Tangerine Gem. They bloom prolifically, but their tiny single flowers are in scale with the small plants. Their foliage is attractively feathery or ferny and has a delightful, surprising lemony scent.

I also am high on *T. lucida*, the Mexican mint marigold, a tender perennial that sometimes survives the winter. It has attractive, licorice-scented foliage. Small, single, yellow flowers appear at summer's end on eighteen-inch plants.

One year a friend gave me plants of the South American species, *T. minuta*. From the name I suspected it was dwarf in stature, but the thing just grew and grew, until it became a narrow column of green at least twelve feet tall, maybe more. It never bloomed, but I later learned that the species name refers to the size of the flowers, not the height of the plant. I haven't grown it a second time, for it's not at all ornamental (though it is decidedly a conversation piece). In South America, however, its leaves have been used as a beverage, a medicinal tea, and a culinary herb since Pre-Columbian times. It, not *T. erecta*, is the source of the oil of marigold that is sometimes used as an additive to tobacco as well as to certain beverages, candies, and relishes. The dried leaves of *T. minuta* are used in folk medicine in parts of the world, and scientific research is taking place today to determine exactly what the medical properties of the plant might be in preventing or curing certain diseases.

❦ Flowers of Achilles

THE YARROW, the genus *Achillea*, embraces some eighty-five species of herbaceous plants native to Europe eastward to the Ukraine and Siberia. One species, A. *millefolium*, has escaped from North American gardens into the larger landscape to become so prevalent throughout most of the United States that it is often considered to be a native wildflower. Several species, A. *clypeolata*, A. *filipendula*, and A. *ptarmica*, as well as A. *millefolium*, would deserve a place in the perennial border just as they occur in nature, except that extensive hybridization and selection have resulted in cultivars of obvious superiority.

The two best known of these are 'Coronation Gold' and 'Moonshine'. Some yarrows get beaten to earth in wind and rain, but these stay solidly erect without staking. 'Coronation Gold' is a hybrid between A. *filipendula* and A. *clypeolatum*, 'Moonshine' of A. *clypeolatum* and the cultivar 'Taygetea', from which it derives the silvery gray of its ferny leaves and their downy texture. Its flowers are a softer and less brash shade of yellow than 'Coronation Gold'. The two plants combine exceptionally well with one another, but other yellow and gold cultivars are worth seeking out, including 'Cloth of Gold', 'Gold Plate', 'Sonnengold', and 'Schwefelblüte'.

The latter two names (respectively translated as 'Sun Gold' and 'Flowers of Sulphur') show that hybridizers in Germany have taken a special interest in achilleas. 'Sonnengold' and 'Schwefelblüte' are both hybrids of A. *filipendula* and A. *ptarmica*, but German breeders have not overlooked A. *millefolium* either. Crossing it with mostly 'Taygetea', the hybridizer Heinze Klose of Stuttgart has produced several cultivars, known collectively as the Galaxy series, that move away from the yellow end of the spectrum toward pink and red. 'Apfelblüte' is dark rose, 'Lachsschönheit' is orange-pink. Cultivar names are not supposed to be changed to appeal to the native tongues of gardeners, but it's not surprising that English and American nursery catalogs list these two as 'Apple Blossom' and 'Salmon Beauty'. They also jazz up 'Hoffnung', not translating it simply as 'Hope' but giving it a nudge in the direction of Charles Dickens, with 'Great Expectations'. There are other Galaxy cultivars, like 'Paprika' and 'Red Beauty'. They all are superior in their sturdy, upright habit to earlier hybrids of A. *millefolium*, which often had weak stems and floppy ways.

Achilleas are rich in their associations with mythology, folk medicine, and superstition. The genus takes its name from the Greek hero Achilles, to whom is attributed the discovery of the healing properties of these plants. According to Dioscorides, Achilles gave his soldiers poultices of yarrow leaves to stop the flow of blood from their wounds and help them heal. Centuries later, European medicine still held yarrow in high esteem for a number of ailments.

John Gerard wrote in *The Herball* (1633) that "the leaves of yarrow doe close up wounds, and keepe them from inflammation or fiery swelling." He recommended them also as "a remedy for the tooth-ache" and asserted that "the leaves being put into the nose, do cause it to bleed, and ease the paine of the megrim." Gerard also, some-what mysteriously, recommended yarrow in matters "spermaticke." "This hath been prooved," he averred, "by a certain friend off mine, sometimes a Fellow of Kings Colledge in Cambridge, who lightly brused the leaves of common Yarrow, with Hogs-grease, and applied it warme unto the privie parts, and thereby did divers times help himselfe, and others of his fellowes, when he was a student and a single man living in Cambridge."

Some of the common names yarrow has accumulated testify to its supposed medical properties—all-heal, soldier's woundwort, nose bleed, bloodwort, and staunchweed. (It also has a variety of nonmedical names, including calico border plant, devil's plaything, thousand-leafed clover, old man's pepper, seven years' love, sweet maudlin, carpenter's grass, and bastard pellitory.)

In the Western world, most plant lore, except maybe a lingering belief that four-leaf clovers bring good luck, has died out, but at one time in England achillea had magical powers. If a young woman wanted to know whom she would marry, she should wrap yarrow leaves in flannel and sleep with it under her pillow. In one version of this procedure, she would dream of the man who was to be her husband. In another, she was destined to wed the first man she saw the next day. (Presumably, fathers and brothers didn't count.)

Yarrow has played an important role in Chinese culture as well as Western. Cast on the ground, its dried stems were held to sym-bolize hexagrams that would then be interpreted by the I Ching. In traditional Chinese herbal medicine, *A. siberica* is used for ulcers and abscesses, snakebites and nasty falls, as well as to soothe stomachaches and painful menstruation. The Chinese may be onto something, as perhaps Achilles and John Gerard were also, for yarrows are loaded with volatile oils like eucalyptol, also such spe-cific lactones as achilleic acid and achillene. (These chemicals give the foliage a bitter flavor that may account for it not being very sus-ceptible to damage from deer.)

The flower clusters of yarrows, particularly of the yellow and gold cultivars, are shaped like half-domes, and the plants themselves have a mounded habit that begs for contrast from plants with a more steepling form, a more vertical profile. Kniphofias are splendid foils for them, also hollyhocks, plume poppies, and verbascums. Blue and purple larkspur with yarrows is a beautiful marriage. Yarrows also indirectly bring motion into the garden, for they attract many species of butterfly. They bring a little music with them as well, since from dawn to dusk they are constantly visited by bees.

❦ Daylilies Are Indispensable

EVER SINCE THE 1920s, when Dr. Arlow B. Stout of the New York Botanical Garden began his breeding program with daylilies, hundreds upon hundreds of hybridizers have spread megatons of pollen to improve the several species of *Hemerocallis*. The work of these hybridizers is one of the great success stories of twentieth-century horticulture, for daylilies are now the backbone of the summer perennial garden. Their range of colors extends far beyond their original yellow and orange to include deep purples, glowing reds, soft melons, pale ivories. By balancing early and late cultivars with the more common midseason ones, gardens can be bright with daylilies for over two months of bloom.

Visitors to my garden at daylily time usually head for the bold cultivars such as 'Ruffled Apricot' and 'Pride's Crossing', but my favorites are increasingly diminutive—the ones the American Hemerocallis Society designates as "miniature," meaning that their blossoms measure under three inches across, or "small-flowered," meaning that they range from three to four and a half inches. Calling daylilies miniature or small-flowered says nothing about the height of their flower stalks. They may be only ten inches high or may tower over four feet. These variations in height and size of flower, combined with the wide range of flower color, assure that perennial borders dominated by daylilies will escape monotony.

All daylilies appreciate fertile soil that is rich in organic matter and like a good drenching once a week in time of drought, but they can survive in poorer soil with less moisture. They thrive in full sun or light shade. Every four or five years they should be divided, and the excess plants shared with neighbors or friends. Daylilies, great or small, can be planted at almost any time during the growing season—even moved in midsummer in full bloom with little harm except some slight bedragglement. Northern gardeners who want to plant them in the autumn should mulch them to prevent winter heaving, especially in areas where there's light snow cover or none at all. When selecting daylilies to grow in the colder regions of the country, keep in mind that those marked "evergreen" or "semi-evergreen" in nursery catalogs generally will not survive harsh winters; pick the ones that are described as dormant, usually abbreviated as "dor." Conversely, gardeners in Florida and other warm regions will want to go for the evergreens and semi-evergreens, for without a period of rest the dormant ones will weaken and decline, even die.

Nurseries specializing in daylilies generally give their flower sizes, making it not much of a chore to pick out the smaller ones. The names are sometimes a tip-off, however, as with 'Raspberry Pixie', 'Little Carnation', 'Bitsy', and 'Little Cherub'—all good ones. Some daylily names, incidentally, are a trifle embarrassing. One cultivar that is ideal for the rock garden—it grows only 16 inches high and is smothered with miniature golden blossoms for three weeks in mid-July—is afflicted with the name 'Little Bugger'. 'Little Wart' and 'Eenie-Weenie' don't sound very nice either, and the names of 'Little Joy' and 'Little Love' are disturbingly ambiguous. But considerable genius went into the naming of a truly excellent red called 'Pardon Me', words that suggest a common quality of many miniature and small-flowered daylilies—their quiet and polite insistence on being noticed once homage has been paid to their gargantuan kin.

True aficionados of daylilies will recognize from the names of the daylilies I grow that I am behind the times and am not growing the ones that currently excite members of the American Hemerocallis Society. They're right. Over 33,000 daylilies have been named and registered since the society was founded right after World War II. Thousands of cultivars are sold by specialized nurseries. Years ago I was faced with a decision—either turn my garden into a daylily patch, or throw out all the ones I was growing and start over. I decided to keep the ones I had and stop collecting, instituting a ten-year moratorium. Ten years are almost up. It's about time to dig into some daylily catalogs. I have some ideas about what I may end up with. A lot will have 'Siloam' in their names, for Pauline Henry of Siloam Springs, Arkansas, has introduced many small-flowered cultivars that honor her hometown. Pictures of 'Siloam David Kirchoff', 'Siloam June Bug', and some others look toothsome.

I may even rejoin the AHS and read its journals. I'll feel like Rip Van Winkle. Everything will have changed. Old names will have disappeared, and everyone will be praising cultivars whose names I haven't yet learned.

Gardeners who would like to grow some daylilies but haven't yet started may feel paralyzed by the thought of choosing from so many kinds, but the AHS offers genuine assistance. It has a list of over one hundred fifty display gardens all over the country, where people can see huge numbers of cultivars, then choose those they like. The society also gives out annual awards for the best plants in several categories—miniatures and small-flowered daylilies, daylilies with contrasting eye zones, and so on. Those that have won the yearly Stout Silver Medal are the cream of the crop. This award generally goes to cultivars about ten years after their introduction. Recent winners are apt to be fairly expensive, but older winners like 'Ruffled Apricot' (1982) and 'Ed Murray' (1981) are reasonably priced. Finally, those who suspect that a new passion has entered their life can join the AHS. Its published membership lists are likely to turn up folks who live just up the street or in the next town. A telephone call is usually all it takes to get an invitation to come garden-visiting at daylily time. As in visiting a display garden, you can see what you like and order it for yourself. But chances are that if you say you admire this daylily or that, you'll go home with it as a gift.

❧ The Feathery Plumes of Astilbes

IT WOULD BE TERRIBLE to look round the summer garden and discover that, as varied as its play of colors might be, there was little variation in plant habit and form—an outcome that is entirely possible. Many popular annuals and perennials (for example, hostas) tend to grow in mounds, little dumpling and gumdrop shapes. Anyone who takes even a quick look around my garden knows that my affection for hostas is unstinting, but I still recognize that every garden needs its vertical accents, its steeples and its spires, its plants that point toward the heavens and inspire us toward higher things. We should contrive never to be without thalictrums (meadow rues), especially *Thalictrum rochebrunnianum*, for its strong central stem, its graceful, columbine-like fans of blue-tinted foliage, and its sprays of pale blue and butter yellow flowers that go on for weeks and weeks in high summer. There always needs to be some yucca on the premises and—unless the garden is too small—some tall miscanthus grasses with their airy plumes. If the climate is suitable, as it really isn't in almost all of the United States, then some tall delphiniums are in order.

Then there are astilbes, virtually indispensable for any proper garden. Some astilbes, to be sure, don't aspire very far. *Astilbe chinensis* 'Pumila' throws in the towel at about ten inches high, but it is still valuable for the spreading habit that makes it a fine ground cover, for its late season of bloom, and for its ability to withstand more drought than other cultivars can tolerate. A. *simplicifolia* 'Sprite', which the Perennial Plant Association named as perennial of the year in 1994, is another low-growing species, but highly desirable for its rich pink flowers and its glossy, varnished-looking foliage. Most cultivars, however, lift their feathery plumes well above their leaves to a considerable altitude, and one, A. *tacquettii* 'Superba', can tower up to four or even five feet high, provided that it gets the heavy fertilization and copious moisture that all astilbes need to be at their best.

Every astilbe is built to a common blueprint—hundreds of tiny flowers in panicles that wave like feather dusters above deeply cut, almost ferny foliage. The color range is pretty much summed up as white, pink, and red. The blooming season is, alas, not very long. It can be puzzling to read in nursery catalogs that cultivars are divided into early, middle, and late varieties and then to discover that the main season of astilbes lasts about three weeks in all, with a lot of overlap in the blooming times of the various kinds. There is an explanation. Although a few species of astilbe are native to North

America, those that figure in our garden hybrids are native to cool regions of China and Japan. The hybrids were bred in northern Europe, including England, where cool summers encourage a prolonged season of bloom, over almost two months. In most of America, high summer heat and humidity arrive as early as the end of May, severely compressing the period of bloom. In my garden, almost all cultivars flower for about two weeks in late June, with A. chinensis 'Pumila' and A. tacquettii 'Superba' following in July.

Americans are accustomed to thinking of Great Britain as the fountainhead of superior garden perennials, not realizing that some of the most familiar and popular ones originated in Germany. Many were hybridized by the plantsman Georg Arends (1862–1952) at his small nursery in the village of Ronsdorf, a few miles from Cologne. He introduced many cultivars of bergenia, dianthus, silene, and other perennials, but his greatest program of plant breeding took place with astilbes, which he worked with from 1897 almost up to the day of his death.

Before he set hands to the task, all astilbes grown in European gardens were a rather dirty white. Arends used as the foundation of his breeding program two species recently collected in East Asia, A. chinensis, with soft rose flowers, and A. davidii, a late bloomer with tall spikes of intense rose-red. Arends later recalled in a memoir published shortly before his death that when the first seedlings bloomed in 1907, "it was very hard to select the best plants from such a wealth of material."

The modern astilbe had been born, but Arends continued his work for decades, interrupted by two world wars, incorporating other species as they became available to him at his nursery. A. japonica, A. grandis, A. thunbergii, A. simplicifolia—all contributed their genes. The final result was the introduction of some seventy-four cultivars. Forty of Arends's astilbes are still carried by European nurseries and about twenty are offered in this country. Recommended cultivars include 'Bridal Veil' and 'Deutschland' among the whites, 'Cattleya' and 'Rheinland' among the pinks, and 'Fanal' and 'Red Sentinel' among the reds.

Astilbes are invaluable for pumping color into partially shaded gardens. In the South they virtually insist on shade, but in cooler regions they may thrive in fairly full sun. They have two absolute requirements. One is an ample and constant supply of moisture (but with good drainage) at least until the end of their flowering season. The other is division every third year at least. Such regular division is a must, as I learned some years back. All the astilbes in my garden had gone five years without this necessary attention. The plants looked terrible—sparse bloom, gawky stems, and an untidy habit, sprawling over other plants and into paths. I decided to get rid of them altogether, rooted them up, and consigned them to the compost heap. Tiny pieces of astilbe roots, however, were left behind. The following year, I had more astilbes than ever, growing lustily, with admirable tidiness, and drenching the summer garden with sparkling white, luminescent pink, and flaming crimson. Fine and sturdy plants had grown from those little bits that had been left behind.

❧ The Hardy Mallows

THE KINSHIP AMONG SPECIES in some families of flowering plants is obvious to anyone who can tell a rose from a lily, but in other families the similarities are barely detectable except by botanists.

Many members of the Primrose or Primulaceae family look nothing like the primroses in our mental maps: I defy anyone to look at a couple of lysimachia—say *L. nummularia* (creeping Jenny) and *L. clethroides* (gooseneck)—and figure out that they share a family tree. But most, though not all, genera in the Compositae, to take an easy case, present no mystery: asters or daisies or sunflowers, their blossoms are all built to the same blueprint, even if goldenrods, on first and even second glance, are difficult to fit in the family.

The Mallow or Malvaceae tribe is another easy family. To the botanist, it is typified by generally bisexual flowers with a calyx of five sepals, sometimes joined at their bases, and with a corolla of five petals, often forming a tube before and sometimes after they open . . . and by other technical similarities. The flowers of members of the Malvaceae, in other words, all look a lot like those of the holly-hock (*Alcea rosea*), and even a small child can see the similarities.

Children, in fact, have long been associated with hollyhocks, although the origins of the name of the genus, which used to be *Althaea*, are a bit grisly, celebrating a highly dysfunctional family, we now might say. Althaea was an ancient Greek princess whose son, Meleager, killed his uncles in a dispute over the possession of the carcass of a boar. Lighting a torch, Althaea announced that he would perish once it went out. It went out. He died. Althaea killed herself with a dagger. But the English word "hollyhock" means "holy mallow," and in medieval times the flower was a symbol of salvation and held to be a sure cure for snakebites.

But children know nothing of this mythology, theology, and folk medicine, and despite the inroads of Saturday morning TV, some kids still make dolls out of hollyhocks. The open flowers resemble long skirts, and the buds pass for heads in hats.

Gardeners who want hollyhocks today are in for a pretty bad time of it. Seed companies offer mostly the double or powderpuff flowers they fancy, although many folks much prefer the more elegant single flowers once common. Other gardeners who have them are the best source of their seeds, which germinate easily in late summer and bloom the next year. It is wise to propagate them anew each year, in fact, as this practice somewhat reduces the distressing and disfiguring rust disease that tends to afflict hollyhocks. If you see hollyhocks you like in someone else's garden, beg for some seeds when they ripen. That's how I got two forms I especially treasure, one with black single flowers, the other with pale yellow ones.

The Mallow family is a large one, comprising among others the following genera of plants both herbaceous and woody, both annual and perennial: *Abelmoschus* (okra, whose pods are reputed by some to be suitable for eating), *Abutilon* (a favorite houseplant in Victorian times), *Callirhoë*, *Gossypium* (cotton), *Hibiscus*, *Lavatera*, *Malva*, *Malvaviscus*, and *Sidalcea*.

All of these genera have species of ornamental value. *Abelmoschus esculenta*, the okra of disputable culinary worth, is pretty for its large yellow flowers with black-red eyes. Its elongated fibrous seedpods are splendid for winter bouquets of dried materials. A.

manihot, a tropical perennial that can be treated as an annual in colder climates, has similar flowers, large and buttery yellow and followed by large, hairy seedpods that are uncommonly handsome when glistening with dew on a crisp day in midautumn. Where it is happy, it will volunteer dependably from year to year, although self-sown seeds do not germinate and spurt into their rapid growth until truly hot weather arrives. It is especially fetching in early October, when flowers and seedpods are often both in evidence.

Callirhoë involucrata, the wine cup or poppy mallow, has not received as much attention from gardeners as it should. Oddly taking its genus name from the daughter of an ancient Greek river-god, although it is native to the dry plains of the American Southwest, it bears flowers that are . . . well, let's say it, magenta—the color that Louise Beebe Wilder once described as "maligned" by people who thought that knocking it testified to their own impeccable taste. But perhaps, on second thought, the color has too much red in it to be truly magenta. Its blossoms are about the size of a jigger and have a delicate silken texture. The plant looks sensational in combination with red-violet forms of *Verbena canadensis* and geranium 'Ann Folkard'. Their flower colors are similar, and they grow together and weave among one another in a pleasantly tipsy way.

Hibiscus I shall pass over quickly here. The kinds I really like, *H. rosa-sinensis* and *H. acetosella*, are tropical plants, best discussed elsewhere, and two of the hardy species, the shrub *H. syriacus* and the perennial swamp mallow *H. moscheutos*, are not plants I much care for. The former is so late to leaf out in the spring that it looks dead eight months of the year. It also is a relentless, prolific self-seeder. Seedlings germinate everywhere, establish quickly, and are a pain to weed. The plant is also subject to spider mite in late summer, and the flowers close up forever toward evening. As for the American rose mallow or swamp mallow, *Hibiscus moscheutos*, it has been crossed with other species to produce strains that cavort around with names like the widely sold Dixie Belle. (Think of Scarlett O'Hara played by Dolly Parton, not Vivien Leigh, and you have it.)

There are other mallows of garden merit, in the genera *Malva*, *Sidalcea*, and others. Cotton, for one, is handsome, first in flower and then in fruit, in autumn when its fat bolls open to reveal their crop of seeds enshrouded in glistening white fiber. But here I will round out my praise of the Malvaceae with the lavateras, two of them.

Lavatera trimestris is an easily grown annual, but you must raise it yourself from seed, as you will seldom find the plant growing in garden-center market packs. It is entirely worth the effort. Seed companies offer three strains. Mont Blanc is pure white, and (no surprises here) Mont Rose is deep pink. But—you figure it—Silver Cup is pink. All three form tidy, two-foot mounds covered with a prolific crop of flowers all summer long and well into autumn.

Then there's the vegetatively propagated cultivar of the tree mallow, *L. thuringiaca*, called 'Barnsley', after Barnsley House in England, where Rosemary Verey lives and gardens and where the plant originated. A shrubby perennial with decidedly woody characteristics, it looks tender, but it has now gotten through several winters for me, dying back considerably, but still returning in the spring. I believe it to be root-hardy, perhaps into Zone 6. That's good news, for this large, very rangy plant is a delight. Its foliage is gray-green and felted, and at summer's height it simply covers itself with medium-sized flowers that open white with a red eye and then fade to pink. It's a real winner.

❦ Lilies

LILIES have loomed larger in the human imagination for a greater stretch of history than any other flower, except the rose. One species, the Madonna lily (*Lilium candidum*), is depicted in frescoes in Crete dating back to about 1500 B.C. Its flowers are a dazzling white. An ancient Greek tradition holds that this lily originated when a few drops of Hera's milk were spilled while she was asleep and suckling the infant Hercules. Hera didn't know she was breastfeeding the child, which Zeus had fathered with Alcmene, a mortal woman, and brought to Hera as she slept. Hercules bit her, waking her violently. The milk that fell in heaven turned into the Milky Way, while that which fell to earth sprang up as milk-white lilies.

Christians were quick to adopt *L. candidum* as their own, giving
it a range of meanings extending from the virtue of chastity to the
toil-free life of Adam and Eve before they were driven out of Eden
for disobedience. But the Madonna lily, as its common name suggests, was preeminently the symbol of the Virgin Mary. If represented amidst thorns, it betokened the Immaculate Conception,
whereby she was freed from original sin. Paintings of the Annuncia-
tion often show the archangel Gabriel presenting white lilies to
Mary, as he proclaims that she will give birth to a Savior, while yet
remaining a virgin. In some paintings there are three lilies in a vase
indicating that she was a virgin before, during, and after bearing
Christ. And depictions of her death and assumption into Heaven
sometimes represented her as being greeted by throngs of angels and
martyrs bearing lilies and red roses.

I like to think that the Madonna lilies I grow, which cease
blooming in mid-June and then go dormant until new rosettes of
leaves appear in fall, bring some ancient testimony to my garden,
linking it with the history of human religion, with Hera and Hercules, as well as with Mary and Christ. But Madonna lilies only initiate a long parade of lilies, blooming in succession from early summer until late August—and most of the lilies in my garden span
geography rather than long stretches of time into the distant past.

There are lilies native to North America as well as Europe, but
Asia is the treasure trove of the lily world. British and European
plant explorers began collecting species in China, Japan, Korea, and
Tibet early in the nineteenth century. One of the most spectacular
of these, *L. auratum*, was introduced at a Royal Horticultural Society flower show in 1862 by the British firm James Veitch and Company, creating a great sensation among English gardeners for its
huge, bowl-shaped flowers with gold stripes coursing up each petal
and numerous spots of crimson and gold.

During the following four decades, hundreds of thousands of
these bulbs were collected from Japanese hillsides and woodland
fringes and shipped to the West. These proved difficult in cultivation and extremely susceptible to rot and viral diseases, but others
were easy. One that is worth not only mentioning but also growing
is *L. formosanum*, which was first found in Taiwan in 1858. It was
introduced in England in 1881, again by James Veitch. Similar in

form to the tender Easter lily (*L. longifolium*), it blooms in late summer, producing clusters of fragrant white trumpet flowers borne on stems to six feet or higher. Since it is highly tolerant of summer heat and humidity, it is in considerable favor today among gardeners in the South. Those who favor growing lilies in masses and having plenty for cut flowers can delight in the Formosa lily's generosity in blooming from seed in its first year. Those who are weary of envying British gardeners for the plants they can grow that we cannot will take an evil pleasure in knowing that this lily doesn't just tolerate summer heat but insists on it. Where summers are cool, it rots away entirely in the fall.

Another easy East Asian lily that can be grown from seed is *L. regale*, the regal lily—which almost cost its celebrated collector, Ernest H. Wilson, his life. In 1903 Wilson discovered regal lilies growing in the rocky, sun-baked crevices of the Min Valley, a habitat notable for intense cold in winter, stupefying heat in summer, and sudden, violent thunderstorms in all seasons. Wilson collected a few bulbs for Veitch. In 1910 he returned to the Min Valley to collect 6,000 bulbs for the Arnold Arboretum, breaking his leg and narrowly escaping death in a landslide on a dangerous mountain path. His accident left him with what he called his "lily limp" the rest of his life.

Decades earlier, gardeners who were not content with the rich numbers of lily species that nature provided began to create hybrids of two or more species. The first hybrid of record was bred in 1830 by an Englishman named Henry Groom, who crossed two Asian species, *L. dauricum* and *L. bulbiferum,* to produce a group of cultivated varieties. They were grown in the United States by Charles Mason Hovey, a nurseryman in Boston, who soon began his own breeding program, crossing Groom's hybrids with the Japanese species, *L. speciosum.* The evolution of modern garden lilies of extraordinarily complicated genetic ancestry was under way, in a process that continues today, when new cultivars are introduced to the market each year.

Garden lilies fall into three main groups. First to bloom, just as Madonna lilies cease, are the Asiatic hybrids. All by themselves, these are wonderfully diverse mainstays of the early summer garden.

Some start blooming in mid-June, others in mid-July, so their season is long. Some bear open, slightly flattened blossoms, others are cupped, and still others have petals that are strongly reflexed or swept back. The flowers of some are nodding and pendant, so that to look them in the face it may be necessary to kneel. Others face outward, and the rest face upward. The range of color is huge—white, yellow, orange, red, lavender, and winey purple are just a few colors to choose from. Some are spotted with brownish-purple for a freckled look, while others have clear complexions. The names of the Asiatic hybrids are legion—'Connecticut King', 'Festival', 'Red Velvet', and many more, including the popular 1950s' introduction, 'Enchantment'—but I've never seen one I didn't like, and in fact, the unnamed seedlings (hybridizers' rejects) that are sold as mixtures by several mail-order nurseries can furnish a garden with an abundance of lilies at very little cost. Something else recommends these mixes, too. Of the three groups, the Asiatics are the most impermanent. Some last only a year or two before the bulbs break down into smaller, nonblooming bulblets that eventually disappear.

In late July the second group of lilies, the Aurelian hybrids, begin. These are tall plants, typically bearing large trumpet-shaped flowers in a somewhat narrower range of color than the Asiatics. The strains Moonlight, Pink Perfection, Copper King, and Black Dragon are widely sold by many nurseries. The Aurelians are irresistible to hummingbirds, who often add their vibrant color and their darting movement to a garden where they are planted. They are, happily, far more permanent than the Asiatics.

The lily season reaches its climax in August, with the group known as the Oriental hybrids, largely derived from crosses among several Japanese species, including L. auratum and L. rubellum. A few are pure in color, all white or all pink, but most of them are like floral tapestries, mixing red, white, yellow, and pink in every imaginable combination of two or more colors. The Orientals often bear strange raised markings called papillae on their waxy and elegant petals. Even at night, when they cannot be seen, these lilies make their presence known by a fragrance matched in its powerful sweetness only by gardenias and southern magnolias. My favorite lily (and one of my favorite summer plants) is the Oriental hybrid

'Casablanca'—a huge and hugely fragrant pure white. It has returned in my garden for over ten years, so it's tough.

All lilies have some things in common. Most are easy to grow, provided that they are given good drainage and moisture. They also take up very little room in a garden, considering the great show they make there. They perform best when the ground is covered with other plants, such as vinca or other low-growing perennials. They thus provide a tiered look to plantings that otherwise might be dull and uninspiring. And they may bring over the years many a surprise, in the form of seedlings cropping up in unexpected places. They may also bring another surprise—disappearance. The culprits are voles.

Oriental lily

❧ Gloriosa Daisies

THE ASSOCIATION OF DAISIES with the enormous family of the Compositae is extremely strong, although not absolute. No one would call the flowers of the composites *Baccharis* and *Solidago* daisies, and the flowers of some plants in other families are somewhat daisy-like, as in the case of *Delosperma cooperi*, a hardy ice plant from South Africa with purple blossoms, which belongs to the Aizoaceae or carpetweed family. Nevertheless, if a flower has a circle of "petals" (actually ray flowers) surrounding a central boss or cone (disk flowers), the chances are that it truly qualifies to be called a daisy. They may be botanically complex, but daisies seem simple flowers, as ordinary and as essential to the good life as bread and wine. They are flowers of exceeding good cheer. Indeed, how could they not be, considering that their common name goes back to Anglo-Saxon and breaks down to mean "day's eye"? They loom large in our affections, for from childhood on we know that they have the power to tell us whether our loves reciprocate our affection or reject it. *Aster, Chrysanthemum, Erigeron, Helianthus, Ratibida* — the names of the daisy tribe as they are found in nature are legion. It would take a page just to list the most familiar genera, omitting the much greater number of obscure ones.

One of the most cheering and giving of all daisies, however, is a human creation, at least in part. It derives from *Rudbeckia hirta*, the black-eyed Susan that spread from its native Midwest in shipments of hay back to the Northeast in the nineteenth century. But shortly after World War II, Professor Alfred Francis Blakeslee, a world-renowned expert on the genus *Datura* and director of the Genetics Experiment Station at Smith College in Massachusetts, took the black-eyed Susan in hand. In his attempt to remake this common wildflower into something grand and elegant, he was as determined as Henry Higgins was with Eliza Doolittle. Using colchicine, a carcinogenic substance derived from the autumn-blooming bulb *Colchicum*, Blakeslee assaulted germinating seedlings of *Rudbeckia hirta*. Hundreds of thousands of them died on the spot, but a few survived. A tiny number of these emerged with double their usual

number of chromosomes. They had changed from diploids to tetraploids.

Human beings are often a bit too proud of the results of
their tampering with the natural order, too quick to claim that
the hybrids they have brought into being are superior to the species
that emerged through evolution, too certain that tetraploids are
superior to diploids. But anyone with a lick of sense and normal
vision can see that some plants as they come from the hand of
nature are far more appealing than they are once hybridizers have
labored for their supposed improvement. Furthermore, tetraploid
daylilies—despite predictions made in the 1960s when I believed in
them with fervent faith—have not driven diploid ones into obliv-
ion. Far from it.

Nevertheless, Professor Blakeslee's tetraploid black-eyed Susans
have deservedly made a place for themselves. Burpee introduced
them with huge fanfare in 1957, christening them gloriosa daisies.
They made a splash that year at the Philadelphia Flower Show, and
Edward R. Murrow even featured them on *Person to Person*. Their
extra set of chromosomes brought the gloriosa daisies extraordinary
diversity of form and color. The central cone is ordinarily dark
brown, but it can sometimes be deep green. Ray flowers may be single or double or semidouble, their colors ranging from dark yellow
to burnished copper to deep mahogany. Gloriosas are extremely
short-lived perennials best treated as hardy annuals. They self-seed
prodigiously, and each year's new crop of flowers contains surprising
changes from last year's crop. They insist on full sun, but they can
take drought in stride. They flower abundantly over a prolonged season, making excellent cut flowers.

Gardeners with small children hope that they will inherit the
passion. They can hardly do better than giving their kids a pack of
gloriosa daisy seeds and helping them plant them. Germination is
quick, growth vigorous, and the wait for the first flowers remarkably
short. Tell the kids that the flowers are theirs, to do with as they
please. They can pick them, make bouquets of them, turn them into
garlands, tear off their petals one by one to tell their loves, or just
study them closely, to see how each differs from all the rest.

In just such ways, the life of a gardener may get its start.

❧ Bee Balm by Oudolf

MONARDA OR BEE BALM is one of our most satisfying North American perennials. Its leaves have a minty fragrance. It flowers over a long period starting in midsummer. Its palette of colors is rich in flaming crimsons and smoldering purples, as well as soft pastel pinks, lavenders, and lilacs. Its common name honors its attractions for bees, but butterflies also visit the flowers, likewise hummingbirds. And best of all, bee balm flowers well in moderate shade, pumping in a lot of highly welcome color. Just a few plants can enliven a collection of hostas and ferns. But there is one problem: it is highly susceptible to unsightly powdery mildew that often strikes just before it comes into flower.

This malady is a variable thing. One year the infestation may be severe, and the next there may be almost none. Weather plays a part. Paradoxically, mildew is worst when the weather is either very wet and humid, or when it's blazing hot and hasn't rained in two months. Culture has something of an influence. Thinning a colony of bee balm seems to help by increasing air circulation. Cultivars vary in susceptibility. Some are highly prone to the affliction, others resistant, and now we have some that are actually immune. One is 'Jacob Cline', which originated in the Midwest and has immense flowers of rich scarlet.

But the greatest improvement in our native bee balm took place not long ago in the Netherlands. There the well-known plantsman and garden designer, Piet Oudolf, launched a frontal attack on monarda mildew, by means that prove seeds aren't obsolete even if we now have tissue culture. Oudolf paid some farmers to plant acre upon acre of monarda plants, all grown from seed. They were thus genetically diverse, showing among other things a wide range of susceptibility to mildew. Like some political dictators, he was letting many flowers bloom in order to eradicate most of them. He ripped up and composted any plant with the slightest trace of disease before it could pass on its genes. Those that remained were crossed with one another and their progeny further winnowed out. In time, the best were selected and named and then propagated vegetatively.

Oudolf's monardas have earned much praise, and it's entirely deserved. They are easy to identify, as they are named either for signs of the zodiac ('Pisces', 'Sagittarius', and so on) or for particular tribes of the native peoples of North America ('Cherokee'). Oh, yes, I might mention: most of them are very tall as well as mildew free.

✿ Lucifer and His Kin

THE TRUTH of the proposition that experts often disagree and that when they do they cannot logically all be right (although they could all be wrong) is evident with what reference books say about the South African genus *Crocosmia* (the name means "like a crocus"). Some authorities say that the crocus in question is *Crocus sativus*, the source of saffron, and that if you crush crocosmia flowers and steep them in boiling water they smell of that spice. Other experts say the flowers don't smell of saffron and that they have no idea how the name originated. This disagreement is easily resolved by empirical experiment and observation. I picked some flowers of crocosmia 'Lucifer', threw them in boiling water, waited half an hour, and sniffed. There was a faint odor, difficult to place, but definitely not that of saffron.

Then there's the issue of the genus name itself. At various points, certain species now considered to be crocosmias have been separated off into other genera, including *Antholyza*, *Curtonus*, *Montbretia*, and *Tritonia*. The upshot is that some experts consider certain cultivars bigeneric hybrids between *Crocosmia masoniorum* and *Curtonus paniculatus*, while others demur in favor of interspecific hybrids of *Crocosmia masoniorum* and *Crocosmia paniculata*.

There's also confusion over the degree to which crocosmias are winter-hardy. Some sources say they're not hardy north of Washington, D.C. Graham Stuart Thomas asserts that their great decline in popularity in England since early in the century is attributable to their tenderness. Some say that in the United States they'll get through fairly severe winters if thoroughly mulched. My own experience with 'Lucifer', 'Jenny Bloom', 'Emily McKenzie', and 'Sol-

fatare', the four I have grown thus far, is that they
never fail to appear in the spring, even
without mulch.

Of these four,
'Lucifer' is the stand-
out. Anyone who has
ever grown it will recognize
it by name on sight. It
makes a vigorous clump
with tall, swordlike, dark
green foliage, and it
enlarges in a few
years to a sizable
colony. Its spikes
of bloom, which
can reach chest
height, are well branched and
bent at odd, somewhat irregular
angles. The individual blossoms, scarlet
with orangey yellow in their throats, last only
a day or two, opening from the back of the spike
toward the tip, but there are so many of them that
the season of bloom, starting in early July, is prolonged, two weeks at least. While in bloom,
'Lucifer' is the most arresting plant in the garden.

Crocosmia
'Lucifer'

There is contradictory information about where 'Lucifer' came
from. In *Perennial Garden Plants* (1990), Graham Stuart Thomas
calls it "one of Alan Bloom's best efforts," thus attributing its origin
to Bloom's nursery at Bressingham. But Leo Jelitto and Wilhelm
Schacht's *Hardy Herbaceous Perennials* (3rd ed.), published in Tüb-
ingen in two volumes in 1985 and appearing in English in 1990,
calls it 'Luzifer' and posits that it originated in Germany. If so, this is
by no means the only example of the British claiming something as
their own that really isn't. 'Autumn Joy', the one sedum cultivar
everyone knows by name, often claimed as British in origin, started
out as 'Herbstfreude', the name given it by its German hybridizer,
Georg Arends, before World War II. The meaning of 'Herbstfreude'? — "autumn joy"!

'Lucifer' is one of those plants that really earns its keep. Its foliage remains attractive after it blooms (unless spider mites get to it, and they may). Harvested in late fall when they have dried, the tall flower spikes make good material for winter arrangements. Although their Satanic competitor outshines them, my other crocosmias are fine in themselves. 'Emily McKenzie' has good-sized dark orange flowers, and those of 'Jenny Bloom' are glowing apricot. 'Solfatare' also has apricot flowers, with the added attraction of handsome, bronzish foliage.

❦ Cat's Whiskers

ONE OF THE MOST fetching plants I've encountered in a long time is cat's whiskers (*Orthosiphon stamineus*). It is by no means a common plant. The genus isn't even mentioned in *The New Royal Horticultural Society Dictionary of Gardening*. From what I can glean elsewhere, there are several species, one of which (*O. aristatus*) sounds as if it would be devilishly hard to distinguish from *O. stamineus*. Orthosiphons (the name means "straight tube") are in the Labiatae family, and various species hail from Indonesia southward toward Australia. Some are prominent in Asian folk medicine, particularly in the form of teas that are said to alleviate kidney and urinary tract disorders.

My interest in cat's whiskers, however, is purely horticultural, not medical. When I spotted it in a garden in Florida, I was immediately taken with it. It is a shrubby perennial about two and a half feet in every direction, and loaded with spikes of white flowers ringing the stem. The blossoms, which open from the bottom of their inflorescence and look much like honeysuckle, have long protruding stamens. There is also said to be a form with lavender flowers.

I brought the plant home with me and, because it is tender, put it in the greenhouse to overwinter and propagate from cuttings. *Orthosiphon stamineus* is a worthy plant that requires little special care beyond a steady supply of moisture and full sun. An impressive flush of flowers that lasts about ten days is followed by a lull of four weeks, then another flood of blooms. This is a plant that hybridizers should take in hand, or perhaps just ambitious home gardeners—those who have lots more room than I do. I have an idea that if it were planted by the many thousands some plants might prove to be constant rather than intermittent bloomers. These could then be selected for vegetative propagation, enlivening the gardens of us all with new and improved forms of cat's whiskers.

If you think Piet Oudolf and his field of monardas gave me this idea, you're right on target.

✿ Tobaccos for Nonsmokers

ITS GENUS NAME honoring Jean Nicot, the French consul to Portugal from whose colonies in tropical America it was introduced to France, this plant inspired passionate and contradictory feelings almost from the moment it arrived in the English-speaking world. In 1633 the English herbalist John Gerard attributed wonderful medical properties to it. For one thing, it "driveth forth wormes of the bellie, if withall a leafe be laid to the Navell." It "doth likewise scoure and clense old and rotten ulcers, and bringeth them to perfect digestion." It also "mitigathe the paine of the gout if it be rosted in hot embers and applied to the grieved part."

But Gerard also described something else people could do with this plant: "The drie leaves are used to be taken in a pipe set on fire and suckt into the stomacke, and thrust forth againe at the nostrills." The stuff could also be smoked, a practice already condemned by King James I in the strongest possible terms. Smoking *Nicotiana tabacum* or tobacco, the king said, was "lothsome to the eye, hateful to the nose, harmefull to the braine, dangerous to the Lungs, and in the blacke stinking fume thereof, neerest resembling the horrible Stigian smoke of the pit that is bottomelesse." The American Heart Association, the American Lung Association, and the American Cancer Society today all concur with His Majesty, as the human race divides itself into crusading nonsmokers and a dwindling band of people who skulk around corners, furtively lighting up. In the

102 • A L L E N   L A C Y

movies twenty years ago, everyone smoked. Nowadays if a character
smokes in a film or a TV show, you can be sure that he or she is otherwise up to no good whatsoever.

Regarding tobacco, a new form of Calvinism has sprung up
among us, and it is not unthinkable that people who want to continue smoking the leaves of Nicotiana tabacum may have to start
growing their own. (Deciding to stop, as I have done after fifty years
of being surrounded by a blue cloud, is of course another, wiser
option.)

Even nonsmoking gardeners, however, may agree that Nicotiana tabacum is a handsome plant. Tall and commanding, with
striking pinkish-green flowers, it is a pretty sight in the ever-
diminishing tobacco fields of North Carolina and southern Virginia.
It would be worth considering as an ornamental plant for the garden, except that the so-called flowering tobaccos are even more
attractive.

The most familiar of the flowering tobaccos are the annual bedding nicotianas, hybrids of Nicotiana alata, the jasmine tobacco of
temperate South America. Common and easily available already
blooming in their market packs in spring at most garden centers,
these are cheerful plants, not at all to be despised. Generally sold in
mixed colors, their flowers may be white, lavender, pink, crimson,
purple, or even pale lime. They will grow in full sun or light shade.
They can take high summer humidity and heat. They bloom abundantly over a long season, and they aren't troubled by the botrytis
that can sometimes plague some other New World members of the
nightshade family, such as petunias. That said, it must also be said
that in "improving" Nicotiana alata, hybridizers have allowed much
of its charm to vanish. Instead of growing to thirty-six inches or even
more, it now gives up at fourteen inches. If any fragrance remains,
it's just a trace — certainly not enough to call jasmines to mind.

For the best flowering tobaccos, it's necessary to seek out the
unimproved species. They're unlikely to be found at garden centers,
and that may be a good thing, too, in encouraging more of us to
grow our own annuals from seed, as all gardeners used to do before
we got hooked on convenience.

Two nicotianas are virtually indispensable in any proper garden.

The first is *Nicotiana sylvestris*, the woodland tobacco from
Argentina, which first made its way to European gardens in 1898.
This splendid annual rises five feet or more above its huge, light
green lower leaves. At the top of its stems and encircling them, there
are clusters or whorls of pure white, tubular blossoms that lift themselves slightly as evening comes on and they begin to pour their
powerful sweet scent into the air to announce their presence to the
night moths that pollinate them. The second, and older in cultivation, *N. langsdorffii* is named in honor of the German botanist

Nicotiana sylvestris

Georg Heinrich von Langsdorff, who brought it back to Europe from Brazil in 1819. Although it has been around for some time, it was only in the 1990s that it became a bellwether plant whose presence in a garden suggests highly advanced tastes on the part of its gardener. This tobacco combines forcefulness with delicacy. It can grow to five feet high and as much across. Its lime-green flowers flare out on their slender tubes like bells or skirts. The flowers repay close attention for the turquoise anthers around their throats. N. langsdorffii is massive, but still airy, as it does not entirely block from view whatever may happen to be growing behind it. It is especially lovely combined with tall yellow verbascums and with Lavatera thuringiaca 'Barnsley', for its fine large pink flowers with a deeper pink eye.

Both of these tender perennials that must be grown as annuals (except in frost-free areas) are reputed to self-seed freely, but so far N. sylvestris is the only one that does so for me. To make sure I am keeping it going (because its seedlings don't show up until the middle of June), I sow its infinitesimal seeds and those of N. langsdorffii indoors in late April. The seeds must be scattered lightly on top of the planting mix without covering, since light is needed for good germination.

❧ The Neglected Cape Fuchsias

CAN THERE BE even a scintilla of doubt that the most mysteriously neglected plants in North America at the moment are the cape fuchsias, two species and several cultivars of Phygelius? I hasten to mention that they aren't fuchsias at all. Fuchsias are New World plants in the Evening Primrose family, or Onagragaceae, distributed from Mexico southward to Chile; cape fuchsias are South African natives, in the Figwort family, or Scrophulariaceae. Both have tubular flowers, but there the resemblances end, and it isn't possible to mistake one for the other.

There is general agreement that the phyg- part of the name Phygelius comes from the Greek word for flight, the same root that gives us the musical term fugue. The meaning of the rest of the name is contested. Some say that *elius* derives from *helios*, for sun (as in *Heliotropium*), and that it refers to these plants' preference for shade. According to another school of thought, phygelius means flight from botanists and refers to the prolonged period of time these plants were unknown. I somewhat favor this second alternative, inasmuch as they are sun-loving, not shade-loving, creatures that remain unknown to a great many gardeners.

There are only two species, *P. aequalis* and *P. capensis*, both native to the Drakenberg, a mountain system in South Africa. Both have tall, upright racemes in which their long, tubular flowers hang down like chimes. The flowers of *P. aequalis* are rusty reddish pink, although there is a selected form, 'Yellow Trumpet', whose name pretty much describes it. The blossoms of *P. capensis* range from red to orange, with yellow interiors at their bases, where they flare out slightly. This species also has a selected form with cultivar status, 'Coccinea'. Neither species has the faintest hint of fragrance. The ornithologically minded gardener will deduce quickly from the tubular form, color in the red/orange part of the spectrum, and absence of scent that the cape fuchsia is not pollinated by insects but by birds, which lack any sense of smell. The deduction is right on the mark; in the Drakenberg these plants are pollinated by the sunbirds that spread pollen as they move from one flower to another searching for sips of nectar. There are no sunbirds in North America, but hummingbirds step in to replace them beautifully.

It was apparently not until the mid-1980s that anyone produced hybrids between the two species. Peter Dummer, head of propagation at the Hillier Nursery in England, finally got around to the task, crossing *P. aequalis* 'Yellow Trumpet' with *P. capensis* 'Coccinea'. The result was 'Winchester Fanfare', which has striking reddish pink flowers. Backcrossed with *P. capensis*, 'Winchester Fanfare' produced two more cultivars of great distinction. 'Moonraker' has soft pastel yellow flowers, while those of 'Salmon Leap' are light orange-pink. From another backcross, of 'Winchester Fanfare' with 'Yellow Trumpet', came 'Pink Elf'. Two more cultivars, 'African Queen' (orange red) and 'Devil's Tears' (scarlet), finish out this group of plants, collectively known as the *P. × rectus* hybrids.

With the exception of 'Pink Elf', which has about half the spread and height of the rest, these are big, bold plants. In areas with mild winters, they are shrubs or subshrubs capable of reaching eight feet or more in height, with a four-foot spread, which may in time widen considerably, as the plants tend to sucker easily. Where they die back to the ground over the winter, they still can rise to four or five feet by the official arrival of summer. They will continue to bloom right up to the first frost of autumn if their flower stalks are regularly cut back once the last blossoms at their tops are spent.

Phygelius

❧ An Unstoppable Passion for Salvias

ONE EUROPEAN SPECIES of sage has been well regarded since Pliny, who may have given it the name *salvia*, which Carolus Linnaeus adopted without change as the name of its genus. Culinary or medicinal sage, *Salvia officinalis*, is a plant of many uses. The herbalist John Gerard was more enthusiastic about it than he was about tobacco. He wrote that it "is singular good for the head and braine; it quickneth the sences and memory, strengthneth the sinewes, restoreth health to those that have the palsie upon a moist cause, takes away shaking or trembling of the members, and being put up into the nosthrils, it draweth the flegme out of the head. It is likewise commended against the spitting of blood, the cough, and paines of the sides, and bitings of serpents." *Salvia officinalis*, which often imparts its strong flavor to dressings for poultry, continues to be a useful garden plant today, especially in the forms with foliage that is golden, purple, or variegated in shades of purple, cream, and green. But it is the purely ornamental species of salvias that are rapidly becoming one of the most exciting tickets in American horticulture, today and for the foreseeable future.

A few standard garden reference books on my library shelves and some current nursery catalogs on my desk together tell the story. The reference books have little to say about salvias. *The Wise Garden Encyclopedia* (1990), which is typical, gives just over a page to the genus and lists eleven species: *apiana, argentea, azurea, coccinea, farinacea, nemerosa, officinalis, patens, pitcheri, sclarea,* and *splendens*. The nursery catalogs are from Canyon Creek Nursery and Plant Delights Nursery. Among them they are offering over seventy-five species of *Salvia*, some of which—*guaranitica, greggii,* and *leucantha*—have several forms and cultivars. (If I tried out only five new salvias a year from these offerings, it would take fifteen years!)

A decade ago, I would have considered that *Wise* gave salvias their due, maybe more than their due. *S. argentea*, the silver sage, is wonderful for its silvery-gray foliage, velvety and as thick as terry cloth, but it gets the mugs in humid weather and tends to die as soon as it has flowered. *S. coccinea*, Texas sage, is a pleasant annual with small red flowers on spikes that are in scale with the rest of the plant. *S. farinacea*, the mealy cup sage, is a common border plant, with either light violet-blue or dirty white flowers and, frankly, is something of a bore. As for *S. splendens*, it is the origin of the hybrid bedding salvias that scream in the American suburban and gas station landscape for months on end, plants I could do without.

Then 'Indigo Spires' entered my life, as a small rooted cutting I got from a mail-order nursery in the spring of 1988. A vegetatively propagated hybrid between *S. farinacea* and *S. longispicata* that originated in the gardens of the Huntington Museum in California, 'Indigo Spires' begins blooming in early summer, when it's no more interesting than its mealy cup parent. But as the nights begin to lengthen perceptibly in late summer, 'Indigo Spires' turns into one of the champion plants of the fall garden. By now a fair-sized bush, the color of its flowers deepens and takes on metallic hints, while its spikes elongate and begin to twist into graceful curves. In a good breeze the plant fairly dances.

'Indigo Spires' was just the beginning of a love affair with salvias that promises to absorb me as long as I am able to garden, for it is impossible to collect plants in this genus without becoming aware that it is remarkable in many ways. First, it spans the globe, with species that are native to Europe, Africa, the Middle East, Asia (including Tibet and Japan), and all three Americas. Second, most species are uncommonly attractive to bees and butterflies, who seek their nectar (which people can easily sip, like that of honeysuckle). Third, the genus has accommodated itself easily to a wide range of habitats. Some species thrive in full sun under arid conditions, while others like things shady and on the moist side. Some are winter-hardy, but a great many are tender. Scented leaves are fairly common, the scent ranging from pineapple, honeydew melon, and lemon to something best described as the essence of dank basements or old shoes. Finally, there is an extensive range of flower color. Shades of blue, red, and purple are most common, but salvias also come in white, yellow, and orange. Their only competitors in covering the spectrum are irises.

Here are some of the salvias that I have grown so far.

S. guaranitica, from Argentina, Brazil, and Uruguay, starts blooming in midsummer continuing into fall. It has slightly rounded, pebbly, dark green leaves and racemes of intense indigo flowers. One cultivar, 'Argentina Skies', has pale blue flowers, somewhat larger than the species. There is also a hybrid between *S. guaranitica* and *S. gesneriiflora* called 'Purple Majesty' that has large flowers of deep royal purple.

Mexican bush sage, *S. leucantha*, rapidly grows from a tiny cutting planted in late spring into a bushy thing that can get well over thirty inches tall and as many across if it's happy. Even out of bloom it is interesting. Its long, thin, sharply tapered leaves have a knobby texture, and their undersides are pale gray. In flower, *S. leucantha* is magnificent. On long, curving spikes it bears long-lasting calyces that are pure purple velvet. The large flowers of the cultivar 'Emerald' are white; those of 'All Purple' are (no surprise here) purple.

Belize sage, *S. miniata*, has smooth, somewhat succulent foliage, and large bracts of scarlet over a long season starting in early July. It is similar in form to *S. vanhouttii*, a large plant that covers itself with clusters of garnet bracts in increasing numbers from early September until the first frost. The two species should never be planted together as I did one year, for their color clash is horrendous.

Pineapple sage, *S. rutilans* (syn. *S. elegans*) deserves a place in every garden. It does not bloom strongly until autumn, when it abounds with blazing scarlet torches, but the scent of its crushed foliage is delicious throughout the growing season. Children soon learn its delights; my own grandchildren always race to it when they visit the garden.

My most recent discovery among salvias is the forsythia sage, *S. madrensis*. Native to Mexico and Costa Rica, it is a magnificently shrubby plant, tropical in appearance at about six feet tall, with eighteen-inch spikes of clear yellow flowers in October, continuing in places like southern Texas almost to Christmas. Those of us who live where winter arrives before this salvia starts blooming can plant it in a container and bring it indoors. It will flower well in a cool, sunny room.

Of the salvias I have grown, only *S. guaranitica* has proven reliably winter-hardy in my garden in southern New Jersey. 'Indigo

Spires' and S. *rutilans* get through some winters, but not others. The rest are entirely tender, with only gardeners who live in climates like that of Southern California being able to count them as truly perennial. But the good news about tender species of salvia is that they root easily from cuttings. People with greenhouses can dig up a plant of those they want to keep. Or cuttings can be taken in the fall, rooted, and grown under lights through the winter.

Much of the excitement over salvias emanates from Yucca Do Nursery in Texas, which has collected a great many species from Mexico. Most are being tested, but a few have been released. I'm set on getting S. *confertiflora*, described in the Yucca Do catalog as growing six feet tall, blooming from midseason till frost with orange flowers and chocolate bracts, and preferring moist shade. I also want some selected forms of both S. *greggii* and S. *microphylla* that were collected in Mexico. And I simply must have S. *regla*, which likes shade, grows three to five feet tall, and has vibrant orange flowers between two and three inches long, which is an enormous size for a salvia. I want to grow S. *discolor* (black flowers set in gray-green bracts), S. *sphacelifolia* (purple flowers that smell like ripe grapes), and S. *clevelandii* 'Aromas' (intensely fragrant flowers and leaves, too). Once the passion for salvias gets under way, it is unstoppable.

III   Summer —
Decks and
Tender Plants

❧ The Joy of Decks

GARDEN DECKS are delightful places, and they are thoroughly American inventions originating, like much else in our national life, in California. The noted California landscape architect Thomas Church once described them aptly as "wandering porches"—porches that "have become detached from houses and wander freely around the property."

Our own deck has its history. Before it came into existence, there was no comfortable place to sit outdoors, just a mean concrete stoop by the back door. That we should have a deck was the notion of Paul, our elder son, who dreamed it up and then built it in the summer of 1980, between his graduation from high school and his entrance into college. His friends helped, also our next-door neighbor Ed Plantan. He gave Paul and his friends instructions in the art of building things that have served them all well in their later life.

When the deck in this stage of existence was finished, we had what I called in an essay written three years later "a kind of viewing platform from which we could contemplate good and proper order"—on those rare days when the lawn was mowed and not a single weed was in sight. Our deck, then twenty by twenty-four feet, changed the way we lived, also the way we gardened. But eventually we wanted to make changes. The deck sat west of the house. We needed shade, so in 1984 we hired carpenters to come in and build a handsome, sturdy pergola covering a third of the deck. We planted

114 • ALLEN LACY

hardy kiwi vines, which grew twenty-seven feet in one season, bringing the cool summer shade we longed for.

My mother died in a nursing home in Texas in the spring of
1993, after nine years of unconscious existence with Alzheimer's disease. She loved gardens, so we wanted to use the small inheritance
she left to improve our own garden. The result was that our friend
Ed Brightly and his son Jimmy, both of them fine craftsmen, spent
much of the summer extending the deck that Paul had built and
building two new platforms that covered most of the south side of
the house. Most of the new construction was at ground level, so
deck and garden flowed together smoothly into a unified space. The
deck became the entrance to the garden, both the woodland garden
out front and the lawn and shady border out back. At the same time,
the garden moved onto the deck, as we began to take up seriously
the pursuit of gardening in containers, about which more will follow shortly. Ed Brightly did one more thing for us, constructing
French doors where no door had been before so that our living
room opened onto the new deck. The thirteen-year evolution of this
transitional space between house and garden was now complete,
and it was wonderful.

A deck, particularly if it is partially covered with a shady pergola
clad in hardy kiwis or other vines, is an enormous creature comfort.
It is a virtual magnet for comfortable chairs and a table for dining al
fresco, for chaise longues, and for hammocks. If it is designed with
protected spots that the sun reaches on chilly days, it extends the
season for pleasant lolling outdoors, and because its wooden surface
dries much more quickly than a lawn, a passing rainstorm is only a
brief interruption in outdoor pleasure.

A deck is an invitation to garden in containers. Even resolute
nonpractitioners will usually place a few potted plants here and
there—brightly colored pelargoniums, Super Elfin impatiens for
shady spots, New Guinea impatiens for sunny ones, and probably
some petunias and marigolds.

Such minimal gardening, somewhat the outdoor equivalent of
interior decorating, can lead to the real thing. Gardening in containers is highly seductive, because the gardener is *in control*, more
than is possible in any other kind of gardening. First, there's soil—

planting mixes, to be precise. Dirt gardeners have to start with what they are given, and what they are given is often pretty poor stuff, filthy with weed seeds and unfriendly pathogens, and desperately in need of organic matter. In comparison, a well-formulated, light weight planting mix comes close to what Adam was given to cultivate in Eden. Then there's liquid fertilizer. Out in the garden beyond the deck I somewhat resist—not always—chemical fertilizers, preferring instead dried manures, cottonseed meal, compost, and the like; but on the deck I spritz freely and frequently during the growing season, using a formula that goes easy on nitrogen but really pours on the phosphoric acid, since it's abundant flower production I'm after, not excessive leaf growth. (I use a liquid fertilizer with an N-P-K ratio of 9–59–8.)

Plants in containers, like living room furniture, can be moved around at will all summer long, as they can't be in the garden. If a scarlet pelargonium blooms next to a crimson verbena to ghastly effect out in the border, it's either pull one of them up or grin and bear it until winter comes along to take care of the visual offense. If they're in pots on a deck, they can be shunted off into different corners, an immediate remedy for their gruesome clash.

Sometimes moving containers around is more a matter of finding a combination of colors, textures, and sizes that works harmoniously than of response to a disaster. In late spring, Hella can fiddle around for a couple of days before she is satisfied with a grouping of plants next to the French doors leading from our living room to the sunniest part of our deck, on its south side. One year the result was a huge pot of rosemary next to an even larger pot of *Euryops communis*, the shrub daisy that is equally remarkable for its dark green ferny foliage and its deeply saturated golden flowers. Somewhat higher, on a step, went a pot of soft pink geraniums. Higher still, in hanging baskets suspended from chains attached to a narrow pergola were a lavender lantana and a large plant of *Lysimachia congestiflora* 'Eco Dark Satin', whose abundant clusters of dark gold flowers with darker throats neatly echoed the large daisies of the *Euryops*. In another year, when a little fountain was installed in the same spot, it was encircled with pots of cigarette plant (*Cuphea ignea*), coleus 'Leprechaun Lace' (variegated cream, white, and green), another coleus with leaves of solid brownish purple, *Fuchsia microphylla*, several fancy-leaf geraniums, all huddling beneath a huge hanging basket spilling over with pink *Diascia vigilis* and trailing white bacopa.

The range of plants suitable for growing in containers on a deck is vast. Virtually all the bedding plants sold in garden centers in late spring and early summer will do—and three petunias or marigolds in a pot make much more of a splash than they do in a flower bed. Experienced or experimentally minded gardeners will want to go far beyond the simplicity of annuals. A deck provides a wonderful opportunity for people who live where winters are severe to grow some of the tender or subtropical plants that their counterparts in Zones 8 and 9 can easily grow outdoors all year long. My own choices include gardenias and Sambac jasmines (two cultivars, 'Maid of Orleans' and 'Grand Duke of Tuscany'), all for the powerfully haunting, spicy perfume, and also night-blooming jasmine, which isn't a jasmine at all but a cestrum, *Cestrum nocturnum*, and which has to be kept in a far corner of the deck because its nighttime fragrance is almost overpowering. Other subtropicals include *Pentas* in red, pink, and white; *Plumbago auriculata*, in both white and pale blue; and a lot of hibiscuses, including one named 'Tammy Faye', which Hella dislikes intensely as being way beyond gaudy.

All these plants used to come indoors in winter, to a cool east-facing bedroom with good light. They were kept unfertilized and barely watered until March, when they got a severe pruning and a heavy dose of fertilizer so they would be ready to burst into growth when they returned to the deck in late April. Now that I have a greenhouse, life is simpler, and winter is full of flowers.

But the true glory of deck gardening in containers lies not in how many plants can be grown separately, in their individual pots, but how many different plants can be crammed into a single large pot. A watering wand used daily, lightweight planting mix, and frequent ample doses of liquid fertilizer make it possible to herd plants together, packing them in as tightly as subway passengers at rush hour. As an example, these plants are growing in merry profusion in just one of the several large urns on our deck: *Helichrysum petiolare* 'Limelight', purple perilla, dusty miller, holy basil, *Fuchsia magellanica* 'Señorita', *Ipomoea batatas* 'Blackie', *Verbena canadensis* 'Homestead Purple', asparagus fern, and *Salvia discolor*.

Containers themselves can be of great interest, besides the strawberry jars, old whiskey barrels, and clay pots of every size and shape that are easily obtainable at every garden center. I haunt flea markets and garage sales in the quest, and I've turned up some dandies, including a cast-iron pig trough, some baskets made of coconut stems that look as if they're undergoing electrocution, and a huge urn from Mexico with a goat's head sticking up on one side.

Because no two houses are exactly alike and certainly no two gardens, it follows with relentless logic that every deck as a transitional space between garden and house will be different.

Here's what mine is like. Part of it sits eighteen inches above the ground, on the west side of the house, and it is partially covered by a pergola that shelters chairs and a round table for dining. At the northwest corner, wide steps lead down into the back garden. Connected to this part of the deck there's another section, on two levels, on the south side of the house. Because there's a gentle slope on our property from east to west, the garden—the real garden, some might say, with its plants growing in the real earth that it is our lot to till and tend—sits right next to the deck. A long-established hedge of mock oranges and lilacs screens us from our neighbors, with a dense planting of ostrich ferns, ligularias, chelones, and other shade- and moisture-loving things growing alongside the deck. At its southwestern corner, where it sits right at ground level, round aggregate pavers lead along a path lined with caladiums, elephant ears, tiarellas, alchemillas, ferns, and epimediums past a huge freestanding copper birdfeeder to our colony of yellow groove bamboo and, just this side of it, our spring woodland garden patch.

❦ More on Container Gardening

THE EXCITEMENT in container gardening, I have said, comes when several or even many plants are planted in the same container. Because competition for moisture and nutrients from weeds and tree roots is absent, an amazing number can be crammed together successfully. But how is it determined which plants go together, which marriages (polygamous ones, of course), are happy and which aren't?

There are three approaches to container gardening. The first involves just grabbing whatever plants are closest to hand and sticking them into the same pot, with no reflection at all. Sometimes it works, but usually the results aren't something the gardener is proud of or hopes to repeat in future years.

The second approach, which can be called copycat gardening, is to visit other gardens that feature plants in containers, to observe them carefully, taking note of combinations you like; then you simply try to reproduce them in your own garden the next year. I've learned a lot this way, by visiting gardens that are open to the public (such as Brookside Gardens in Wheaton, Maryland, or Wave Hill in the Bronx). I've heavily borrowed ideas for good combinations from such places; for example, putting black mondo grass (*Ophiopogon planiscapus* 'Arabicus') in a large clay bowl with golden creeping Jenny (*Lysimachia nummularia* 'Aurea') as an underplanting.

The third approach is much like the second, except that it calls for thought and analysis. It involves looking at a combination that seems to work and then trying to figure out the principles it embodies, saying, "Yes, this works, but why does it work?" Take that duet of black mondo grass and creeping Jenny. The plants are similar in some respects. They're both small. They're both herbaceous, not woody. They both bloom, at roughly the same time, just as summer arrives officially, but the flowers are inconspicuous: both are better understood as foliage plants. But they also differ from each other in some respects. Black mondo grass is perky and upright, and its leaves are narrow and grassy. Creeping Jenny has fairly tiny leaves, but they are round, not narrow. The plant creeps just above the surface of the soil, and trails downward wherever it can. Its habit of growth is lax. But the most striking difference between these two plants is the color of their foliage. The mondo grass is very dark, almost charcoal black. This form of creeping Jenny is a brilliant chartreuse that sets the other plant off, makes it leap to the eye. There seems to be a principle at work here: *contrast* is an important element in attractive combinations.

Another agreeable combination was one of my own devising this summer. It involves two adjacent containers, plus another plant growing on a nearby trellis. There are three plants to consider here. One is *Cuphea ignea*, growing in that goat-headed Mexican urn; another, in a pot that sits slightly higher on our deck, is the *Fuchsia triphylla* hybrid 'Gartenmeister Bonstedt'; the third is the superb native honeysuckle, *Lonicera sempervirens*. These three plants differ in some respects, but they have in common an abundance of similar flowers that are long, narrow, tubular, and brilliant scarlet. In both color and form, they echo one another. Here, *similarity* is the twin brother of contrast.

Tubularity is but one of the forms that flowers take. A great many flowers have the daisy structure of petals (ray flowers) surrounding a central boss (disk flowers). Most of these are in the Asteraceae family, but similar construction occurs in the Ranunculaceae (*Anemone blanda*) and the Aizoaceae (*Delosperma cooperi*). Flowers may also be trumpet-shaped, cup-shaped, saucer-shaped, and so on through many forms. Color, obviously, is diverse.

As with flowers, so with foliage. Leaves may be shaped like hands, hearts, or kidneys; like blades, lances, needles, shields, spatulas, or spears. They also differ in the way they are arranged on their stems—opposite one another, alternating with one another, and so on through the great litany that botanists use to construct their keys of plant identification. Color? There is almost as much variety in foliage color as in flower color. Besides green, there are copper, gray, chartreuse, gold, purple, and the many different degrees and kinds of variegation that today fascinate many gardeners. There are also differences of texture, ranging from fine and feathery to bold and assertive.

Plants may also be classified according to their growth habit. Some droop and trail. Some form compact mounds. Some aspire upward, like steeples or spires. Some climb, whether by tendrils, or by spiraling, either clockwise or counterclockwise, around whatever support they can find.

In container gardening there is only one absolute, fixed rule for plant combination. To thrive, any plants grown in the same container should have similar requirements of light, nutrient supply, and moisture. If for some reason you'd like to arrange a marriage between cattails and cacti, just stick them in separate but adjacent containers.

Container gardening gives gardeners the chance to experiment and to play. It teaches us stuff. Here's an example. One year recently I removed a couple of hostas from a shady border, potted them up, and put them on the deck. It was an impulsive but a happy thing to do, because the slugs in my garden haven't yet learned to climb very far. At the end of the season, the hostas on the deck were in perfect condition while those in open ground were in their usual tatters. I also discovered that hostas work well as pot plants, even apart from relative immunity to slugs. 'Patriot', one of my favorites, a middle-sized cultivar with apple-green leaves splashed in white, nicely mirrored the similar coloration of an adjacent nameless tradescantia found in the produce department of our grocery store. It also contrasted beautifully with the feathery plumes of the woody houseplant *Asparagus setaceus* that sat nearby.

It was a combination I decided to repeat in future years. So was another ensemble of two ornamental grasses and two grasslike

plants. The grasses are *Hakonochloa macra* 'Aureola' and *Pennise-tum setaceum* 'Atropurpureum'; their grassy-looking companions are the sweet flag *Acorus calamus* 'Variegatus' and a cultivar of New Zealand flax, *Phormium colonsoi* 'Maori Sunrise'. These four plants offer an overall feeling or impression of similarity that also embraces noteworthy differences in form and color. The leaves of the hakon grass, variegated green and yellow, arch down with uncommon grace. Those of the adjacent phormium arch somewhat and are spectacularly colored apricot, pink, and bronze. The dark-leaved pennisetum arches only slightly and shows no variegation. The sweet flag has upright, swordlike leaves, somewhat reminiscent of *Iris pallida* 'Variegata'. This foursome punctuates a mixed planting of purple heliotrope, petunias, lantanas, plectranthus, and gaura, lending it rhythm and giving it a sense of unity. (I should mention though that this pennisetum and the phormium are not winter-hardy in New Jersey, something that readers who want to try this combination should keep in mind.)

On a hot summer evening as we sit on our deck and sip tall glasses of iced tea, we contemplate our garden of plants in contain-ers with a satisfaction that is entire and complete. Decks or terraces and containers are made for each other; they also enhance the pleasure we gain from observing our plants intimately.

❧ The Great Coleus Comeback

AS ONE CENTURY and one millennium ends and new ones begin, an intriguing trend in American gardening is the great revival of interest in plants that our Victorian forebears adored—plants that William Robinson and Gertrude Jekyll, whom we have regarded for decades as arbiters of good taste, either scorned or ignored. Cannas are back—and more spectacular than ever—since some of them, such as 'Pretoria', 'Tropicana', and 'Durban', now have highly colorful variegated foliage as well as huge flowers in glowing colors. Alternantheras have returned from aesthetic exile, especially *Alternanthera dentata* 'Rubiginosa', which has superb leaves of deep red-purple. Ornamental grasses are in a rerun, albeit with new species and cultivars unknown one hundred years ago. Elephant ears and caladiums are turning up in the gardens of the horticultural cognoscenti. No one is surprised any longer to discover, as I did one year, elephant ears, cannas, pennisetums, and even culinary asparagus planted cheek by jowl at Wave Hill in the Bronx, one of the most admired gardens on this continent. Here, the garden's creator, Marco Polo Stufano, has repeatedly shown himself to be a genius in the art of combining plants. He has also revealed a sense of humor. The combination just described is a botanical pun, for the plants making it up are all monocots.

But the greatest revival has taken place with coleus, whose scientific name used to be *Coleus*, but now has been changed to *Solenostemon*. If anyone had asked me in 1990 if I had the slightest interest in growing coleus, I would have answered, "Absolutely not!" And if I had been feeling a little peckish that day, I might have responded with a rhetorical question, "What, are you crazy or something?" Coleus were uninteresting plants, somewhat on the gaudy side, maybe okay for window boxes, but not plants that anyone would want especially to grow. They were of some historical interest, having been extremely popular with gardeners during the Victorian era, but in and of themselves they were hardly desirable.

Things have changed. Starting around 1993, I began to notice that coleus plants were beginning to turn up with surprising frequency in the gardens of people of unquestionable good taste, even some who could be considered in the horticultural vanguard. When I took a close look at some of the coleus they were raising—and were passing along to other passionate coleophiles—I was hooked. Today, if you ask me about my favorite plants, coleus will be high on the list. Today, if you come to my garden you will see coleus plants galore.

I haven't changed, however; but the coleus has. A decade ago, the only ones I knew were seed-grown mixed strains, like Wizard and Rainbow, which were dull plants, hardly able to stir even a flicker of attention. Today many dozens of fascinating cultivars are available. The revival has proceeded on two fronts, with what might be called "garden-center coleus" on the one hand and "collector's coleus" on the other.

The garden-center coleus originated in the South, particularly at Texas A&M University, which has introduced 'Burgundy Sun' and 'Plum Parfait', two vegetatively propagated cultivars that can take full sun and high heat. Other garden-center coleus include 'Volcano' and 'Alabama', both strong reds. These are all best grown in groups of three or more, for the greatest color impact.

Garden-center coleus—some of which are trademarked, maybe even patented, for heaven's sake—come to us through the bedding plant industry, just like impatiens and marigolds. Collector's coleus pass from one eager and enamored gardener to another, and also are found in specialized mail-order catalogs. These cultivars much resemble those that enchanted the Victorian gardener, but most of them probably haven't actually been around since Victorian times. Two that may possibly have come down from them are 'Pineapple Beauty' and 'Pumila'. The egg-shaped leaves of 'Pineapple Beauty' are soft golden yellow from midsection to tip, purple from midsection to stem. The venation is purple. So is the stem, and even the sap. 'Pumila' also runs around as 'Rob Roy', 'Trailing Red', and a couple of other names. It may be the species *Coleus pumilus* (before the name change), instead of a cultivar. Whatever. It is a low and spreading plant, ideal for hanging baskets in combination with more erect things like *Fuchsia magellanica*. The small, rounded leaves are burgundy-brown, with deckle edges of pale green. It is the exception among coleus in having interesting flowers—small, but brilliant blue and abundant on their spikes.

Coleus are another example of plants that offer intellectual beauty, the pleasure of contemplating the variations that occur in the genus. Plants vary in size from small to enormous. Leaf size similarly varies, as do leaf shape, venation, and emargination. Leaf color may be chartreuse, yellow, gold, several shades of green, pink, russet, and something that may reasonably be called purple. Beyond these single colors, the degree of variegation is enormous, everything from the merely bicolored to something right out of Jackson Pollock.

Some fine coleus came to me without names. Some are selfs or monochromatic. One has enormous leaves of chartreuse, borne on a plant that can reach three feet high and as many across. Two others, also large plants with large leaves, are purple. One has egg-shaped leaves only slightly deckled. The other has deeply incised leaves that are heavily ruffled. Another anonymous cultivar, likewise a huge plant, bears ruffled leaves that are solid purple when they first unfold. Scarlet deckles that glow like stained glass form all around the leaves as they mature.

I am happy that many fine coleus came to me with names. 'Mars' (a.k.a. 'Red Duckfoot') has small palmate leaves on multiple stems. Their color in shade is a washed-out brown, but in sun they are a luminous maroon. 'Inky Fingers', a vigorous spreader, has small, hand-shaped leaves, green at their tips, blotchy maroon at their centers. 'The Line' has elegant, lance-shaped, pale gold foliage with thin maroon midribs. 'Leprechaun Lace' is a real beauty, with narrow pointed leaves that are mottled yellow and bright green when they first appear, then turn to pale green and cream with pink veins. 'Dipped in Wine' is golden-yellow, overlaid with purple patches. About 'Max Levering' I can't quite make up my mind. It's kind of a paisley thing, irregularly patterned in blotches of several shades of green, a couple of yellows, and the reds of bloodstains both fresh and old.

Coleus are tender tropical or subtropical plants, mostly from Java, that cannot withstand the least amount of frost. But they root with legendary ease, either in water or in moist potting soil. By taking cuttings in the fall and overwintering them indoors, there is no difficulty at all about keeping those you especially favor, year after year.

✱ In Praise of Plectranthus

IT WOULD BE wonderful if fine, useful, and attractive plants were always accompanied by solid and unambiguous names, but we live in an imperfect world. Take the genus *Plectranthus*. It includes some of my favorite tender ornamental plants, but both scientific and common names (where there are any) are terribly mixed up.

I place various plectranthus species and cultivars second only to coleus as foliage plants, but at one time there was no distinction between them, as taxonomists regarded all plectranthus as species of *Coleus*. The second edition of *The Wise Garden Encyclopedia* (1970) lists just two kinds of coleus, *Coleus* × *hybridus* (the many colorful sorts we all know today as coleus) and *C. amboinicus*, which it calls Spanish thyme. In *Hortus Third* (1976), Spanish thyme was still considered to be a species of *Coleus*, but the genus *Plectranthus* was also listed, and described under the common names Swedish ivy and Swedish begonia. Both of these names are deeply puzzling, for the plants in question are neither ivies nor begonias, and they certainly aren't Swedish, given that this genus is native to tropical and subtropical regions of Africa, Asia, and Australia.

Swedish ivy is a common houseplant, an ideal subject for hanging baskets in sunny windows. Many gardeners have grown it for decades, long before any other plectranthus started moving into our orbit. It's a classic passalong plant, for it roots in water almost overnight. But I haven't got the faintest idea what to call it if I want to be precise and use a Latin name. Depending on the reference source I choose, it could be *Plectranthus australis*, but it might also be *P. ciliatus*. Or *P. oertendahlii*. Or *P. nummularius*. It's not at all clear what's going on here. It might be that four different species share the same common name. That's perfectly possible, for such doubling or quadrupling up is one of the problems with supposedly gardener-friendly popular names. Or it could be that there's just one species, which has one correct scientific name but has also accumulated three others that are invalid. Sometimes a problem of this kind can be sorted out by consulting the scientific literature, but not here, as far as I can tell.

In the interval between the publication of *Hortus Third* and *The New Royal Horticutural Society Dictionary of Gardening* (1992) there was a major change in nomenclature (already mentioned in the previous piece) that affected coleus as well as plectranthus. Coleus was maintained as a common name, but abolished as a genus in favor of a brand-new genus, *Solenostemon*. At the same time, Spanish thyme, once *Coleus amboinicus*, now became *Plectranthus amboinicus*. By now, it also had collected a whole passel of common names, including Mexican thyme, Cuban oregano, Mexican mint, Indian mint, and French thyme, all referring to the genuine culinary uses of its leaves in various regional cuisines.

The species name *amboinicus* refers to Ambon, one of the islands in the Moluccas (or Spice Islands). The name is somewhat misleading, for although this plant may grow there, it is native to tropical Africa, one of a number of species of Labiatae, some with medical properties, that are known collectively as African mints. This species has soft green leaves, but there is also a cultivar, *P. a.* 'Variegatus' which I acquired—or so I thought—about ten years ago at Fearrington Village in North Carolina. It was widely planted there and also sold in the garden shop as a double-duty plant—a culinary herb as well as a highly ornamental subject for containers.

The common name under which it was sold at Fearrington was Cuban oregano, but I was a bit puzzled. The leaves had such a nasty smell that I wouldn't even dream of cooking with them. Nevertheless, I valued the plant highly for its branching habit and bold foliage—large, fleshy, downy, dark green leaves with broadly deckled edges of somewhat dirty white. It proved to be easy to propagate by cuttings, and I passed it along to others, under the common and the scientific names I had been given.

Some doubt set in when a friend mentioned that the true Cuban oregano had pure-white leaf edges, whereas an imposter that sometimes went around under its name had smudgy white edges. The imposter was *P. forsteri* 'Marginatus'. When I found the real

P. a. 'Variegatus' in a herb nursery in Florida, I realized my mistake. There were other differences between the imposter and the real thing. True Cuban oregano has smaller, less downy leaves and a highly agreeable scent.

Over the years, I have collected additional species and cultivars. Some of them I cannot identify satisfactorily, including one of my favorites. This one has paddle-shaped opposite leaves about the size of a penny. They are intensely fragrant if touched only lightly. The aroma is minty, with just a hint of cinnamon or perhaps cloves. The plant clumps up into a thick little grove about a foot high. I'm not absolutely sure that what I have is a plectranthus—I'd be more confident if it would bloom—but it seems a reasonable guess.

There's no doubt whatsoever about my *P. discolor* 'Lemon and Lime', a low and spreading cultivar with strongly variegated leaves of several shades of green and greenish-yellow and gold. This one, which flowers constantly, is a fine plant to combine with upright forms of coleus in hanging baskets. So is *P. coleoides*, which seems also to run around as *P. madagascariensis*. Under either name, it's useful for its tiny scalloped leaves with prominent white edges and attractive veining.

I acquired one of my very best plectranthuses through theft, although it wasn't my doing and I didn't know it at the time. It's the Australian species *P. argentatus* 'Longwood Silver'. One of my horticulture students saw it growing in the conservatory at Longwood Gardens, thought (correctly) that I would like it, and swiped (wrongly) and rooted cuttings for both of us. 'Longwood Silver' is quite simply an indispensable plant. Its large, pebbly, fleshy leaves are a silvery gray that looks either bluish or greenish depending on the light. It is a rampant grower once summer heat sets in for real, and it is equally effective in containers and in borders with other plants.

There's a brand-new plectranthus on the market now, 'Athens Gem', and it's a dilly. Said to have originated as a sport of *P. amboinicus* 'Variegatus' in the garden of Professor Allan Armitage in Georgia, it has large leaves that are boldly variegated with blotches of dark green against margins of pale chartreuse. I love it, but suspect that it's really a mutation of *P. forsteri* 'Marginatus', for the leaves are quite large and have an unpleasant smell.

❦ Dismal History — But Great Beauty

THE EVENING NEWS recently carried word that people in Florida are concerned about daturas and brugmansias, which are so closely related that they used to be in the same genus. It seems that some teenagers are smoking the leaves of these plants to produce altered states of consciousness. This isn't a desirable practice, since one possible altered state is known as death. Thus, some municipalities are passing ordinances forbidding growing these plants. There aren't any such ordinances here in our part of the world, and we've got a lot of brugmansias, and daturas, too. Some are in pots on the deck, others in pots stuck here and there in the larger garden.

Daturas (including brugmansias) have a pretty dark and dismal history. As Professor Amos G. Avery pointed out many years ago in his chapter in the classic monograph *Blakeslee: The Genus Datura*, the Arabs in the eleventh century used it in small doses as a hallucinogen and in larger ones as a poison. The Aztecs called it "ololiuhqui" or magic plant, thought it sacred, and used it to get in touch with the spirit world. Native Americans in western South America, Professor Avery reports, gave it "in large doses with tobacco to women and slaves to deaden their senses before burial alive with their dead husbands or masters." The heroine of the opera *Lakme* committed suicide with something she brewed up from daturas, and they may also have been what Sister Angelica used to the same end in Puccini's *Suor Angelica*.

One weedy North American species, *D. stramonium*, figures prominently in an early episode of our national history. The British soldiers sent to Jamestown in 1676 to put down Bacon's Rebellion ate some of its seeds and, in the words of a later historian, "turned natural fools for several days. One would blow up a Feather in the Air; another would dart Straws at it with much Fury; and another stark naked was sitting in a Corner, like a Monkey, grinning and making Mows at them; a fourth would fondly kiss, and pat his Companions, and snear in their faces, with a Countenance more antick, than any in a Dutch Droll." As a result, the plant became known as Jamestown weed, later changing to jimsonweed.

Jimsonweed is nothing to mess with for it is loaded with the toxic alkaloids atropine, hyoscine, and hyoscyamine. Symptoms of poisoning by ingestion include dry mouth and unquenchable thirst, glassy eyes, pounding pulse, fever, and nausea. They may go on to include delirium, seizures, coma, and death. People who have tried to get a jump on tomato season by grafting the tops of tomatoes to

Brugmansia

jimsonweed rootstocks have regretted it long afterward. Snow White's wicked stepmother would have loved the resulting poisonous fruit.

I don't grow jimsonweed, but that's because it's ugly. Daturas and brugs, which are known collectively as angel's trumpets, are another matter. I wouldn't grow them if very small children were on the premises. But once they've reached a certain age, children can understand that they should put nothing in their mouths unless they are assured it's okay. Our grandkids have all passed this age, and accordingly our angel's trumpets are the glory of our deck from midsummer until frost.

Brugmansias, tender natives of South America, are small evergreen trees in frost-free regions. Where winter temperatures do not drop below 25°F, they are root-hardy, but those of us who live where winters are real may grow them in containers. They are the perfect adornment for decks and terraces, where the great beauty of their immense, pendant, trumpet-shaped flowers and their delicious nocturnal perfume may be enjoyed up close.

There are five species in the genus *Brugmansia* and a considerable number of hybrids. Among the species, *B. versicolor* is the most widely grown and perhaps the loveliest for its enormous tubular flowers with fluted petals. Like all brugmansias, it comes into flower in early evening. The flowers open a creamy white but quickly— within half an hour—change to luminous salmon pink. By day, the blossoms are unscented, but at night they advertise themselves to their pollinators with a strong, fruity scent that carries far on the still air.

All species hybridize freely among themselves to produce a wealth of superb cultivars. Sometimes the parentage is known. *B.* × *insignis* 'Pink' and *B.* × *i.* 'Orange' are crosses between *B. suaveolens* and *B. versicolor*. *B.* × *candida* 'Double White' has *B. versicolor* and the yellow-flowered *B. aurea* in its bloodline. Most cultivars, however, have such complicated parentage that it's pointless to try to figure it out.

I started out with only two brugmansias, *B. versicolor* and a hybrid called 'Jamaica Yellow'. The latter is a luxuriant, well-branched plant with luminous flowers of soft creamy yellow. It is a profuse bloomer; I have counted as many as sixty blossoms open at the same time on a plant eight feet tall. In time, I acquired three more kinds. 'Betty Marshall' is a good white, with especially fragrant flowers that reach ten inches in length. 'Charles Grimaldi', named for a landscape designer in California and popular on the West Coast, bears large flowers of yellow-orange with petals that flare outward and upward. 'Ecuador Pink' blooms abundantly and like some other brugmansias has on its petals odd, rather whiskery protuberances that turn upward at night.

Brugmansias are thirsty and hungry creatures that require a lot of water and regular fertilization from early spring until the end of July with a liquid fertilizer that's low in nitrogen but high in phosphorous and potassium. Their blooming habit is peculiarly cyclical. A great flush of flowering is followed by a period of rest, after which bloom recommences. I have heard it said that flowering is synchronous. That is, if a particular kind of brugmansia is in bloom in Key West, it will also be in bloom in Kuala Lumpur; and if it is resting in San Diego, it will also be resting on my deck in New Jersey. I do not know whether this assertion is true, but I have also heard it said that the cycle of bloom corresponds with the cycles of the moon. I believe that there is no correlation whatsoever, and it also flies in the face of the fact that 'Ecuador Pink' may be at a peak of flowering while 'Jamaica Yellow' has stopped for a while.

I have friends in North Carolina who have successfully overwintered brugmansias in the open ground, but they also report that it takes them so long to come into bloom that it's preferable to bring them indoors during the winter. Fertilizer should be withheld by the first of August and the plants brought inside to a cool, dim room before the first hard freeze. They should be watered sparingly if at all. The foliage will yellow and drop off as the plants enter a state of semidormancy. In late winter, cut the plants back very severely, and resume fertilizing and watering. The plants may be brought outside as soon as all danger of frost is past, and as warm nights return vigorous growth will occur.

For gardeners who don't want to go to the trouble of overwintering mature, full-sized plants, there's an alternative. Tip cuttings taken in midsummer root easily in water. The trick is to take the cuttings from stems that have matured enough to have lots of little dots on them. Remove all leaves but the newest ones on the ends of the cuttings, and plunge them into a glass of water in a spot out of direct sunlight. When the little dots start swelling into pimples (incipient roots) pot the cuttings in growing medium. These can be potted up in early fall and kept in a warm, sunny window. Regular watering and fertilizing will produce plants that will grow to flowering size by the time the next growing season rolls around.

There are both similarities and differences between the *Datura* and the *Brugmansia*. Both have trumpet-shaped or tubular flowers. Both are loaded with those toxic alkaloids. But even to an eye not trained in botany, brugmansias and daturas are difficult to confuse with one another. Where climate permits, brugmansias are woody plants, and daturas are herbaceous, either annuals or perennials, depending on the species. It is the flowering habit, however, that is the instant tip-off: the flowers of daturas point up, and those of brugmansias hang down.

All five species of *Brugmansia* are ornamental, but the same thing cannot be said of the eight species of *Datura*. It is difficult, however, to fault *D. innoxia*. This rangy, well-branched plant has musty-smelling, gray-green foliage and large flowers of purest white produced in abundance for about a month in late summer. A chancy perennial as far north as North Carolina, in New Jersey it is an annual that self-seeds so reliably that once it finds its way into a garden it will become a permanent fixture. Its seedpods, about the size of a pullet egg, bristle with thorny armament.

D. metel is another species worth growing, and like brugmansias it is a fine container plant for a deck. The range of floral color is fairly wide, embracing white, yellow, and shades of blue and lilac. I am particularly taken with 'Cornucopaea', a double-flowered cultivar. It is nowhere near as floriferous as *D. innoxia* or any of the brugmansias, but the flowers are stunning when they do appear. The season of bloom is much longer than that of *D. innoxia*, and in fact will continue throughout winter if plants are brought into a warm greenhouse. The tubular buds are almost black and swell to six inches in length before opening. The petals, as flounced and frilled as petticoats, are spotted with purple on their backs, soft lilac-purple on their facing side. The blossoms have to be hand-pollinated to produce seed, and to my surprise the doubling of the flowers is inherited in the next generation.

✿ I Will Plant Gourds

THE MAIN PERGOLA—the older one—above our deck allows us no choices. It's covered with kiwi vines, period. The other one, the newer and smaller one, does offer choices. One end is occupied by a splendid red swamp honeysuckle vine, but the other end is where we try annual vines—one year moonflowers, another rhodochiton, and so on. This year I will plant gourds.

I got the idea from a photograph of a gourd walk at Helmingham Hall in Suffolk, England. Here gourds of many shapes, sizes, and colors have been planted on a long trellis above a walkway so that their fruits hang down in great profusion from the end of summer well into fall. The effect is somewhat like a laburnum or a wisteria walk, except that the display goes on for many weeks instead of only a few days. And there is a dividend, in the form of the fruits.

According to their common names—and also their likely locations in the produce sections of grocery stores—gourds are easily distinguished from some other members of the Cucurbit family. They are in fact distinct in genus from cucumbers (*Cucumis sativa*) and watermelons (*Citrullus lanatus*), but matters become more complicated with squash and pumpkins. Despite their different culinary uses, they share the same botanical name, *Cucurbita pepo*, which also applies to a large group of small, decorative gourds, including apple gourds, pear gourds, flat fancy gourds, and warty-skinned fancy gourds. All of them have the yellow flowers of zucchini and pumpkins. Not all gourds are *Cucurbita pepo*, however. The large calabash or white-flowered gourd is *Lagenaria siceria*, which goes about under several common names indicating either the form of the fruits or their uses. Among these names are Hercules' club, bottle gourd, birdhouse gourd, swan gourd, dipper gourd, and a good many others. Then there's *Luffa aegyptica*, whose value lies not in

Gourd walk

an exterior rind that eventually dries to become as hard as wood but in its fibrous interior, from which vegetable sponges are made. And finally, there's the snake gourd (*Tricosanthes cucumerina* var. *anguina*), whose bizarre, twisted, cylindrical fruits turn bright orange on ripening.

It might be thought that all gourds differ from squash and pumpkins in that squash and pumpkins are edible and gourds are not, but that isn't the case. Calabashes and luffas can be eaten when they are very small and immature. Some strains are indeed unpalatable, thanks to high concentrations of cucurbitacin, the chemical that occasionally in lower concentrations makes a cucumber bitter.

The act of planting gourds unites us with much of human history and many other cultures. What other fruit has so many uses? Gourds may end up as rattles, dippers, and drinking bowls. In Turkey, the calabash, grown in a form that confines it and determines its shape, is one source—briar and a claylike substance high in magnesium are the others—of the meerschaum pipe so closely associated with Sherlock Holmes. Some gourds become musical instruments. South Africa has its thumb pianos, mbiras and kalingas, with sounding keys made of steel affixed to a gourd for resonance. One of the most ancient Chinese instruments is the sheng, which employs a large gourd as a windchest. In Hawaii, the hula is traditionally danced to the sounds of the ipu and the ipu heke, dried gourds of different sizes that are struck with a stick or slapped with the palm.

Gourds also have their religious uses, as in the gourd dance of the Kiowas, a circle dance performed to the sound of gourds shaken with ever-increasing intensity, a dance believed to call down divine blessings on the participants and onlookers. In several cultures, gourds are used as ceremonial masks.

The gourd also figures prominently in one bit of African American folklore and history. The song "Follow the Drinking Gourd" (meaning the Big Dipper) embodied specific geographical and astronomical instructions for slaves from Mississippi and Alabama making their way northward through Tennessee and Kentucky on the Underground Railroad to freedom. (The song ends, "For the old man is a-waiting for to carry you to freedom/If you follow the drinking gourd.")

Calabashes are reputedly beloved of purple martins. If a sufficient number of the gourds are dried, have holes of the proper size cut in them for entry, and are then suspended from timber frames ten feet or higher off the ground, a martin colony may—or may not—take up residence, to take care of many an unpleasant or noxious insect.

Since prehistoric times gourds have been objects of art as well as utility. Among American artists and craftspeople, particularly in the Southwest, there is much interest in gourds, which are carved, incised, burnished, painted, and stained to a pleasing result. They

Gourds

end up in art galleries and museum shops, at some fancy prices that may be entirely justified.

I will plant gourds this year, primarily for amusement and ornamental value. The vines grow rapidly to a considerable height, upward of fifteen feet or even more. Whether I will try to harvest and keep any of the fruits is yet to be decided. Gourds dry slowly as the water content of the ripe fruit is about 90 percent. They should be stored in a cool, dry location for several months—best off to themselves somewhere, since they may produce an objectionable odor while drying. Mildew on their rinds is almost inevitable, but it can be removed with a rag dipped in a weak chlorine solution. Some people just leave it, admiring the patterns it forms, much like frost flowers on windows in winter.

People who are passionate about gourds may join the American Gourd Society (P.O. Box 274, Mt. Gilead, OH 43338), which at present claims some 5,000 members. Founded in 1937 to bring together people interested in gourds and their history, mythology, cultivation, and uses, it sponsors gourd shows and sells books on gourds. Some one hundred genera of plants are classified as gourds, but the A.G.S. concentrates on the genera *Cucurbita*, *Lagenaria*, and *Luffa* and their varietal forms. The society is a good source of seeds, either mixed or specific kinds. It publishes a quarterly newsletter.

I might just become a member.

❧ Color and Flounces and Frills

IN THE LIVES of many gardeners, the evolution of taste and preference follows a common pattern, sometimes beginning in childhood. We begin with flowers; after all, isn't that the whole point of making a garden, a place that will be awash with bloom from the first crocus to the last flaming chrysanthemum? We want our flowers to be enormous, and preferably double, if that's possible. We feast our eyes on what they couldn't miss if they tried—dahlias as big as dinner plates, for example, and in every shade of the spectrum except blue and green. (We don't covet green in dahlia blossoms, but we may hope blue will come along one day.)

We start out wanting color, lots of it, and we prefer to have it mixed. There's a seductive mysteriousness in a package of zinnia or larkspur seed in mixed colors. The unpredictability of the result is exciting: we can hardly wait to see what we get. The things that catch our eye in mail-order catalogs are vividly colored, sometimes in several colors at a time. We set our hearts on cannas, gladiolas, tigridias.

Our hero is Luther Burbank. After all, he gave us Shasta daisies, both double and single (but big enough to count), so we wouldn't have to make do with common field daisies ever again. Our favorite word is "hybrid" (and, once we learn it, "tetraploid": twice as many chromosomes double the joy). We rejoice in the idea that in our gardens we don't have to settle for plants as they occur in mere nature, for nature needs improving, and our hybridizers are aces at making improvements.

Then things change.

We reject our first loves. We get sensible.

Foliage becomes as important as flowers—more so, in fact—because foliage stays the course for much of the year and flowers fade and wither. We come to disdain double flowers, particularly those that mock others, such as dahlia-flowered zinnias. The only dahlia we can stand to have around is *Dahlia merckii*, one of the species that the dahlia-improvers had to work with, which has single flowers of soft pink. It's unobtrusive, not like those in-your-face dahlias that the folks down the street insist on growing in plain view, causing pain to anyone with the good taste we are starting to display in our own gardens.

We want to think about color in advance, not be assaulted with it when it happens. We are *pure*. (Some say, we are *snobs*.)

That's pretty much the road I've traveled, but at summer's height there's a reversion to childhood: *tuberous begonias are irresistible*.

First hybridized in England and France in the 1890s from a complex assortment of South American species, including *Begonia boliviensis, B. veitchii*, and others, the present-day plants are the embodiment of my childhood dreams as a beginning gardener and everything that a tasteful mature gardener—a garden snob if you prefer—should reject as if they were sin itself. They are double (except the male flowers). Their flowers are so enormous that the plants can break off at ground level under their weight when they are moved. They come in the deepest shades of apricot, yellow, orange, scarlet, crimson, and pink. Even in dim light they glow, and when backlit by the lowering sun toward evening, they are absolutely incandescent. They are the triumph of the hybridizer's art and science. They couldn't survive ten days in the native habitats of their ancestors. Luther Burbank had nothing to do with them, but I bet he'd wish he had, were he still with us.

It's possible to spend serious money on tuberous begonias—as much as $32 apiece for some imported from England, where the firm of Blackmore & Langdon, which also deals in delphiniums, has been breeding, naming, and propagating tuberous begonias for almost a century. But I get mine on the cheap from a local greenhouse for about $3 each, already in bloom. They come without pedigree, being the seed-grown strain called Non-Stop Mixed Hybrids, but these mutts are radiant nonetheless.

Shade—the very idea of it as well as the reality—is wonderful during the torrid part of summer, but it can be fairly gloomy unless some thought is given to brightening it up with color. Tasteful plants won't do the job. We need colorful things like coleus and caladiums, and like these begonias in all their bright tones and warm hues, their flounces and frills resembling party dresses at a 1950s prom.

❧ Delightful Diascias

DIASCIAS, OR TWINSPURS, are among the most exciting new plants
to come along in recent years, especially for hanging baskets.

I say this with some confidence, despite the certainty that some
readers will say, "Been there, tried that, no thank you, not again."

I first got interested in the genus *Diascia*, which hails from
South Africa and is a member of the Figwort or Scrophulariaceae
family, when I heard the late Professor Gerald Straley, curator of the
University of British Columbia Botanical Garden in Vancouver, lavishly praise diascias. I admired Straley's judgment enormously and
proceeded to grow 'Ruby Field', the only diascia I could get my
hands on at the time. When it started to bloom in mid-May, I was
impressed. It covered itself with a multitude of little flowers, somewhat reminiscent of the male flowers of begonias, but with two little
spurs, like those of columbines, protruding from the backs of their
upper petals. The blossoms, slightly smaller than a dime, were
borne in loose racemes at the ends of their lax or trailing stems. In a
gentle breeze they jiggled and fluttered attractively, like tiny butterflies looking for a place to land. The flowers looked a bit like those
of nemesias, or maybe flattened snapdragons. (Neither of these
comparisons is at all surprising since diascias, nemesias, and snapdragons are in the same botanical family.) The color of the flowers
of 'Ruby Field' was hard to describe—pink, but what kind of pink?
Salmon pink, maybe, or shrimp pink. 'Ruby Field', I decided, was
nice.

Then June arrived, and with the heat and humidity 'Ruby Field'
quit blooming. It revived slightly (but not much) when cool weather
returned in September. I decided that Dr. Straley's high opinion of
disascias was probably justified for gardeners in the Pacific Northwest, but not the Atlantic Northeast.

I grew diascias again the following summer, however, and
revised my opinion considerably upward. I grew the species *D. fetcaniensis*, *D. rigescens*, and *D. vigilis*. All three are trailing or weav-
ing plants, with flowers in the shades of pink that typify most species
and cultivars. All three flourished without halting throughout the

summer. The following winter was too mild for adequately testing the winter-hardiness of anything, but *D. vigilis* and *D. fetcaniensis* survived with a little protective mulch.

In a certain sense the genus *Diascia*, which is closely related to the alonsoas of tropical South America, isn't really new. Botanists described and named several species in the nineteenth century, including *D. barberae* 'Pink Queen'. A half-hardy, seed-grown, strain of this species has been planted in England as a bedding annual for many years. It also figures in the ancestry of the vegetatively propagated hybrid cultivar 'Ruby Field', which is the diascia most widely grown in America.

The modern history of diascias begins in the late 1970s and early 1980s, when two British botanists, Olive Hilliard and Brian Burtt, identified and named several new species, perennial in varying degrees, that they discovered in South Africa. These species included *D. anastrepta, D. integerrima, D. lilacina,* and the aforementioned *fetcaniensis, rigescens,* and *vigilis.* Although diascias held little interest for South African gardeners because their season of bloom is limited to spring and extremely short, some plants were imported to England and Scotland. The change of climate transformed diascias altogether, for in the British Isles their season of bloom continues unchecked for six months or longer.

In the United Kingdom and elsewhere outside their native South Africa, diascias will not set seed because the bee that is their specific pollinator did not accompany them on their journey to the Northern Hemisphere. Numerous hybrids among the species listed, as well as another species, *D. mollis,* that came along a little later, have arisen — thanks to Hector Harrison, an Englishman with a hybridizer's brush and a passionate interest in the genus and its improvement. Harrison has introduced a great number of cultivars and has worked to extend the color range beyond shades of pink and rose toward apricot, grayish blue, and other hues. For several years in a row, Harrison's diascias have attracted fervent attention at London's Chelsea Flower Show.

Although some diascias have upright tendencies, or at least grow vertically until they finally flop under their own weight, their growth habit is basically lax, which makes them ideal for hanging baskets, especially in combination with plants with higher aspirations. I have grown them effectively in such baskets with *Fuchsia magellanica* 'Señorita', pentas, rosebud impatiens, and several cultivars of pelargoniums.

Considering the enormous climatic differences between the Pacific Northwest west of the Cascades and the rest of the country, it would be surprising if the success that gardeners have had with diascias in British Columbia, Washington, and Oregon were to prove pertinent for eastern gardeners, particularly in the Southeast. Gardening friends in North Carolina have in fact told me that their experience with these plants has been either notably disappointing or unhappy. But Dr. Allan Armitage, of the University of Georgia, has successfully tested many diascias. For southern gardens, he recommends the species *integerrima*, *fetcaniensis*, and *rigescens*, as well as eight cultivars. (He doesn't mention *D. vigilis*, which I like a lot.) The cultivars are 'Blackthorne's Apricot', 'Joyce's Choice', 'Langthorne's Lavender', 'Lilac Belle', 'Lilac Mist', 'Rupert Lambert', 'Salmon Supreme', and 'Wendy'. About 'Ruby Field' he is notably contemptuous, writing in his assessment of diascias for southern nursery managers that it's "one of the poorest performers" and "the runt of the litter." I must agree. Here in New Jersey it makes a fine showing in May, then, as I have already pointed out, sulks the rest of the summer, much like bedding lobelias.

Diascias are far too new in American gardening for anything other than a tentative and hesitant assessment. I have a wait-and-see attitude about their winter-hardiness in most of the country, and plan to take cuttings soon of those I grow, keeping some in my greenhouse and others in open ground with lots of protection. I also am perplexed by what seems to be parity between their performance in England and here and a lack of parity between their performance in South Africa and here. That they should be considerably more than spring-bloomers in England isn't surprising, but I am surprised that they don't give up the ghost as early here as they do in their native habitat. If someone would explain this matter to me, I would be extremely grateful. But diascias call for a lot of experimentation to find out which ones are suitable for what climates.

❧ Scented and Fancy-Leaf Geraniums

WITH A COUPLE of notable exceptions, there's one annual chore I just skip when the time rolls around in late autumn—storing my tender geraniums (by which I really mean pelargoniums) for the winter. I simply put them in the compost pile after the first good freeze, and then buy new ones the next year. There are good reasons, all having to do with a vast, international geranium industry whose workings are generally unknown by those of us who trot to the nearest garden center in May to bring home geraniums. For one thing, every large company dealing in these plants employs breeders who are constantly at work to improve them—to increase the number of flower clusters and the size of the flowers, to increase the quality of the foliage, and to develop new flower colors.

Even more importantly, geraniums are highly susceptible to a formidable array of ills. They are plagued by vascular wilts, fungal diseases, bacterial blights, and more than fourteen viruses that are spread by aphids, thrips, and other insects, and even the undisinfected hands of human beings who have touched tobacco. Considering that the value of the annual geranium crop in the United States alone exceeds $200 million wholesale, it is not surprising that commercial growers have strict and complex protocols to reduce the threat of disease. The process involves highly technical things, like meristeming and enzyme-linked immunosorbent assay, as well as rigid rules about greenhouse sanitation and insect control. The upshot is that I can rely on large companies like Oglevee or Fischer to provide healthy, and perhaps new and improved, geranium plugs or rooted cuttings to local growers each spring. There's no reason beyond frugality to hang last year's plants upside down in a cool room, keep them in a sunny window, or allow them valuable space in my greenhouse.

Now for those exceptions, the pelargoniums that I do carry over from one year to the next. These are geraniums whose main attraction lies in their foliage, not in their flowers. There are two major kinds.

First, the fancy-leaf zonals, whose main attraction lies in their foliage, fall into several categories. Bicolors, not too surprisingly, display two colors in their leaves, and tricolors three. Gold leafs are entirely golden yellow or chartreuse. Silver leafs are edged or banded in cream or white. Stellars can also be bicolors or tricolors or gold leafs, but their leaves are oddly shaped, more angular and pointed than rounded, perhaps handlike or fanlike.

You can't just run down to a garden center in May and pick up a bunch of fancy-leaf geraniums. They aren't part of that $200 million annual geranium crop. They are collector's items, to be hunted down and acquired one by one. (Only one fancy-leaf is in large-scale commercial production, 'Wilhelm Languth', which makes a sizable plant with red flowers and green leaves with wide white margins.)

I have come by the plants in my small collection of fancy-leaf geraniums piecemeal, running across one or two at a time unexpectedly in greenhouses in several parts of the country. My first was 'Vancouver Centennial', a stellar with pale yellow-green leaves washed with reddish brown centers. It cascades somewhat and shows to best advantage when placed where its trailing ways can be admired. Its flowers are bright scarlet, open in form, with jagged petals. Another stellar, acquired later, is 'Bird Dancer', a curious, compact little plant with tiny olive green leaves overlaid with a jagged-edged central band of brown that has a faint suggestion of red. Both of these cultivars are of recent origin, but others were favorites in Victorian times. These include, I believe: 'Mr. Henry Cox' (pale yellow leaves, ringed inside with two shades of red, salmon flowers); 'Skies of Italy' (yellow-edged leaves ringed with red and brown, single red flowers); 'Occold Shield' (golden leaves with brown centers and red flowers); and 'Ben Franklin' (green leaves with broad creamy margins and red flowers). Some fancy-leaf cultivars are impossible to describe fully, as adjacent leaves can vary enormously. On my plant of 'Mrs. Pollock' one leaf has an irregular yellow margin with a perfect butterfly image in two shades of green at its center. Right next to it, there's a leaf with margins of a much deeper shade of yellow, and instead of a butterfly the center has rings of two shades of green watermarked with crimson.

I also have an ever-increasing collection of geraniums with scented leaves, which abound in the genus *Pelargonium*, the greatest olfactory mimic in the plant kingdom. The leaves of many species ape other scents in the natural order. The scent of apples is found in *P. odoratissimum,* and *P. grossularioides* smells like coconut (some say coconut-oil suntan lotion). *P. crispum* is redolent of lemon, *P. citriodorum* of orange. Some people swear that the foliage of *P. scarboroviae* has the unmistakable perfume of ripe strawberries in the noonday sun.

As for *P. graveolens,* the fragrance of its leaves is so close to that of rose blossoms that its essential oils are extremely valuable in the perfume industry. Then there is my favorite species, *P. tomentosum,* whose large leaves I prize equally for their strong suggestion of peppermint and for their wonderful, velvety feel. Crosses among these and other species, such as *P. capitatum* and *P. scabrum,* have yielded cultivars with names like 'Atomic Snowflake', 'Dr. Livingston', 'Clorinda', and 'Chocolate Peppermint' (which I like not only for its smell of after-dinner mints but also for its large, fuzzy, green leaves with darker markings at their centers). Among the scented geraniums of hybrid origin, some people claim to find scents of eucalyptus, of nutmeg, of citronella, of Old Spice after-shave, and even of Juicy Fruit chewing gum.

The industrially produced zonal and ivy geraniums sold in garden centers to the tune of many millions of dollars seem at first to be extremely diverse, but for the most part that diversity is only a matter of flower color. It is almost trivial in comparison with the great variations of plant habit and leaf size and form among the scented geraniums.

Writing in 1932 in *The Fragrant Path,* Louise Beebe Wilder devoted a chapter to what she called "sweet leaved geraniums." Fondly recalling her childhood in Baltimore, she remembered a small commercial greenhouse "owned by an apple-cheeked old Englishman whose name was Unwin." Mr. Unwin had a large collection of scented geraniums, which Wilder and her father often visited. "No notice was taken of me," she writes, "and so, left to my own devices, I would snip as I went, a leaf here, a leaf there, until finally with my hands and pockets full of aromatic leaves I would subside on an upturned tub to sniff and compare the different scents to my heart's content. It was a very good game indeed, as well as valuable nose training."

Wilder goes on to assert that once upon a time hundreds of varieties of these geraniums could be had in England and America, but in her day they were so badly neglected that it was impossible by diligent searching to come by more than two or three kinds. She feared that most had been lost forever, yet hoped that perhaps "plants that have been hiding away in obscure greenhouses, in farm kitchens and shabby parlours, will be brought to light and once more slipped and exchanged, sniffed over and exhibited as of yore."

Mrs. Wilder's hopes were realized, not her fears. Thanks to a few specialized growers in North America, Great Britain, and Australia many heirloom varieties, both fancy-leaf and sweet-leaf, have been preserved. I have been able gradually to start a collection by picking up cultivars one by one whenever one turns up in local nurseries or garden centers. Several mail-order specialists also list many scores of different "sweet-leaf geraniums" (as well as fancy leaf ones).

❦ The Sweet Scent of Jasmines

ANYONE WHO PLANTS a jasmine is also planting a link with an ancient and romantic part of garden history. The very word *jasmine* conveys a sense of poetry and aristocratic privilege. Jasmines loom large in the folklore and religion of India, where they have long graced shrines and temples sacred to Vishnu. The delicious sweet and spicy scent of jasmines pervaded the air in the gardens of Persia and Samarkand, whose poets sang the praises of the plant at every opportunity. Boccaccio did the same in his *Decameron,* and Louis XIV insisted that his gardeners plant jasmines in the grounds of his pleasure palaces at Marly and at Trianon.

Native to Africa, Asia, and Australia, the genus *Jasminum* has long been transported throughout the world by its passionate admirers. One species, *J. sambac,* was brought by the Moors to Spain, and even today its perfume mingles with the equally heady scent of orange blossoms in the Alhambra and other historic Spanish gardens. Marco Polo discovered jasmines growing in the gardens of China, and later Venetian traders brought them to Europe, along with silks, teas, spices, and gunpowder.

Most jasmines have white flowers, but there are exceptions. *J. beesianum* bears pink flowers, *J. nudiflorum* and *J. mesnyi* yellow ones. The latter two have no fragrance whatsoever, and the same is true of *J. rex* (named for the king of what used to be called Siam), *J. multiflorum*, and—its name notwithstanding—*J. odoratissimum*. Considering that highly fragrant species are easy to come by, it seems advisable to concentrate on these and forget the others, except for *J. nudiflorum*, which is by far the most winter-hardy species (to Zone 6) and one to be treasured for its long period of radiant bloom in January and February.

Many fragrant jasmines remain, all with white flowers. *J. polyanthum*, collected in China earlier in this century by George Forrest, is a tender winter-blooming species, profuse in flower and powerful in scent—if, that is, it blooms. It is a short-day plant that will not initiate bloom if the least bit of light reaches it at night for even a brief moment. Furthermore, its vining tendencies make it difficult to keep in check. I once owned a plant, but ultimately discarded it after years of never seeing it in bloom.

Next to *J. nudiflorum*, the hardiest jasmine species is the poet's jasmine, *J. officinale*, which can survive in a somewhat protected location in Zone 7 as far north as the North Carolina Piedmont. This jasmine is a shrubby vine capable of attaining a height of thirty feet in areas with mild winters. One of its cultivars, *J. o.* 'Grandiflorum', is of great importance in the perfume industry. In the south of France many acres are dedicated to its cultivation, for the sake of the attar that is extracted by coating the flowers with a grease that absorbs their essential oils.

The subtropical species *J. sambac* is my favorite jasmine, for many reasons, starting with its place in my childhood memories of Texas. My mother always contrived to have it growing in large pots on the patio right next to the house, where she could enjoy its rich and spicy perfume. She planted it with red hibiscus and blue cape plumbago for a pleasant color combination with a distinctly tropical effect. There are two cultivars. 'Maid of Orleans' is a compact plant with glossy green leaves. Named for Joan of Arc, it blooms intermittently throughout the year, producing a good crop of dime-sized, pure white flowers that fade to magenta as they age. 'Grand Duke of Tuscany' (so named, legend has it, because the Grand Duke's gardener stole it for his lover) is less attractive to the eye than 'Maid of

Orleans'. It is stiff and ungainly, and its double flowers, which are not particularly abundant, look a bit like cottage cheese. (There are said to be forms with flowers four inches across that look like white carnations, but I haven't seen them.) 'Grand Duke of Tuscany' undoubtedly has the headiest perfume of all jasmines—a musky scent of sweetness and spice that travels far on the air on a warm, still night.

Some so-called jasmines aren't jasmines at all, but jasmine-imposters. Cape jasmine is a gardenia, any one of several cultivars of *Gardenia augusta*. Night-blooming jasmine (*Cestrum nocturnum*), a member of the Nightshade family, is a tender shrub that explodes into bloom at intervals, producing large numbers of greenish-white flowers. They have no scent whatsoever by day but become increasingly fragrant as dusk changes to dark. I find its odor cloying, like cheap soap.

'Maid of Orleans'

Two "jasmines" that are beloved of many southern gardeners are the confederate jasmine and the Carolina jasmine, respectively *Trachelospermum jasminoides* and *Gelsemium sempervirens*. Contrary to common belief, confederate jasmine is not named for the Confederacy of Robert E. Lee and Scarlett O'Hara but for the former Confederation of Malay States, where it is native. It is a handsome vine with waxy, dark green leaves and fragrant creamy blossoms. As for Carolina jasmine (or jessamine), genuine danger lurks in its common name. The flowers of true jasmines are edible, often finding their way into teas, but every part of this native jasmine-imposter is so loaded with toxic alkaloids that tea from its flowers could be deadly.

❧ The Nose-Twisting Nasturtiums

IN RECENT YEARS nasturtiums have become an endangered species of the garden. Find a gardener who is still growing them, and you have found a patient soul who is willing to go to the trouble of ordering them by mail and growing them from seed. You have also found a gardener who knows that a wooden half barrel spilling over with the piquant, spicy leaves and radiant flowers of nasturtiums is one of the most sensuous delights of a garden, from high summer well into autumn.

Nasturtiums, like gloriosa daisies, are fine plants for initiating children into the pleasures of gardening. The seeds of these annuals are large, about the size of a pea, but corky. Children know for sure that they are planting something, with none of the perplexity that

Nasturtiums

accompanies planting seeds of nicotianas or petunias, which might as well be specks of dust. If the weather is warm when they are planted—as it ought to be to avoid rot and poor germination—the seeds sprout in about a week, which is just under a child's threshold of patience. They grow quickly, blooming in six or seven weeks.

Nasturtiums have had an illustrious list of grown-up admirers ever since 1569, when the Spanish physician and botanist Nicolas Monardès introduced them to Europe from South America. The English herbalists of the seventeenth century were fairly potty over them. In *Paradisi in Sole* (1629) John Parkinson wrote of the plant he called both "larkes heeles" and "Indian cress" that it was of "so great beauty and sweetness withal, that my Garden of delight cannot bee unfurnished of it." Nasturtium nibbling is also a venerable American tradition. Early in the nineteenth century, Bernard M'Mahon wrote in *The American Gardener's Calendar*, the first truly American comprehensive book on gardening, that the nasturtium "is very deserving of cultivation, as well on account of the beauty of its large and numerous orange-colored flowers, and their use in garnishing dishes. The green berries or seeds of this plant make one of the nicest pickles that can possibly be conceived; in the estimation of many, they are superior to capers." Thomas Jefferson thought so, too. At Monticello, he always had nasturtiums in his kitchen garden, and one year, after a crop failure, he borrowed seeds from a friend, so that his summer salads would not lack their accustomed peppery zip and zing.

Claude Monet also was ardent about nasturtiums, planting them abundantly at Giverny, where in midsummer they grew up turquoise arches and sprawled along gravel walks. I have not gone on pilgrimage to Monet's garden yet, but late one winter I saw nasturtiums used to fine effect in the atrium garden of the Isabella Stewart Gardner Museum in Boston, where they grew in pots in high open windows below pointed Venetian arches. The plants trailed down a stone wall twenty feet or more, a curtain of soft green foliage jeweled with crimson-orange blossoms.

The name given to these annuals—nasturtiums—sounds like botanical Latin, but it isn't. *Nasturtium* (which means "nose-twister" and was coined by Pliny) properly applies to European watercress, *Nasturtium officinale*. Watercress and garden nasturtiums aren't even related; watercress is a Crucifer, and nasturtiums are in another family altogether, the Tropaeolaceae. Botanically, nasturtiums are *Tropaeolum majus*, a name bestowed by Linnaeus. The genus name contains a metaphor of war; it comes from the Greek word *tropaion*, for trophy—as an emblem of victory the captured shields and helmets of the vanquished were displayed on poles erected at the scene of battle. Linnaeus thought that the rounded leaves of nasturtiums looked like shields and the flowers like golden helmets stained with blood. The military overtones of nasturtiums endured into the nineteenth century, when books about the language of flowers claimed that nasturtiums were symbols of patriotic pride.

Modern hybridizers have given the nasturtium considerable attention, a plus for both enlarging the range of flower color to embrace pastel shades and increasing the length of flower stems. Longer stems make nasturtiums useful as cut flowers and also prevent the flowers from blushing unseen beneath the luxuriant foliage. But breeders have also worked for double flowers on compact plants, as they have done with marigolds and zinnias. Like many other gardeners I prefer single to double nasturtium flowers and enjoy seeing the plants cascade or trail, according to their wont. We turn, therefore, to older strains such as the heirloom 'Empress of India', which combines a cascading habit, large round leaves of lovely blue-green, and long-spurred single flowers of radiant vermilion to a stunning effect.

If one strange report is true, nasturtiums have a curious property: under the right conditions they ignite or light up at night. In 1762 the daughter of Linnaeus claimed to have seen wondrous flashes of light streaming from these flowers on a sultry Swedish summer evening. Perhaps. I thought once I had seen the same thing, but it was only fireflies, resting on our nasturtiums.

❦ The Great Verbena Revival

EVIDENCE OF A GREAT resurgence of interest in verbenas may be found by comparing the listing of species and cultivars given in Allan Armitage's *Herbaceous Perennial Plants* (1989) and those offered today by mail-order nurseries such as Plant Delights in Raleigh, North Carolina. Professor Armitage serves up a mere five species and three cultivars, not including 'Homestead Purple'. After his book was published, he and Michael Dirr found this popular, much-planted cultivar at an old homestead in Georgia and introduced it to the nursery trade. Plant Delights' current catalog lists two species, the tall V. bonariensis (a fine front-of-the-border plant for its skinny profile) and the fiery red V. peruviana (which figures prominently in the ancestry of the annual bedding plants that were the only verbenas on the market about fifteen years ago). The catalog goes on to describe another sixteen cultivars, identifying some as forms of V. canadensis, V. ternera, or V. tenuisecta, but refusing to speculate about the parentage of others, such as 'Blue Princess', 'Snowflurry', and 'Texas Appleblossom'.

There's a new craze for verbenas set loose in the land, and it's accompanied by a strong sense of déjà vu, a replay of passions that sprang up in England in early Victorian times. Between 1826 and 1837 V. incisa, V. peruviana, and V. tweedii were introduced to Europe from South America, following the earlier introduction of V. bonariensis in 1726. Hybrids of the more recent newcomers, known collectively as V. × hybrida and often given individual fancy names, were soon available in the hundreds and much used in the carpet bedding landscape style of the mid-Victorian era. But even William Robinson, a staunch opponent of carpet bedding and its gaudy excesses, had nothing to say against verbenas. In the fifteenth and final edition of The English Flower Garden (1933), he wrote, "Their wonderful diversity and brilliancy of colour and their many flowers combine to make them most effective plants." His words still hold today. Verbenas come in almost every color but yellow, orange, and a true blue. There are blazing reds, soft roses, wonderfully sullen purples, whites, and many lilacs and lavenders; and they bloom unstintingly and abundantly from early May well into autumn. (Some, however, including 'Homestead Purple', tend to bloom themselves to death. I have found it useful to prune them severely in early August and give them a breather, after which they will burst back into renewed bloom.)

I'm not exactly sure when and how the resurgence of verbenas in American horticulture began. I first became aware of it in the

152 • ALLEN LACY

early 1980s, when the former Montrose Nursery offered several cultivars of *V. canadensis*, identified only by color. The one called 'Red-Violet' was especially luminous and combined beautifully with the similarly trailing, purple-leafed *Tradescantia pallida* 'Purpurea'. Montrose also sold *V. tenuisecta* 'Edith', named for Edith Eddleman, the co-curator with Douglas Ruhren of the splendid herbaceous border at the North Carolina State University Arboretum, now the J. C. Raulston Arboretum. Montrose played a major role in the new rise of verbenas in our garden landscape.

There have been other players, including Greg Grant of Lone Star Growers in San Antonio, Texas. With Dr. Jerry Parsons of the Texas Agricultural Extension Service, he discovered 'Texas Rose', a superb deep pink verbena with delicately incised foliage, growing in a roadside ditch near Batesville, Texas. Grant also introduced 'Blue Princess', a fragrant cultivar that he imported from England.

'Blue Princess' is not the only cultivar of these mostly South American tender perennials to originate across the ocean. 'Sissinghurst' is a fine deep rose with somewhat lacy foliage that got its name by sheer mistake. Possibly derived from *V. ternera*, the plant was collected, perhaps in Tenerife (the matter is far from clear) by the director of the Institute for Greenhouse Crops Research in Sussex, who gave it to Pamela Swerdt and Sibylle Kreutzberger, head gardeners at Sissinghurst from 1959 to 1991. They sent the plant to the Royal Horticultural Society for identification, with a label indicating where it came from. The label was misunderstood to be a cultivar name, but it stuck after the plant won an Award of Merit from the RHS in 1982.

Verbenas have many virtues, and also a few faults. Besides their abundant and colorful bloom, they are highly tolerant of drought, once established. They insist, however, on full sun and good ventilation, and if these needs are not met, they can be plagued with unsightly but harmless powdery mildew. They may be attacked by spider mites, particularly if grown in nutrient-poor soil. I should add one thing. Many verbena cultivars today are being marketed as perennials. That may be true of some cultivars as far north as Washington, D.C., but I have yet to get one through even a mild winter. 'Homestead Purple', however, has survived in the garden of a neighbor who has it planted on a berm. (Drainage, drainage, drainage!) It's probably best to consider verbenas as tender perennials, and either replace them every year or try to overwinter cuttings in a cold frame.

New recently at garden centers is a somewhat mysterious strain of verbenas marketed under the trademarked name "Tapien." There are four cultivars, all named by color: 'Powder Blue', 'Rose', 'Lavender', and 'Blue' (which isn't blue at all but purple). The series is being propagated in this country under license from Suntory, a conglomerate in Japan that started out as a distiller of whiskey. The plants are identified as hybrids, but there's room for doubt.

My effort to find out more about the origin of the Tapiens has produced only sketchy results. Suntory is said to have sent a research scientist to tropical South America to study techniques of winemaking in frost-free climates. He spotted some interesting verbena species and suggested that his company hybridize them and go into the bedding plant business. Whatever the case, the Tapiens are sensational. Their very dark green foliage is delicate and ferny. The plants lie prostrate, with almost no vertical dimension. In hanging baskets they trail downward to considerable length, three feet or even more by summer's height. They are ideally suited for planting in large urns with other plants, for they will spill over the sides and hang down, softening the lines of the container with beautiful foliage and flowers. They are, happily, resistant to mildew.

The flower clusters of the Tapiens are small compared with those of 'Homestead Purple' or 'Sissinghurst', but they are produced in prodigious numbers. The Tapiens root along their stems as they grow and are exquisitely easy to propagate, rooting in about a week with no hormone dip. (Their trademarked status means you can't sell them under the Tapien name without permission.) They are said to be hardy to 14°F, and a friend of mine in Oregon reports that those she got in the fall, somewhat in advance of their formal introduction, came through the winter just fine, even escaping from her flower beds to take up residence in her lawn.

Verbenas have some strange-sounding, nonhorticultural resonances among a tiny segment of the population. They are celebrated in various ways by groups with names like the Cult of Final

Ecstasy, the Divine Circle of the Sacred Grove, the Order of the Eternal Dawn, and the Celestial Chorus. The verbena that these cults venerate is not one of the New World species or cultivated derivatives, however, but the European herb *Verbena officinalis*, the blue vervain, which has a long history of religious and occult associations. Its name in Greek meant "sacred plant," for it was used to purify dwellings from evil. The Romans crowned statues of Venus with wreaths of verbena and myrtle. The plant was particularly important in certain Druid rituals and has had a long association with sorcery and witchcraft, which in some quarters continues even today.

There's a final thing to report, and it's slightly disturbing. If certain taxonomists get their way, we may have to learn not to speak of 'Homestead Purple' or 'Sissinghurst' as a verbena at all. These botanists want to reserve that name for *Verbena officinalis* and only a tiny number of New World species. *V. canadensis*, *V. tenuisecta*, and the others that bring such beauty to our gardens? We'd have to learn to put them in the genus *Glandularia*.

❧ *Play-Pretties of the Gods*

ITS COMMON NAMES are multitudinous and tinged with theology, medicine, and metaphor. It's Aaron's rod, Jove's beard, Jupiter's eye, and thunder plant; healing blade; houseleeks, live-forever, and hen-and-chickens. Botanically it's usually *Sempervivum*, a literal translation of "live-forever" into scientific Latin. But part of the genus, the part that includes Jove's beard, has been split off and put in a separate genus of its own, *Jovibarba*, another literal translation of a common name.

I'm not sure why, but sempervivums have long been considered play-pretties of the gods, especially Zeus, his Latin counterpart Jupiter or Jove, and the more Teutonic Thor and Wotan. What these sky gods have in common is that they like to fool around with lightning and thunder; it was long believed that they drew the line at hurling a bolt anywhere near a fine clump of sempervivums. The belief didn't die with paganism. Far from it. The Christian emperor

Charlemagne commanded his subjects to plant the species S. *tecto-rum* on their rooftops to guard against lightning. Thus arose the common name houseleek, which generally applies to other species, and the specific epithet, *tectorum*, meaning "of rooftops."

As for medicine and the name healing blade, folklore holds that the crushed leaves of this succulent genus of perennials can ease minor burns, somewhat like those of *Aloe vera*, and that they can bring down fevers if applied to the forehead. I've heard rumors that they also remove warts and freckles, and take care of chigger and mosquito bites, but I ignore them.

The main thing is, sempervivums are fun. I remember them fondly from my own childhood when the only name I had for them was hen-and-chickens. It was a good name. We could start with just one plant, and soon tinier versions of it were popping out all around the mother rosette of leaves, just like the baby chicks around their mother Leghorn or Rhode Island Red out in the henhouse. Each little rosette could be detached and given its own spot to brood, and soon it too would have its chicks. It was one of my earliest lessons in reproduction, if not of sex.

I've said already, more than once, that I find intellectual beauty in coleus and several other sorts of plants because they embody great variations in expressions of common themes. (Bach's "Goldberg Variations" comes to mind.) So it is with the genus *Sempervivum*— great differences of effect, within strict limits. All sempervivums are built to the same plan. But some are large, spreading, and open; some are tiny, closed, and somehow inhibited; some are as cob-webby as a neglected upper shelf in an old bookcase, but others are downy, satiny, or smooth and glossy. Some have tubular or quilled leaves. Foliage color varies: pale green, forest green, rose, gray, wine, purple, and almost black are all possible, plus suffusions of several colors on one another. Some mound themselves up into tight clumps, but others spread to form a mat. And sempervivums are real toughies. I have had them sail through a rough winter, like that of 1993–1994, in shallow terra-cotta trays left unprotected in an exposed location on our deck. Their main requirement is perfect drainage.

Considering that the dominant method by which semps repro-duce is chastely vegetative (a trick humans have not yet managed), it is always a surprise when in midautumn sex raises its head, in the form of peculiar starry blossoms in shades of pink and cerise and celadon, atop strange little fleshy stalks, the whole thing looking like a life form that evolved on some other planet or at the bottom of the sea.

Sempervivums are classic passalong plants that usually are handed on from one gardener to another without the myriad fancy names used by some nurseries selling them. The names don't matter particularly. I've never seen a semp I didn't like, never had one that some other gardener didn't ask for a piece of. (Generosity comes easy, considering that semps multiply as readily as bacteria.)

I thought I had enough. But then a catalog arrived from Porterhowse Nursery in Oregon offering 424 named cultivars of *Sempervivum*, and over fifty of *Jovibarba*. Some names were intriguing: 'Hooker' (let's hope for Sir Joseph!), 'Ashes of Roses', 'Edge of Night', 'Jelly Bean', and 'Sassy Frass'. I was in the mood for more sempervivums—but how to choose? Fortunately, I didn't have to. Porterhowse would do it for me, in the form of a "collector's case" of twenty plants in four-inch pots. For the really far gone on these darlings of the gods, this catalog advises that up to ten cases may be ordered without a single plant being duplicated.

✿ The Tender Tropical Mallows

I MUST START with the Chinese hibiscus, *Hibiscus rosa-sinensis*, a subtropical shrub that will not survive winter temperatures much below freezing. But this mallow is extraordinarily fine for its glossy deep green foliage and for a palette of colors that Gauguin would have loved: rich reds, radiant pinks and lavenders, burnished oranges, lemon yellows, pristine whites, and blends of two or more colors. Sometimes the blossoms are double, but as with hollyhocks, I prefer the singles.

The only faults of the tropical hibiscus are that its flowers lack any trace of fragrance, that they last only a day, and that the plant itself will not return where winters are serious. These faults are not

Hibiscus

important, however. The sheer opulent colors of hibiscus treat the eye to a feast, even if the flowers offer nothing to the nose. The flowers may be evanescent, but the plant blooms freely, and each blossom remains beautiful for hours, even out of water.

Winter isn't really much of a problem for me in keeping these hibiscus through to another year. In fact, it's no problem at all, since I now have a greenhouse; but even when I didn't, we just brought the plants inside in late September and kept them in a cool room until spring, watering them very lightly and occasionally. Other gardeners may want to simply treat them as annuals, buying new ones every year. They bloom well when only twelve or eighteen inches high.

Too often overlooked is the red shield plant, a form of the African species *H. acetosella* with maplelike, maroon-purple foliage. The flowers are generally so insignificant as hardly to be noticeable, but the leaves are beautiful and are borne on plants that rapidly grow seven feet or higher once the weather warms up in early summer. A tropical perennial, red shield is winter-hardy only to Zone 10, but in colder areas it can be grown as an annual from seeds planted indoors in late March. It makes a fine quick-growing screen, as well as a bold accent plant in a sunny herbaceous border.

I said that generally the flowers of red shield aren't much, but I got a clone in North Carolina the year our greenhouse went up that proved a fine exception. Inside the greenhouse it started blooming in December and kept it up until April. The many flowers were an inch and a half across, a lovely old rose with a dark maroon eye. I was puzzled, because every flower formed a seedpod in the absence of any perceptible pollinators. A botanist friend offered the probable explanation. My red shield hibiscus is apomictic—a female plant that produces seeds without sex. Each seed will germinate to bring forth a daughter that is a perfect genetic copy of the plant that produced it.

The parlor maple or flowering maple is no maple at all, but a member of the Malvaceae, in this case *Abutilon*. Abutilons are another Victorian favorite now enjoying revived interest. There are many vegetatively propagated cultivars, 'Moonchimes' and others, but I'm delighted with a new seed-grown strain called Summer Sherbert that was introduced in 1998 in the United States, and in 1999 in Europe and Great Britain, where it's called Bella. These were bred in Costa Rica by Claude Hope, who many years ago brought into being the modern impatiens hybrids that bloom their heads off from late spring until the first frost of autumn in almost every American garden.

These new abutilons are really fine plants. Burpee touts them as an annual and suggests that unlike all other abutilons heretofore their flowers face upward and outward. Neither of these claims is exactly on the mark. They bloom very soon after the seeds have been sown and have germinated—flowers three inches across can appear on plants under six inches tall, with only four to six leaves, a curious sight indeed. Within a couple of months the plants are eighteen inches tall and covered with typical Mallow family blossoms in a wide range of pastel shades of pink, yellow, creamy white, apricot, and copper. Their quick bloom from seed and their profusion of blossoms over a prolonged period make them as useful as true bedding annuals, but they are woody plants that can be held over from one year to the next as houseplants or greenhouse sub-jects. As for flowering habit, their blossoms are not entirely pendant, like most other abutilons, but the most I can say is that they face slightly outward—not upward.

There's some good news about Summer Sherbert, perhaps. Abutilons are tender plants. Rumors turn up from time to time about winter-hardy cultivars, but so far they have all turned out to be unfounded. In Zone 7 at least, Summer Sherbert does produce occasional plants that overwinter successfully outdoors. They don't even lose all their leaves! I base this report on my experience and the experience of friends following the winter of 1998. It was, of course, the warmest winter on record in much of the country, including New Jersey. It may be that some plants in this seedling strain will prove more susceptible to cold temperatures than others, but these abutilons will bear watching for signs of true immunity to the worst that winter can dish out.

IV Fall and Winter

✖ Carousels of Spider Lilies

I ALWAYS GET A BIT HOMESICK for Texas in late August, when I know that spider lilies *(Lycoris radiata)* are blooming there on their leafless stalks. Because I live just outside the northernmost limit of their winter-hardiness I can't grow them. But when early fall rolls around, these bulbs still bloom in the imaginary garden in my head. I remember the farmwomen of my childhood, who grew them in their front yards, usually planted in big circles, with nothing in the middle. They reminded me somehow of merry-go-rounds, and so did the dusky red flower clusters themselves. Their individual florets were arranged circularly, facing outward, for a carousel look. Their slightly twisted petals were reflexed upward, and from the base of each one the extremely long pistil and stamens jutted out in an upward curve, ringing the entire cluster with the spidery "legs" of its common name. (Their scientific name, incidentally, comes from Roman history: the actress Lycoris was Mark Antony's mistress.)

Soon after Japan was opened to the West in 1854, Captain William Roberts, an associate of Commodore Perry, brought three shriveled spider lily bulbs to a niece in New Bern, North Carolina. The bulbs took their own sweet time in getting established, but right after the Civil War they bloomed and began to increase prodigiously, spreading

Lycoris radiata

quickly throughout the South as they passed from gardener to gardener.

Red spider lilies spring up almost overnight soon after the hot days begin to abate, giving grounds for hope that the fall rains will soon come to wash away summer's dust and grime, cool the air, and refresh our spirits. Their flowers have a complex beauty that no other bulb can match. Only the climbing African lily, G*loriosa roth-schildiana*, comes close with its own twisted and reflexed petals, striped yellow and scarlet, like tongues of fire.

Two species of *Lycoris* are winter-hardy at least to the lower Midwest and to coastal New England. One of them, *L. sprengeri*, is scarce and hard to find, but the other, *L. squamigera*, has been around in this country since the late nineteenth century and is often offered in bulb catalogs. *L. squamigera* has accumulated several common names, two of which are inappropriate. Some people call it Hall's hardy amaryllis, for it went around for a time under the name *Amaryllis halli* or *hallii*, after Dr. George Hall, the New Englander who in the nineteenth century introduced many Asian plants into American horticulture (including, alas, Japanese honeysuckle). Even though *L. squam-igera* looks much more like an amaryllis than spider lilies do, it's not an amaryl-lis at all, and anyway

Lycoris
squamigera

that genus has been dashed to smithereens, most of its species now being reclassified as *Hippeastrum, Brunsvigia, Rhodophiala,* and so on. (All that's left now is *Amaryllis belladonna,* the Jersey lily.) Some people, especially in the Upper South, call *L. squamigera* Guernsey lily, another misnomer, since that common name belongs to an entirely different bulbous plant, *Nerine sarniensis.*

L. squamigera has two equally valid common names, magic lily and resurrection lily, although again it helps to remember that the plant isn't a lily at all or even in the Liliaceae. The adjectives in both common names refer to the sudden appearance of the flowers seemingly out of nowhere, a trait characteristic of all the lycorises. (My friend Joanne Ferguson, who was born and raised in Arkansas, reports that her grandmother's washerwoman called the plant "Rexrise lily.") To the casual eye, magic lilies don't much resemble spider lilies. Their flowers are simpler, being upward- and outward-facing trumpets, and there are fewer of them in a cluster, generally only four or five. The color is an odd shade of lavender-pink, veering toward blue. Magic lilies bloom earlier, too, three or four weeks before spider lilies.

❧ Dazzling Dahlias

THE DAHLIA HAS GONE about under several names. The Aztecs, who domesticated it from wildlings growing in the mountains of central Mexico, called it cocoxochitl. (The name in Nahuatl, the language of the Aztecs, means water pipe. The hollow stems of one species were used to bring spring water to cities.) If the Aztec name had passed into European languages along with the plant itself, we would probably call it cocoxochitos, considering that their word for tomato was tomatl.

The Spanish botanist Antonio José Cavanilles (1745–1804) named the genus *Dahlia* for Andreas Dahl (1751–1789), a student of Linnaeus, but for a time it was also named *Georgina,* a name proposed by Carl Ludwig Wildenow, a German botanist who mistakenly believed that the name *Dahlia* had already been given to another plant altogether. Georgina is still occasionally used as a common name in Germany, and in fact the first plants that reached the United States came from Germany, labeled as Mexican georginas.

Hernán Cortés and his soldiers in 1518 were the first Europeans to spot dahlias, growing in hedges in the central highlands of Mexico. They may have admired the plants for their lustrous green foliage and their small, single, red flowers, but Spanish botanical literature is strangely silent about dahlias until 1798, the year of their formal accession to the collections of the Madrid Botanical Garden. Once the historical record begins, theft and dahlias are conjoined, at least according to one apocryphal but often repeated story. As this tale has it, the royal gardeners at El Escorial, the large monastery built by Philip II outside Madrid, guarded their dahlias zealously, being peculiarly unwilling to see them fall into the hands of either commoners or foreigners. But a French visitor to the monastery swiped some seeds and gave them to the Empress Josephine, who valued them almost as much as the roses she grew at Malmaison. She was just as jealous of them as the Spanish royal gardeners had been. Theft made its second appearance in this tale of the dahlia when one of Josephine's courtiers stole some tubers for her lover. Josephine then flew into an imperial snit. According to Tyler Whittle's *The Plant Hunters* (1970), she had all her dahlias dug up and chopped to pieces instantly and commanded that no one even mention them from then on.

The truth about the early career of dahlias in Europe is much more straightforward. Vincente Cervantes, a botanist at the Mexican Botanic Gardens, sent seed in 1789 to Cavanilles at the Royal Botanic Garden in Madrid. He in turn sent seed to other European botanists, including some in France, sometime around 1802.

But the story about Josephine does have a kind of poetic truth, teaching the lesson that dahlias may arouse extreme emotions. Some passionate lovers of dahlias grow almost nothing else and refuse to describe themselves as gardeners. Dahlias, moreover, like hostas and daylilies, are plants that have fostered fellowship among the like-minded. The American Dahlia Society is a large and thriving institution with a great many local chapters all over the country, but especially in the Pacific Northwest. Australia, Great Britain, and

South Africa also have their national societies of breeders, growers, exhibitors, and just plain enthusiasts. To these societies we owe a system of classification that sorts dahlias into various classes, according to size (nine categories in all, from under two inches to more than ten), form (eighteen possibilities—formal decorative, ball, pompon, and so on), and color (fifteen in all, virtually anything except blue).

The breeding of dahlias got under way in England and France around 1814, when the first double-flowered cultivars turned up. By 1826 there were sixty named varieties, and 1,200 were listed by the 1840s. Hybridization received new impetus in 1872 when *D. juarezii*, with its genes for cactus-flowered forms, was introduced to Europe from Mexico. Breeding continues today at a lively pace, with a truly bewildering number of cultivars available commercially through specialized nurseries.

Their real aficionados may not care to grow other plants, but for those of us for whom dahlias are just one worthy plant among many, they are, with one exception, problematic. The dahlia is difficult to integrate with other plants in a herbaceous border. Henry Mitchell put the matter very well in *The Essential Earthman* (1981): "When all is said and done it looks best in a sunny field among the corn and pumpkins."

That exception? Any dahlia with handsome leaves so dark a red-purple that they verge on black. These cultivars characteristically have single or semidouble flowers in shades of crimson or scarlet. There are several plants in this category, including the recent introduction 'Fire Mountain', but the much older 'Bishop of Llandaff' is difficult to surpass. Its burgundy foliage is handsome even in early summer before flowering starts, and it combines well with almost any plant in a herbaceous border.

❧ A Hardy Begonia

IT'S ALWAYS A SURPRISE when we encounter a winter-hardy version of plants we associate with death by frost. I was a doubter when I first heard about a hardy fuchsia, but I tried *Fuchsia magellanica* 'Señorita' anyway. It came back the next spring and I've grown it

Hardy begonia

ever since—lots of it, for it roots easily from tip cuttings and is superb in containers as well as mixed borders. Same thing with a begonia: *Begonia grandis* ssp. *evansiana* has proven entirely winter-hardy. It is an exceptional species in its large genus, composed almost entirely of tropical and subtropical species. Originating in northern China and Japan, it is fully winter-hardy at least to Zone 6 and possibly even colder regions in a protected location with mulch or snow cover. Plants form woody tubers just below the surface of the soil, and they also produce tiny bulblets about the size of BBs in their leaf axils. They don't sprout till late May, but they grow rapidly to flowering-sized plants by the end of summer.

   B. grandis is handsome as well as hardy. The venation on the back of the pale green leaves is attractive. In some forms, those with pink flowers, the veins and the underside of the leaves are both deep red; and in others, those with white flowers, they are green. Like other species in the genus, B. *grandis* bears both male and female flowers on the same plant, the males being slightly smaller than the females and also having fewer petals. The flowers, whether white or pink, male or female, are translucent and slightly frosted, like satin glass. They begin to appear in August, increasing in number right up to the first hard freeze.

This begonia does best in soils of only moderate fertility and moisture. In a richer and wetter setting it becomes highly territorial, even weedy, although it's fairly easy to control with a few swipes of a hoe in early summer. So far.

❧ The Bulbs of Autumn

NATURE SOMETIMES PLAGIARIZES herself, producing plants that look like close kin, perhaps siblings, although they're not even in the same family. Thus it is with certain kinds of cactus and their look-alikes among the Euphorbiaceae. And so it also is with the cup-shaped flowers of autumn crocuses, colchicums, and sternbergias. They closely resemble one another in both form and season of bloom, but crocuses are in the Iris family, colchicums are in the Lily family, and sternbergias are in the Amaryllis family.

People can garden for many years, hearing rumors of species of crocus that bloom in the fall, but never seeing any. Because cro-cuses are so strongly associated with spring, the autumn ones have the charm of the unexpected when they pop out almost overnight. There are quite a few species, subspecies, and variant forms, but most American garden catalogs list only three, if they list any: *Crocus sativus*, *C. speciossus*, and *C. goulymyi*.

The first, *C. sativus*, has enormous historical and economic significance for it is the saffron crocus. In the ancient world it was the source of an important dyestuff. It was held sacred both in the Egypt of the Pharaohs and in the Minoan civilization of Bronze Age Crete. In former times, though not today, tinctures and powders made from it were used to treat depression and hangovers, among other maladies. Of it, William Coles wrote in *The Art of Simpling* (1656), "There is not a better Cordial amongst herbes than Saffron is, for it doth much comfort the Heart, and recreateth the Spirits and makes them cheerful that use it." Other English herbal writers of the seventeenth century advised that saffron was beneficial in treating diseases ranging from jaundice to smallpox and plague.

Crocus sativus remains important economically today mainly for its roasted stigmas from which come saffron, a spice that can be worth its weight in gold, depending on the market in precious metals. A lover of paella, I value this crocus highly for its flavor. But its pale purple flowers aren't especially exciting. They have weak necks, and their anthers loll out of their cups in an unattractive way. *Crocus speciosus*, the first to bloom in my garden every fall, is much more fetching. Its color ranges from blue-lavender to light purple. The form I have looks blue from a distance, but closer inspection shows it to be pale lavender, with complex stipples or featherings of a darker shade. The prominent stamens are a rich shade of gold, and the flowers have a light lemon scent. One of the best things about this plant is that it produces huge numbers of little cormlets that can be removed and transplanted where wanted. It also self-seeds prolifically, so it springs up every year in new and surprising spots. Several cultivars of *C. speciosus* occasionally appear in American bulb catalogs. 'Conqueror' is sky blue, 'Oxonian' is dark violet, and 'Albus', not surprisingly, is white. The third of the most commonly grown crocuses of autumn, *C. goulimyi*, is my favorite. Discovered by Dr. C. N. Goulimis in southern Greece in the early 1950s, it has excellent form, looking something like a little lavender-pink lollipop. It rapidly develops into thick clumps and also self-seeds abundantly. It blooms for well over a month, starting in early October.

This trio by no means exhausts the inventory of fall crocuses — and of others that bloom so late (or is it early?) that they are better classified as winter bloomers. Here are some choice fall-bloomers, which I have seen in gardens other than my own. *C. banaticus*, sometimes called the iris crocus because its violet-purple hue and the disproportion in size between its inner petals and its outer ones makes it somewhat resemble *Iris reticulata*, is lovely. *C. banaticus*

'Albus' is lovelier still. Both of these bloom in September. C. *longi-florus* blooms in October producing large, fragrant flowers. C. *laevigatus* blooms intermittently starting in late November. Its pale mauve blossoms are delicately scented. Even later is C. *ochroleucus*, which is white with a golden throat. The autumn-crocus lover who wishes to proceed farther in collecting species will find many to covet. That's the good news, especially for people who have devoured the delightful twenty-eight-page chapter E. A. Bowles devotes to some fifty autumn crocuses in *My Garden in Autumn and Winter* (1915). The bad news for such far-gone crocus-devotees is that they must continue their search by mail order from specialized nurseries in Great Britain—at prices that are often startlingly high.

The crocuses of autumn are lovely little episodes in the seasonal garden, but they lack the drama of their look-alikes in the Lily family, the colchicums. Their immense chalices burst from the earth, seemingly out of nowhere, with no advance announcement. One day there is nothing, the next there are buds, and the day after that there are flowers. Colchicums are among the strangest bulbs on earth, in that their leaves and their flowers do not coincide. Their common name in English, since the sixteenth century at least, naked boys (or sometimes naked ladies), refers to their odd trait of producing flowers in the autumn and foliage in late spring.

I grow only five cultivars of *Colchicum*, four in the lavender-purple to pink range of the spectrum. 'Waterlily' is a gorgeous double. Just four or five bulbs make a grand display. 'Lilac Wonder' and C. *bornmuelleri* are both splendid, producing flowers that seem to glow from within from their own radiance. 'Autumn Queen' is a pale purple, tesselated or checkered with a darker hue, like some fritillaries. As for C. *autumnale* 'Album', its enormous pure white cups are breathtaking when they leap forth from an underplanting of black mondo grass (*Ophiopogon planiscapus* 'Arabicus').

Colchicums are sometimes offered as "autumn crocus," and sometimes as "meadow saffron." This confusion goes back at least as far as John Parkinson, whose herbal devotes fourteen folio pages of text and three full-page plates to colchicums and crocuses, including both spring- and autumn-flowering sorts. The confusion continues today, with several standard horticultural reference books giving autumn crocus as one common name for colchicum. This mistake is not just incorrect, but potentially dangerous, because colchicums are fatally toxic in every part.

The burnished golden goblets of *Sternbergia lutea* are beautiful indeed, but it can be tricky to establish. If it grows successfully, it is spectacular, as on a hillside overlooking the Winterthur Museum in Delaware, where it occurs in huge colonies that gleam and capture the eye from half a mile away. People who already have it growing in their gardens should consider themselves lucky, but the rest of us should refrain from buying bulbs. On the Mediterranean hillsides where it grows, it is being harvested rapaciously. Rare and endangered species like *S. greuteriana* are being dug up and sold as the more common *S. lutea*. Even *S. lutea* resents being transplanted. I wouldn't buy a single bulb unless I were absolutely convinced that it was not only nursery grown but also nursery propagated. ("Nursery grown" can mean that a bulb was harvested in the wild, grown in a nursery for a season or two, and then sold as if it had never been collected.)

The same stricture applies to my undoubted favorite plant of autumn, *Cyclamen hederifolium*, the ivy-leafed cyclamen, one of some nineteen species of varying degrees of winter-hardiness in this genus in the Primrose family. This is one of the very easiest species in the genus, provided that it gets the dry shade it likes during the summer, before it emerges from dormancy. It is a cheering plant in every way. Its tiny, swept-back, pink or white flowers, which look like little butterflies, begin to appear before the leaves, in late summer or early fall. The flowering period goes on for a couple of months. The foliage—dark green, beautifully patterned and mottled in pewter and silver—almost rivals the flowers in appeal.

It is difficult to find *Cyclamen hederifolium* nowadays. Most reputable bulb companies don't sell tubers imported from Western Europe because they are likely to have been collected in Turkey and elsewhere in the Mediterranean region, on a scale sufficient to contribute to their endangerment in the wild. In 1976, 256,000 tubers were collected and sold. Nine years later, the toll had increased to 6,632,000. What's worse, cyclamen species that are almost vanishingly rare in their native habitats are often mislabeled as less threatened ones. Rather than risk selling hardy cyclamen that may have been collected, many bulb companies have chosen not to offer them at all.

There used to be—for ten years, anyway, but not for long enough—a source of cyclamen that gardeners could turn to with a clear conscience. It was Montrose Nursery. It sold small but blooming-sized specimens. Gardeners could grace their shady spots with these tiny charmers without exploiting them. But Montrose was itself an endangered species. Fall 1993 was its last shipping season. I am glad that I have dozens of cyclamen plants. Some are fifteen years old. If I were to dig them up for inspection (unthinkable, unless I were about to move to a new house and garden!), I would probably discover that the tubers are now the size of pancakes. Each produces more than a hundred flowers a year, instead of the ten or twelve when first planted.

❧ Some Kind Words for Goldenrods

A FEW YEARS AGO, when his Holbrook Farm and Nursery was still in business, its owner, Allen Bush, sent me several perennials he had just imported from Germany and wanted to test for winter-hardiness in various regions of America. Three of them not only got through the winter splendidly but proved to be indispensable for the late-season garden. Two of these three, hybrids of *Helenium autumnale*, are champions for a long period of bloom stretching from late July to the middle of September. 'Kugelsonne' is a clear primrose yellow, 'Feuersiegel' a brighter yellow splashed with scarlet. Both of these daisies grow about thirty-six inches tall, producing an abundance of flowers that are good in bouquets as well as in the herbaceous border. The third plant was an aster, *Aster lateriflorus* var. *horizontalis*, which I discuss later in this book.

The essential point about all three of these perennials is that they are hybrids or selected forms of plants native to America but overlooked by gardeners here in our quest for more exotic fare. Other plants are in the same category. Many an aster of the field or roadside makes a fine plant for the garden. Starting with Joe Pye weed (*Eupatorium purpureum*) in early August, there is a long procession of wonderful eupatoriums for the late border, not ending until white sanicle (*E. rugosum*) puts in its final word in late October.

But the genus we most neglect is *Solidago* or goldenrod. We think we know all about goldenrods. They are basically perennial weeds that spread viciously by both seeds and underground roots. They are much of a muchness, a muddy yellow in color. And they cause hay fever. Nothing of what we think we know is true. To start at the end of the list, goldenrods are innocent. Thousands have said it before, even if millions still pass on the old, unfounded prejudice. Goldenrods are innocent. The tip-off is the huge number of bumblebees and other insect pollinators that buzz around their flower heads and wander across them, gathering nectar and transporting pollen grains too heavy to float in the air where they might torment the allergic.

People wary of goldenrod should take a look at ragweed. Its flowers are as inconspicuous as flowers can be. They aren't luxury restaurants for bees, which just ignore them. Ragweed has evolved as a plant that depends on its immense production of extremely minute grains of pollen. They float huge distances through the air in the great sexual dance of ragweed plants calling to one another as their biological clocks wind down at the close of the growing season.

To continue my goldenrod defense, although some are a muddy—or sometimes jarringly brassy—color, the range of yellows is broad, from lemon meringue to deep gold. Admittedly, some species are vicious takeover artists. But for gardeners daring enough to take chances with solidagos—and enjoy them fall after fall— a few safe choices are *Solidago altissima*, *S. sempervirens*, and *S. rugosa*. 'Fireworks', a cultivar of *S. rugosa*, the rough-stemmed goldenrod, is special for its handsome branching habit, with secondary stems borne horizontally in almost geometric precision. I'm also partial to 'Golden Fleece', which was introduced by Dr. Richard Lighty. A dwarf, early-blooming selection of *S. spharecephala*, it grows to about eighteen inches tall, produces wands of pale yellow flowers, and has unusually attractive, somewhat rounded leaves. The sweet goldenrod, *S. odora*, is not an especially assertive plant, nor the most magnificent species in the genus. (*S. sempervirens* holds that honor for its height of up to seven feet, its red stems, and its evergreen tendencies south of New York City.) But the leaves of sweet goldenrod have the scent of licorice, and they can be made into a tea of gustatory delight and historic significance. In 1773, Bostonians dumped British tea from Asia into Boston Harbor. To make do, they drank "liberty tea" in its stead. Its main ingredient was the leaves of sweet goldenrod. Following the example of the patriots of Massachusetts, I sometimes steep some leaves from my own garden. I lift my cup, quaff it down in satisfaction, enjoy the anise or licorice flavor, and offer a toast to sweet goldenrod and all its autumnal kin.

❧ Asters — Lords of the Late Season

IT IS ONE OF THE CURIOSITIES of garden history that the multitudinous North American species of aster and their hybrids are more likely to turn up in an English or a European home garden than in their equivalents on this side of the Atlantic Ocean. Sometimes there's a reason for our neglect. The so-called New York asters, a race whose ancestry involves not just the New York aster per se (*Aster novi-belgii*) but such other species as A. *cordifolius* and A. *laevis*, are important garden plants in England. Hundreds of cultivars are available there. They were bred for a climate far gentler than ours, however, and they do not do well in our gardens. They are terribly subject to many fungus diseases, none of them pretty to behold.

New England asters, hybrids of mostly A. *novae-angliae*, are a different cup of tea altogether, able to thrive and bloom beautifully not only in New England, but also in our Southeastern states. German as well as British hybridizers have taken an interest in this species, and it shows in such cultivar names as 'Herbstschnee' ('Autumn Snow') and 'Septemberrubin' ('September Ruby'). One of the first New England asters to bloom, 'Andenken an Alma Pötschke' ('Thoughts of Alma Pötschke'), was introduced in Germany in 1969 but has been common in the North American nursery trade only since about 1985. It is spectacular for the vibrant, deeply saturated cerise of its flowers.

Next comes 'Hella Lacy'—a familiar name! I found this New England aster growing in my neighborhood, lovely but nameless. I sent plants to friends in the nursery business. They praised it highly and thought it was distinctive, so I named it for my wife and let it loose into the world. In just a decade it has become one of the most widely grown perennials in the country. It has purple flowers with yellow centers, much resembling the native species, but its vigor is phenomenal.

Only recently did I learn the exact story of 'Hella Lacy'. I got it from my neighbors, Ed and Jean Plantan, and somehow thought that it was a plant they had brought from their birthplace in Johnstown, Pennsylvania. Ed has now corrected me. 'Hella Lacy' came into being in the garden of the neighbors on the other side of the Plantans. Early in the century the principal of the school just down the block was a plant lover. He was also poorly paid. Until his retirement, he rented a room in the house the Plantans now own. After retirement he moved into a little shack next door. He had a garden there, where he grew perennials from seeds. The plant I named for Hella was one of his creations.

The blooming season of New England asters has been extended greatly by two cultivars introduced by Montrose Nursery. 'Our Latest One' blooms throughout October, with medium violet-blue flowers on arching three-foot stems. 'Fanny's Aster', which came simultaneously to Montrose from an old garden in South Carolina and another in Pennsylvania, is a November bloomer, with darker violet-blue flowers than 'Our Latest One'. (The reason that 'Our Latest One' really isn't our latest one is that it was named before 'Fanny's Aster' showed up.)

Of late, there has been increasing interest in other species and their cultivars. One is the A. *lateriflorus* var. *horizontalis* that I got from Allen Bush. He thought I would love it, and he was right. It is low (about twenty-four inches) and wide-spreading. Its slightly succulent foliage, which is immune to mildew, becomes smoky purple in late summer. Even a first-year plant produces so many hundreds of flowers over a month of bloom starting in early September that they completely hide the leaves. The blossoms are tiny, with white ray flowers and raspberry disk flowers. From a few feet away the plant looks like a cloud of mauve mist. I mentioned earlier that Allen Bush imported it from Germany. But A. *lateriflorus*, of which *horizontalis* is a varietal form, is no more German than the Fourth of July or sweet corn. It has naturalized in Europe, but its native home is a wide area of the United States stretching from Minnesota and New Jersey all the way to Texas and Florida. It is available at several mail-order nurseries, as is the British cultivar 'Coombe Fishacre', which blooms earlier and has darker flowers.

Other asters have passed muster in my fall garden. A. *cordifolius*, commonly called bee-tongue, has rosettes of heart-shaped leaves from which rise thirty-inch sprays of lavender and light yellow daisies that gradually change to purple. There is also a white form. A. *divaricatus* produces a multitude of little starry white flowers on two-foot wiry black stems. I also like the heath aster, A. *ericoides*, a bristly-leaved, rather shrubby low species that produces white flowers with pink overtones by the hundreds. The cultivars 'Ring Dove' (lilac flowers), 'Esther' (pale lavender), and 'Silver Spray' (the name says it all) are welcome variations. One especially graceful native aster is A. *patens*. Its blue-purple blossoms are large, about two inches across, and they weigh on the willowy stems so that the plant arches down, draping itself on shorter plants, like chrysanthemums. A. *oblongifolius*, a very late bloomer, has aromatic foliage and large numbers of striking blue flowers. 'Raydon's Favorite', another Holbrook Farm introduction, is a cultivar of A. *o.* var. *angustatus*, named for Raydon Alexander, a horticulturist in San Antonio, Texas.

Not all worthwhile species of asters are American natives. I could not go without the tartar aster, A. *tataricus*, from Siberia and Mongolia. It is somewhat awkward in habit, at seven feet tall, with pale blue flowers growing in a tight bunch atop its sturdy stems. But its long season of bloom, from late September well into November, makes it a champion, a plant that says farewell to autumn and greets the onset of winter. Because of its ungainliness, I keep it at the rear of a border so that other plants can conceal its lower stems. In late October, it is spectacular combined with another very large plant, the perennial sunflower *Helianthus angustifolius*, which looks like the spectacular shower of gold that Zeus sometimes assumed to dazzle nymphs or mortal young women. This aster and sunflower combination was a favorite of Elizabeth Lawrence. There is also 'Jin Dai', a shorter form of A. *tataricus* that stops at around five feet instead of ascending to the heights. Rick Darke, then of Longwood Gardens, found this form at the Jin Dai ("Ages of God") Botanical Park near Tokyo.

The most astonishing of all perennial asters, however, is a southeastern American species, A. *carolinianus*. It is a woody climber (more of an upward-sprawler than a vine) that unlike other perennial asters must not be pruned back to the ground in winter. It blooms very late, well into November, producing great masses of pale pink flowers with a wonderful fragrance. On a warm, sunny late autumn day, this climbing plant fills the air for a considerable distance with the delicious scent of marzipan.

Browsing in nursery catalogs that offer perennial asters can be confusing. A cultivar that is listed in one catalog, say, as being derived from A. *cordifolius* may be listed as some other species in another catalog. Tidy minds will object, but those of us who have learned that gardening is often an exercise in ambiguity will just forget the confusion, back off from nomenclatural anxiety, and enjoy even those asters with questionable identities.

Asters are easy in culture. They generally prefer a sunny site (although A. *tataricus* does quite well for me in partial shade). They dislike both parched soils and soggy ones. Locating them where they will benefit from good air circulation cuts down on fungus infections. They increase rapidly and must be divided every two or three years, discarding the center of the old clumps and propagating the newest plants around the edges. Regular watering once a week, especially in the dog days of August, helps reduce unsightly yellowing or loss of leaves at the bottom of the stems. The taller cultivars of A. *novae-angliae* may need cutting back by half in mid-June to keep them tidy and manageable in size.

Asters vary from species to species in suitability for cutting. New England asters are poor subjects in bouquets, but A. cordifolius is superb—and widely used in the florist business, as is × *Solidaster luteus*, a bigeneric goldenrod/aster hybrid. Both have extremely long-lasting flowers.

❧ Butterflies — and Beetles

AN INCREASING NUMBER of American gardeners realize that, with a little forethought and effort, we can contrive to have our gardens at their very best in the autumn, the ripening season of the year. We need not depend solely on potted chrysanthemums from local nurseries and roadside stands to brighten a garden with abundant bloom and radiant color. As already seen, we have at our disposal many asters, goldenrods, and autumn-blooming bulbs. In addition, we have toad lilies (*Tricyrtis*) and turtle-heads (*Chelone*). We must not forget several of the tender species of salvias, such as *S. leucantha*, *S. madrensis*, *S. mexicana*, and *S. regla*, that withhold their bloom until the autumn equinox is nigh or has already passed.

But no matter how abundant its flowers may be, an autumn garden gets even greater majesty and power from its setting, from the natural order. At this time of year, we cannot fail to be transfixed by the beauties of field, woodland, and roadside—by maples bursting into flame, beeches assuming quiet but radiant tones of pale gold; by goldenrods of many species suddenly transforming wastelands with their gift of bloom; by flocks of honking geese making their V-tracks across the clear blue sky as they fly south to places that winter never touches.

We also turn in amazement to the insect kingdom that seemed, only a short time ago, to be mostly a source of vexation and distress. The gnats, the biting flies, and the mosquitoes that plagued us in June and July are strangely—and blessedly—absent. Our only annoyance, if we live where they are prevalent, comes from yellow jackets, those insects with the same tastes in food as humans (for fruit ripe with sugar and for meat rich in protein). Gifted with the sense of smell, able to detect in the air molecules of interest from far away, they arrive almost instantly when a ripe peach or a salami sandwich is served forth outdoors.

But for many of the insects of this season—those that attract our attention—we feel only admiration. Butterflies are among the loveliest creations of nature. We wish now that we knew all their names, not just monarchs and swallowtails and skippers, but all the rest. We see a host of monarchs dancing over a purple aster, and it brings up thoughts not only of present, undeniable beauty, but also of transformation. Our tastes run not at all to caterpillars, pupae, or chrysalises, and we will leave it to entomologists to speak of instars, but few of us can look on a butterfly without wonder.

Ancient tradition holds that certain insects have lessons to teach. The bee symbolizes industry and diligence. The ant, knowing that winter will not stay its hand forever, represents prudence and foresight, while the grasshopper stands for foolish prodigality. The crickets' songs celebrate the joys of hearth and home—and if our imaginations were shaped in childhood by the fables of Walt Disney (as they hardly can fail to have been), we may even see a cricket as the embodiment of conscience.

We pick and choose among members of the insect kingdom. We delight in a few—the iridescent dragonfly, the firefly that lights up the night winking out its messages in the code that others of its kind understand, the ladybug dressed in brilliant scarlet and dotted with black. Others are strange life forms as odd as anything that might be dreamed up for a planet in another galaxy—the praying mantis, the walking stick.

We divide insects into beneficial and harmful, as is perfectly natural, and if we are gardeners, our special interests show. Gypsy moths, mealybugs, white flies, and aphids are our enemies; any insects that feast on our enemies are our friends. Meanwhile we remain unaware of the vast number of insects too tiny to perceive: a single tablespoon of soil teems with thousands of these microscopic and submicroscopic creatures. There are said to be at least a billion insects for every human being.

As gardeners, we sometimes assume that the beauties and benefits of the kingdom of plants—the brilliant play of colors that capture and please our eye, the sweet perfumes that greet our nose and gladden our soul, the fruits and grains that nourish our bodies—somehow exist for us, with our good in mind. The assumption is natural and easy to understand, but it happens not to be true.

Long before we appeared on the scene, plants and insects worked out their extremely complex system of interrelationships, transactions in which, roughly speaking, plants provide food to those insects that serve as their particular pollinators. When we take pleasure in the perfume of a fragrant flower, we are really eavesdropping on a message it is sending to an insect pollinator in a chemical language that uses volatile molecules instead of words.

Some plants play to other pollinators than insects. Grasses, oaks, and conifers are married to the wind that lifts and spreads their prodigious clouds of pollen through the air; over 8 percent of the world's flowering plants are pollinated in this way. Slightly under 2 percent are pollinated by birds, bats, mammals, and other vertebrates, less than 1 percent by water currents. All the rest, out of an estimated 240,000 species of angiosperms or flowering plants, are insect-pollinated. We tend to give major credit to bees, butterflies, and moths, for we see them at their work, and we also hear in our gardens the music of flowers abuzz with bees. The work of these particular insects is not inconsequential; together, they carry out one quarter of the pollination that takes place on earth (including pollination of many of the food crops on which we depend).

The surprising champion pollinators of the world, however, turn out to be beetles, the largest order of insects in the animal kingdom, with a quarter million species, 28,000 of them in North America. This piece of news is hardly cause for rejoicing. Bees take nectar and pollen from plants, but generally do not eat them. Some beetles will feed on every part of almost every plant. We may regard ladybugs and fireflies, both beetles, as congenial, but we lose no love for Japanese beetles, Colorado potato beetles, or the bark beetles that spread Dutch elm disease. Not everything in nature is to our liking.

❧ Soapwort Gentian

MY BOTANIST FRIEND Sandy Bierbrauer knows where the fall-blooming pine barrens gentian (*Gentiana autumnalis*) grows in moist
spots in the sandy, almost unpopulated, region of southern New Jersey from which the plant takes its common name. But she won't tell
anyone, not even me. This plant, one of North America's loveliest
wildflowers, is highly esteemed for its funnel-shaped blossoms of
bright blue suffused with tints of bronze. It may not be officially
endangered, but it can't exactly be described as common, either.
Like many, perhaps most, of the roughly four hundred other species
in this geographically far-flung genus, *G. autumnalis* has evolved to
survive in the specific conditions of soil, moisture, and climate that
characterize its native habitat (not only New Jersey's Pine Barrens
but also other moist, sandy meadowlands southward to the Carolinas). T. H. Everett once described the pine barrens gentian as
"notoriously unamenable to cultivation," meaning that if I tried to
gather seeds or—too horrible even to contemplate—collect plants
from the wild, I would never be able to establish it in my garden.
That's the way with most gentian species. If they grow naturally at
6,000 feet in glacial till in the Alps or the Andes or the Himalayas,
they're not going to be happy someplace else, particularly someplace else where summers are hot and humid and last a good four
months.

   Happy to say, a handful of gentian species aren't so persnickety
about where they will grow. I have not grown the summer-blooming
central Asian species *G. septemfida*, but it is equally known for the
exquisite beauty of its sapphire blue flowers and its ability to withstand the worst that summer can throw its way. The European willow gentian, *G. asclepiadea*, is often referred to as easy to please. I
have not discovered this claim to hold true in my own garden; but in
the brief time between planting it and watching it sneak off to Beu-
lah Land, I have admired this species for its attractive foliage and its
elegant, arching stems somewhat reminiscent of tricyrtis. Its flowers
are deep indigo, spotted inside with red-violet. There are also forms
with white flowers and with pink ones.

There is one gentian that I have found for over a decade to be spectacularly easy to grow and utterly reliable as an autumn perennial. It is the soapwort gentian, *G. saponaria*. I presume that its English common name and its Latin species name alike testify to the use of its roots in former times to make soap. I have not run across information to this effect in any of the literature in my library, but I do know that the roots of bouncing bet, *Saponaria officinalis*, were once used for such a purpose. I also know that the roots of some species of gentian are used in folk medicine and in a particularly bitter form of schnapps favored by especially courageous Germans.

Gentiana saponaria, a North American native species that occurs in moist woodlands from New York westward to Minnesota and southward to northern Florida, is one of the closed or bottle gentians. Its flowers do not open into the distinctive upward-facing trumpets or cups found in many other species. Instead, they remain closed, their stigmas barely showing above their fused petals. Emerging from a bronzy green calyx, the flower's petals are green-gray at their base, changing higher up to pale mauve with parallel stripes of dark lilac. From a short distance, the flowers appear to be solid Wedgwood blue. Their interiors, which can be seen only if a flower is dissected, are grayish white with medium purple stripes. The flowers are borne in clusters, first at the ends of the stems, then later in the season in the leaf axils.

This gentian grows to about two feet tall, but slightly lax to begin with, it spreads outward and downward under the weight of its blossoms. Flowering begins in mid-October, continuing well into November, by which time the leaves turn to a rich apricot, a gorgeous foil for the flowers of teal blue.

The soapwort gentian is not only beautiful but also tolerant of a wide range of growing conditions. Moist woodlands may be its original home, but it is perfectly content in my garden in full sun six hours a day at summer's height and in sandy soil that never stays moist very long. It seems to be immune to any kind of disease, and slugs and insects leave it strictly alone. It is extremely well-mannered, as it neither seeds itself around promiscuously nor travels through the soil by stealthy stolons.

The soapwort gentian can be propagated by division in very early spring or by seeds. Unlike some other gentians it does not require stratification for germination. Its abundant crop of dustlike seeds sprout almost immediately if planted as soon as they ripen. There is, however, almost no advantage in sowing them in late fall, for the tiny plants just sit on top of the planting mix until the days begin to lengthen with the arrival of spring.

❧ Mum's the Word in Autumn

AMERICAN FLORISTS MIGHT well pay homage to 1789, the year the first chrysanthemums were imported to Great Britain from Japan, starting a huge craze for the plants first in England and then in the United States that lasted throughout the Victorian era. But we westerners are Johnny-come-latelies to chrysanthemums, which were venerated in China as early as the fifth century B.C. For the Chinese, and later the Japanese, chrysanthemums were far richer in symbolism than roses or lilies were in the West, being tokens not only of autumn but also of a long and happy life.

Although the ancient Chinese and Japanese monkeyed around with chrysanthemums a whole lot, developing forms not to be found in nature, they would not approve, I believe, of what our florists have done with these plants. By artificially mimicking the shortening hours of daylight of late summer, which initiate the formation of flower buds, the florist industry has given us mums 365 days a year, removing all trace of autumnal significance. Having become flowers of every occasion, from a christening to a funeral, they are thus deprived of any association with long and happy lives. I don't like chrysanthemums on Valentine's Day, any more than I cotton to tulips at Halloween. So I ignore potted and cut flower mums in florist shops and concentrate on those that bloom in my garden at their proper season, which is autumn.

Even people who don't garden very much seem to have a great affection for these plants, which I insist on calling mums, despite the purists who demand hearing all four syllables of the botanical

name issue from our
lips. Garden cen-
ters and even gro-
cery stores do a
brisk trade in
potted mums
during early
autumn, for
customers
who use them to
flank entrance-
ways or to fill
empty places
in flower beds
where much
of the bright
color of sum-
mer has van-
ished. It's easy
to understand
why most people
have so much affection
for their mums (and I don't
mean their mothers). They aren't
in the least bit temperamental, being

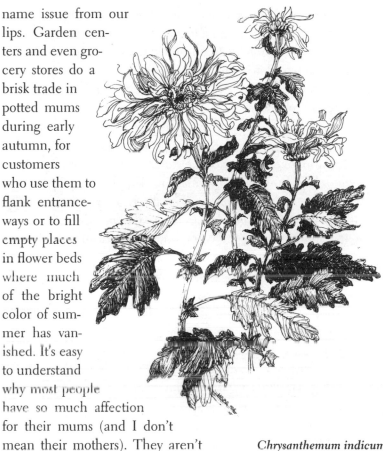

Chrysanthemum indicum

one of the few flowers that can be transplanted when in full bloom
without the slightest wilting. They come in a wide range of colors,
from pristine whites and sunny yellows and golds through russets
and reds, right into the smoky and smoldering end of the spectrum,
the lavenders and lilacs and deep purples. They also vary enormously in the shape of their flowers. Some look like single daisies.
Others are doubled, quilled, reflexed, incurved, and so on, through
over a dozen types.

But some things about chrysanthemums are fairly mysterious.
For many years of gardening I puzzled over one of the oddities of
their behavior. Among the potted ones I planted in the fall, some
simply vanished during the winter, while others came back lustily

the following spring. To be frank, I didn't really mind losing a good many, with casualties amounting to about 50 percent, because those that did come back always had multiplied to more chrysanthemums than any small garden could absorb. One of the less enjoyable chores of spring is ripping out the excess plants and hauling them off to the compost heap.

Finally, a friend in the nursery business solved the mystery for me. Some chrysanthemums are perfectly winter-hardy. Others, bred to be grown in greenhouses for the florist trade, are not. The large wholesale chrysanthemum growers who supply both florists and retail nurserymen don't bother to keep the two sorts of plants separate. It's not entirely a matter of carelessness, either. Customers who buy potted mums that then die on them over the winter will be customers again next fall.

If someone wants chrysanthemums that will be truly hardy perennials, there are two ways to go. One is to buy chrysanthemums in the spring from one of the many mail-order nurseries that offer them as rooted cuttings and guarantee them to be hardy in most of the United States. The other trick is to inspect potted mums very carefully before buying them in the fall. If there are little rosettes of tiny leaves surrounding the stem immediately above the soil, the plant is likely to be hardy. If there's no rosette, it almost certainly will winter kill.

I would like to put in a special word on behalf of a chrysanthemum that was highly popular in America in the 1930s, but nowadays is not often planted. It is the Korean chrysanthemum, widely hybridized fifty years ago. It is bone-hardy, comes in the full range of chrysanthemum colors, blooms in late October when flowers are especially welcome, and produces enormous numbers of single daisy flowers. It is easily raised from seed, but the seeds are extremely hard to come by, a fact that will annoy anyone who has ever seen the magnificent display devoted entirely to Korean chrysanthemums in Manhattan's Conservatory Garden in Central Park. The Park Seed Company used to offer seeds, but does so no longer, at least not the single kind. Any seed company that would step into the breach would do American gardeners a huge favor.

❦ Heaths and Heathers for Yearlong Bloom

SOME HIGHLY SATISFYING GARDENS, starting with the Zurich Botanical Garden in Switzerland, are composed almost entirely of heaths and heathers, plus the occasional dwarf conifer to lend vertical interest. The unity of such gardens is virtually guaranteed by the similarity of their dominant plants—their mounded shapes, the fine texture of their foliage, and their tiny closed or bell-shaped flowers in clusters. Yet within this overall unity there is a comfortable diversity of blooming season, floral color, and foliage color. (Heaths and heathers keep their leaves all year round. Evergreen foliage is the rule, but some cultivars are yellow, bronzy green, or gray instead, and others undergo striking, even dramatic, seasonal color changes.)

Heaths and heathers are a closely related group within the family of ericaceous plants that includes blueberries, huckleberries, sourwood trees, and mountain laurel, all of which thrive in the coastal plain of New Jersey. The well-drained, acidic soils, low in organic matter and nutrients, that typify this region are ideal for heaths and heathers. Several genera, including *Duboecia* and *Andromeda*, are classified as heaths or heathers, but two are the most important as garden plants. First, there is ling or Scotch heather, *Calluna vulgaris*. Although there's only one species in this genus, it has over 1,000 cultivars. Second, there is the heath, *Erica*, which has over 700 species worldwide. Chief of them, for horticultural purposes, are *Erica carnea*, with many cultivars, and the hybrid *E.* × *darleyensis*, similarly varied.

The anatomical differences between heathers and heaths are of interest primarily to botanists. From a practical standpoint, what distinguishes each from the other is that heathers bloom from midsummer into fall, heaths from late fall until midspring. A garden composed mostly of these plants, if carefully selected, will be in bloom all the time, except for a brief lull in early summer. Since during that lull many other plants will be blooming lavishly, it takes but a moment's reflection to understand that any garden with both heaths and heathers in it may claim to have bloom a full 365 days a year. It's

188 • ALLEN LACY

a claim that those of us who live where winters are real might not otherwise be able to make.

These plants are not apt to turn up at local garden centers, and only one cultivar of the heather *Erica carnea*, 'Springwood White', is likely to be found there. This means that, except for people who live near one of the handful of American nurseries that specialize in heaths and heathers, and offer mature specimens in containers, an instant garden featuring such plants is an idle dream. The best way to lay hands on a varied selection of cultivars is the mail-order route. Plants will be small and juvenile. It will take three to five years for them to mature, but once they do, if they are set one to two feet apart, depending on their ultimate spread, they will form a superb groundcover that is impenetrable by weeds. Once they have some age to them, heaths and heathers come closer to permitting low-maintenance gardening than any other plants. They are drought tolerant, happy in lean soils, and seldom in need of more than light cosmetic pruning.

❦ *Winter Color*

ONE DIFFERENCE BETWEEN people who garden and those who can hardly tell a lily from a liatris is that nongardeners think of winter as the season when gardens have nothing to offer. Gardeners know better, and with experience they learn how to make the most of the season. They pay special attention to shrubs with colorful berries that persist almost till spring such as nandinas, hollies, and pyracanthas. They appreciate woody plants with brightly colored stems such as red-twig dogwood and coral bark maple, which are particularly cheering on bright winter mornings when fresh snow is on the ground.

They realize, furthermore, that winter's floral treasures are all the more valuable for their relative scarcity. Every New Year's Day Nancy Goodwin writes me from North Carolina to tell me what was in bloom for her at Christmas. One year it was *Crocus laevigatus, Cyclamen cilicium, C. coum, C. mirabile, Erysimum alpinum Galanthus caucasicus, Iris unguicularis, Narcissus cantab-ricus, N. romieuxii, Phlox subulata,* and many different violas. "It is a joyous time," she went on to write, "for each flower is so important!"

I can't match Nancy's Homeric catalog of winter-bloomers, but I do have some flowers in this season. I've already mentioned winter heaths. I don't grow *Galanthus caucasicus,* but the more common snowdrop *G. nivalis* blooms faithfully for several weeks starting right after New Year's. It has self-seeded throughout the garden. From a kitchen window I enjoy the native American swamp honeysuckle, *Lonicera sempervirens,* not only for its large, translucent, pale red fruits but also for its ever-blooming tendencies. Flowering from mid-December through March may be sporadic, but it's welcome when it happens. Then there are the hybrid Asian witch hazels, *Hamamelis* × *intermedia,* of which the best known (and the one I grow) is 'Arnold Promise'. A small tree, growing to about fifteen feet high and as many across, this hybrid between *H. mollis* and *H. japonica* covers itself from early January to the middle of February with an abundance of whiskery, clear yellow flowers from which emanate clouds of perfume reminiscent of honey and ripe plums. The tree is gorgeous when the early morning or late afternoon sun shines through its branches, and a few twigs brought inside will scent an entire room deliciously, as will other hybrid Asian witch hazels such as 'Jelena' and 'Ruby Glow'.

In March shortly after 'Arnold Promise' finishes its bloom, another remarkable winter-flowering tree begins its season. It is the Japanese flowering apricot, *Prunus mume* (pronounced MEW-may). Mine came years ago as a small seedling in one of J. C. Raulston's distributions from his arboretum in Raleigh. Out of bloom, it is unremarkable, even awkward-looking, with untidy, thorny branches. But in March it is marvelous, especially when its dime-sized pink flowers stand out against a cloudless, azure winter sky. Its beauty is almost indescribable on those early mornings when the blossoms are encased in ice after freezing rain during the night. The flowers are intensely fragrant, like almond candy and jasmine mingled with a hint of baby powder. This apricot—whose blossoms are what many take to be the "plum" blossoms so common in Japanese paint-ing and pottery—is more celebrated in Japan, where there are over

250 named varieties, than even the flowering cherries. The flowers of this ornamental fruit tree may be single or double, and pink, red, or white. The tree has ancient associations with literature and scholarship. It was traditional in olden times for poets to share cups of rice wine with mume flowers floating in them to add fragrance.

A few of these cultivars are available in the United States, such as 'Benishidon', a double dark pink, and 'Omo-no-mama', a semi-double white. Others were bred in the 1920s by the California nurseryman W. B. Clarke—'Dawn', a single pink, for instance, and 'Clarke', a double pink. Still others have been grown and selected by Dr. Clifford Parks, the owner of Camellia Forest Nursery in Chapel Hill, North Carolina. One of his cultivars, 'Bridal Veil', has a weeping habit and white flowers. J. C. Raulston was very fond of *Prunus mume* and did his best to bring this plant to public consciousness. He often pointed out in his many lectures and articles that he regarded it as one of the finest Japanese ornamental plants, and that it was sadly overlooked in America. He was right on both counts; this little shrub or small tree is still overlooked, its mere existence unknown to most gardeners who live where it is winter-hardy (Zones 9 through 7, possibly parts of Zone 6 with protection from wind). Why do we neglect it? Its flowering season is over when most of our garden centers open in April. We don't see it, and we can't want something we don't know. Garden centers don't sell plants people don't want.

Even if winter were completely flowerless, it would yet have its peculiar beauty, thanks to a number of plants, both woody and herbaceous, with handsome, persistent, variegated foliage. Many evergreen conifers are lugubrious on gray, dreary winter days, as well as some broad-leafed evergreens. (Consider rhododendrons, whose dour, dark green leaves roll up like wet cigars on especially chilly days.)

Leaves that are splashed with cream or yellow, however, reflect the least bit of sunshine and bring cheer to the winter landscape. I am thinking here in particular of some of the variegated cultivars of *Aucuba japonica*. My hands-down favorite is 'Picturata'. Its bold, lustrous leaves—with a large, irregular, buttery yellow blotch at their center—light up the garden from many feet away. A moderate-sized shrub, it ultimately gets four feet tall and as many feet across.

Aucubas are much planted in the South, where they are valuable middle-sized shrubs for fairly dense shade—even for that bane of any gardener, dry shade. (In their native Japan, they are shrubs of woodland understories.) Some standard reference books list them as winter-hardy only to Zone 8, but I have seen them survive and thrive in Zone 6 gardens. They are extremely easy to propagate: branches brought inside for winter arrangements root as easily in water as pussy willow. Aucubas generally bear male flowers and female flowers on separate plants. The doorknob-shaped scarlet fruits on female cultivars like 'Picturata' and 'Salicifolia' are so handsome that care should always be taken to ensure that they're planted with a male variety, such as 'Golden King', in the vicinity. One cultivar, however—'Rozannie'—is self-fertile. Originating recently in Holland, it is a dwarf only three feet tall with leaves that are entirely green.

Some of the ornamental grasses have interest in winter. *Carex morrowii* 'Variegata' deserves a place in any garden for its white-striped leaves that form a graceful, swirling mound. It ought to be planted in groups of three or more for the greatest visual impact. *C. phyllocephala* 'Sparkler' is another good one, one of the taller carexes at about twenty inches. Its striped leaves fan out at the top of its spikes or stems, something like the little paper umbrellas used to decorate cakes for parties. About two of the New Zealand carexes there is room for argument. The blades of both *C. buchananii* and *C. flagillifera* are bronze-tan all year long. Some people think they're handsome. Others think they look dead. My opinion wavers back and forth, but there's another grass, surely the least grass with the most name, that I really fancy. It's *Arrhenatherum elatius* ssp. *bulbosum* 'Variegatum', or bulbous oat grass. This perky, tufted little plant is a delight for its narrow leaves striped in several shades of green alternating with pure white. From a few feet away, it looks velvety and soft, a complete deception: up close, its blades are so glossy they fairly sparkle, and their sharp edges can nick unwary fingers. A cool-season grass, it goes partially dormant in midsummer, producing fresh new growth when cool nights return with the advent of autumn.

Also dormant in summer, one of the best groundcovers, *Arum italicum* ssp. *italicum*, has enormous appeal in the other seasons. In October, it puts up gorgeous, silver-marked, arrow-shaped leaves of rich and shining green that remain fresh-looking until mid-June. It blooms in May, with green and pale mauve flowers much like those of jack-in-the-pulpit. After the leaves die down for the summer, the flowers are followed by spikes of large, intense orange-red fruits that are spectacular for a month or more. This aroid is often sold as A. i. 'Pictum', but the name is invalid and risks confusion with another species altogether, A. pictum.

Liriope muscari is a classic passalong plant from one gardener to another. Even in its ordinary, unexciting form, it is useful as a solid groundcover or planted in rows as a low divider marking off one part of a garden from another. Many cultivars have plain green leaves, but 'Gold Banded' and 'John Burch' are variegated. 'PeeDee Ingot', a splendid plant that originated in Coastal Gardens in Myrtle Beach, South Carolina, isn't nearly as well known as it deserves. It has fetching chartreuse-gold foliage. It self-seeds, passing its bright color down to its progeny.

Finally, there's another fine groundcover, Vinca minor 'Aureo-Variegata', also a passalong plant someone gave me that I have passed along to many friends over the years. Its golden variegation is so unstable that it is difficult to find two leaves that are identical. It spreads rapidly by runners to form a low carpet that makes a lovely background for larger plants. Its flowers of pure white are just as delightful in early spring as its foliage is throughout the sunless days of winter. Most vincas are ho-hum plants, but not this one.

❧ It May Not Bloom Through Snow — But So What?

I RECALL THE FIRST WORDS that I read about gardening, all five of them: "It blooms through the snow." I was about eight at the time. The plant in question was the Christmas rose (Helleborus niger), and the words were in an advertisement for Wayside Gardens. An accompanying black and white photograph showed the large white flowers of this hellebore sticking out of a snowdrift.

It made a huge impression on me. I wanted Christmas roses immediately, even though we seldom had snow in my part of Texas. The ad fudged the truth badly. *Helleborus niger* doesn't really bloom through the snow. What happens is that it blooms and then snow falls on it. And it's much more likely to bloom in January, February, or even March than at Christmas. (Christmas got in its name, I suspect, because in German the species is called *Christrosen*—Christ's roses. German plant lore holds that an angel took pity on a little shepherd girl who visited the Infant Jesus in his manger, her hands empty of a suitable gift. Angelic intervention transformed some handy weeds nearby into this beautiful flower of late winter.)

Grownups often realize their childhood desires, so there's no surprise in my having a colony of *H. niger* in my back garden under a tall dawn redwood—a perfect spot, since the tree loses its leaves in the fall to provide good sunlight, and then leafs out again in spring to give protective shade.

Besides the Christmas rose, my other hellebores include the Lenten rose (*H. orientalis*, although it's more properly *H.* × *hybridus*), which blooms about a month later than *H. niger*. It is one of the most elegant of all perennials. The foliage is a dour black-green, itself most handsome against a background of snow. The colors of the single, five-petaled blossoms are strangely wonderful—many shades of green, pure white, pink, cream, mauve, and purple, often stippled or spotted with contrasting colors. The flowers of some winter-blooming plants may be of value only because of the time they blossom, but hellebores would make us rejoice even if they bloomed in July.

There are several hybrid strains of Christmas and Lenten roses. They may be raised from seed although the wait from seed to flower will not please impatient souls whose motto is "Now!" The seeds take their own time, often a year or more, to germinate, and the seedlings are slow to establish. But once a colony of hellebores is happy, it is virtually permanent.

I can think of only two things to say against hellebores. First, their history has its dark side. Their genus name means "food that kills." Every part of the plant is poisonous, containing a nasty chemical called helleborin. In the Middle Ages the roots of several species were used to produce a cardiac-disease medicine that was often more lethal than the condition it purported to cure. Somewhat later, according to some rumors, hellebores were dear to the heart of Lucretia Borgia. Second, whenever I think of hellebores I swiftly go on to think, "Dammit, the Brits are ahead of us!" British books are loaded with pictures of hellebores I've never seen. British gardeners can grow named cultivars, like 'Potter's Wheel'—basically *Helleborus niger*, but with immense flowers of snowy white. They can choose hellebores with yellow flowers and hellebores with double flowers. (I'm not sure I'd fancy double ones, but I'd like to see for myself and decide.) The flowers of the hellebores that have been growing in my garden for years face downward, but British gardeners can choose some that hold their blossoms upright and outward, so that they may be appreciated from on high.

I don't like thinking that British gardeners are ahead of Americans, at least not as concerns the availability of plants. There's nothing we can do about our disadvantages of climate, compared with the prolonged springs, gentle summers, and bearable winters that the Gulf Stream (*our* Gulf Stream) gives England, despite its high latitude. Plants, however, are another matter. Provided that something will grow here, as hellebores certainly will in almost all parts of the country, we should have it available, not waste our energy in envy.

But of late there has been good news for American hellebores lovers. Several mail-order nurseries have begun offering vegetatively propagated hellebores from named clones developed in both England and Europe. They are also selling strains derived from seeds of *Helleborus* × *hybridus* from the gardens of Margery Fish, Elizabeth Strangman, and Robin White in England, and of Gisela Schmieman in Germany. One nursery is offering several species grown from seed collected in Greece and the former Yugoslavia.

In 1995 I bought four plants grown from Gisela Schmieman's seed. At $29.95 apiece, they seemed almost unreasonably expensive, but when they bloomed the following winter they were worth every penny. One was unspotted white, tinged green. Two were pinks, one pale, one dark, and both spotted. The fourth was a wonderfully sullen black-purple, unspotted. Three of them (all but the darkest-flowered) had outward- and slightly upward-facing flowers. They all had flowers twice the size of the ones I have been growing for years.

I thought that hellebores could never be divided, but Nancy Goodwin told me that this common belief is dead wrong, so in the fall of 1998, strictly following her instructions, I divided all four of my prized plants in late August, taking care to have at least three buds or eyes on each piece. Four plants yielded sixteen, thus much reducing my initial investment. I worried that dividing the plants might cost me a year of bloom, but the following spring they flowered lavishly.

Thus far, I have not said anything about the bears claw or stinking hellebore, *H. foetidus*. Were I writing a couple of years earlier, I would surely have praised it. It is a commanding presence in any garden for its fairly towering height, its deeply cut dark green leaves, and its large inflorescences of apple-green flowers in late winter. It is, however, an extremely prolific self-seeder. It is much more short-lived than either *H. niger* or *H. × hybridus*, so perhaps its reproductive prowess represents compensation for the brevity of its existence. In a recent year, I removed enough plants from our back border to fill two garbage cans. With some regret, I am now banishing this plant altogether. But I feel that the decision is correct. Nancy Goodwin has lately told me that the bears claw hellebore has become one of the worst weeds in her woodland garden at Montrose. She was puzzled for a while that it spreads from seeds as easily uphill as down, but now she speculates that slugs—which are immune to many neurotoxins, as they have no nervous systems—feed on the seed capsules. The seeds stick to their slimy bodies, and they cart them in every direction as they slither around.

❦ *Winter Jasmine*

EXCEPT THAT IT LACKS the exquisite perfume of *Jasminum officinale*, *Jasminum sambac*, and most of the other species in this heady genus, winter jasmine (*J. nudiflorum*) is an almost perfect plant. It blooms over a prolonged period, starting in early to middle January.

Its crop of bright yellow flowers appear on naked stems. Since the stems are rich green, like those of *Kerria japonica* and a few other shrubs, it is attractive all winter. To say that the flowers are bright yellow is an oversimplification. The backs of the petals are washed with the red of fresh blood, changing as the flower ages to the rusty red of an old bloodstain. The phalliform glossy buds are tipped with crimson.

Once established, winter jasmine is fully hardy well into the colder reaches of Zone 7. But gardeners should never be intimidated by such statements about any plant. If I lived in Zone 6 or even in Zone 5, I would still try this unassuming shrub that brings such cheer to winter. The worst that might happen is that I wouldn't succeed, and given the proper microclimate (such as next to a stone or brick foundation on the south side of a house), it might just get through colder winters than we have here. This jasmine doesn't keep blooming no matter what the weather is doing. Zero temperatures will blast its flowers somewhat, especially if combined with fierce winds. Under such conditions, it just retreats a bit, and when the weather gets slightly more friendly, it comes back into bloom.

The arching stems of this somewhat sprawling shrub will root where they touch the ground. This amiable habit of self-layering means that there are always a few little plants to give to visitors who want their own touch of cheer in January and February. It also lends winter jasmine a taint of weediness. Left to itself, especially in areas warmer than Zone 7, it can march across a considerable stretch of garden, becoming rather too much of a good thing. A stern hand is called for two or three times a year, pulling up and discarding whatever amount of the plant exceeds the gardener's wishes. It's not really much of a chore—nothing like the backbreaking job of removing a flowering quince or a forsythia, for *Jasminum nudiflorum* is shallow rooted.

This jasmine is a fine cut flower, and its branches can be forced inside in late December. I prefer to wait to cut it until it comes into bloom naturally, in its own rhythm. It blooms for me about two to three weeks after the winter solstice. I take it as a sure sign that the days are lengthening, by slow but reliable degrees.

❧ The Search for a Weeping Mulberry

OUR TOWN WAS FOUNDED in the early nineteenth century and developed gradually over almost two hundred years. It has none of the postwar subdivisions that typify much of New Jersey, including some nearby towns. There aren't many vacant lots left, but the town's slow growth means that it's a visual encyclopedia of residential architectural styles stretching back from split levels and ranch houses all the way to the Federal Period. Victorian houses dominate my own street. Most of them are "landscaped" in the twentieth-century manner, meaning that they are half hidden by the once little shrubs—mostly conifers and rhododendrons—that were planted at their foundations and then grew to monstrous size. A few, however, have been restored to a more Victorian style of planting using cast-iron urns and bedding plants in bright colors.

But one favorite plant of the late Victorian era is still in evidence even in many of the houses of that era that cower behind gigantic rhododendrons and blue atlas cedars that reach to the eaves. It is the weeping mulberry, one of the most graceful of all small trees. Its pendulous branches sway in a summer breeze, covered with large, glossy leaves of a deep, clean shade of green. Handsome in summer, it becomes transcendently beautiful in winter, a living piece of sculpture that looks like a frozen waterfall. (Even dead weeping mulberries are gorgeous, during the many years it takes their iron-hard wood to rot.) This mulberry is *Morus alba*, the same tree used in China for silkworms. The weeping form is Teas' weeping mulberry, which originated as a chance seedling on the grounds of John C. Teas in Carthage, Missouri, around 1883.

For almost a quarter century I drove by these trees in my neighborhod with longing in my heart for my own frozen mulberry waterfall. If one had turned up in a nursery catalog or garden center, I would have snapped it up immediately, but no mulberry ever appeared in either place. Then a friend tipped me off that I didn't need to buy a mulberry to have one. They root almost as easily as coleus. I should just ask a neighbor for some tip cuttings of last year's growth, five or six inches long, bundle them together, stick their bases in damp sphagnum moss, wrap the whole thing in plastic film, and then put it in the refrigerator until March. The cuttings would root almost overnight. When they started growing, I should tie each cutting to a stake to establish an upright trunk that would support the weeping growth habit that would follow. In this way I could have enough Teas' weeping mulberry for everyone in the neighborhood who wanted one.

It sounded simple, but I never got around to trying it. A fine little weeping mulberry just turned up one day at Home Depot in Durham, North Carolina. Martha Blake-Adams bought it for us. It now grows out by our front gate.

❦ Twisted Hazel's Odd Appeal

THE COMMON NAME of *Corylus avellana* 'Contorta', Harry Lauder's walking stick, doesn't mean much anymore, since few among the living can recall the Scottish vaudeville comedian whose strangely bent cane was always good for a laugh. This shrub is at its worst during late spring and summer, for its foliage is coarse and unappealing. But in the winter, it is lovely to see. The twigs and branches spiral and twist and turn in an irregular way, as if the plant is of several minds about which way to grow.

Botanists describe hazels as monoecious, meaning that they bear separate male and female flowers on the same plant, rather than having flowers that are bisexual or bearing male and female flowers on different plants. My twisted hazel, however, has to my knowledge never borne a female flower and certainly never produced a cob or hazelnut for baking or eating out of hand, but its waxy male catkins help measure the progress of winter toward spring. Tiny at first, they steadily grow longer, until by mid-March they reach five or six inches. They sway and dangle in the slightest breeze, and finally one morning, when they release their ripe pollen, the air nearby shimmers with what seems to be gold dust. The twisted hazel is attractively odd even as a small plant, only a couple of feet tall. It grows slowly, but eventually, in about twenty years, a contorted hazel will become a shrub some twelve feet tall and eight feet across. It should be placed where people can see and enjoy it to the fullest when out of leaf. Ours grows out by the sidewalk, next to the mailbox. At Christmas we decorate it with hundreds of tiny lights that we sometimes don't get round to removing for a couple of months.

If we were ever to move to a new house, one of the first things we would plant would be a twisted hazel.

V Reflections on Gardening and Its Work

❧ The Only Rule of Gardening

In a perennial border, put tall plants at the back, medium-sized ones in the middle, and short ones up front. At all costs, allow nothing in your garden of the magenta persuasion. Whatever else you do, your home garden must feature low conifers around the foundation of your house and a verdant lawn out front, which must be open to the street for the enjoyment of people driving by. Insects and weeds are the gardener's enemy: spray them, and let not one of them escape you! Give your bulbs a nice feeding of bone meal every year.

THESE ARE but a few of the rules of gardening that I was once taught, but have discarded or learned to ignore in the course of time, under the dictate of experience. Some of these rules are little more than long-honored superstitions. Here I would place the one about staircasing plants in a border according to size. It assumes that we look at borders from a single fixed position, as in a still photograph. But we have legs, after all, and can walk around a tall plant to see what's behind it. (At the moment, in the vestibule of autumn, there's a hugely handsome specimen of the Japanese bush clover, *Lespedeza thunbergii* 'White Fountain', blooming right at the front of a border in my back garden. It sways and trembles in the slightest breeze and I want it close at hand, not stuck behind other things.)

Some other supposed rules—such as reaching for a spray gun at the first sight of a weed sprouting or an insect peering out from behind a leaf—are downright harmful. Some once made sense but no longer do, as in the case of bone meal. In the days of great estates and their gardens in England, ground-up bones from the dining table with some flesh still clinging to them made a reasonable if ill-smelling fertilizer, but commercial bone meal, steamed to remove gelatin and sterilize the stuff, has virtually no nutrient value in a form that plants can use.

As for extirpating magenta wherever it pops up, I take another course. Following the lead of the people who write copy for those fancy color nursery catalogs, I call it something else—"wine-rose," or "light reddish-purple." (I'm not about to do without *Lychnis coronarius* or *Callirhoë involucrata* because magenta has a bad name it doesn't deserve.)

The notion that we've got to have lawns and foundation plantings isn't really a rule of gardening, but a piece of suburban American etiquette traceable to Frank J. Scott's disastrously influential *The Art of Beautifying Suburban Home Grounds of Small Extent* (1870) and to the later work of his disciple, Frank A. Waugh, who taught landscape architecture at the University of Massachusetts early in this century. Scott wrote that it was "unchristian and unneighborly" to hedge off a front garden or deny passing strangers the thrilling sight of our lawns. Waugh agreed, adding that foundation plantings were "fundamental to the whole of American domestic landscape architecture." (He failed to mention how quickly they ascend to the eaves, plunging the interior of a house into the gloom of Styx.) Everywhere I look in my neighborhood I see that their ideas have triumphed. The consequence is that the much more sensible idea that gardens should be enclosed, private retreats from the world has not been given its fair chance.

After over fifty years of the gardening life, I have come to the conclusion that there is only one rule that counts: you have to garden where you are, not someplace else. As real estate salespersons are wont to say, location is everything.

Latitude and its consequent expression in day-length during the growing season; average rainfall and its actual amount and distribution within any single year; soil composition and chemistry; number of frost-free days—these and similar things are the framework of gardening wherever it is attempted. They set limits, and they provide opportunities. Reason demands that we understand this principle and hew to it firmly.

But as Blaise Pascal once taught us, the heart has its reasons that reason does not know. Gardeners are not entirely rational beings, who moderate their desires according to what is possible. If we live in Biloxi, Mississippi, we crave the sumptuous double peonies and *Cornus canadensis* our climate denies us. If we live in Boston, we long for camellias, oleanders, and crape myrtles. If we live in New Jersey and grew up in Texas, we find it a nasty piece of fate that we can't have gardenia hedges. Many Americans wish more than almost anything else to have an "English garden." We go on pilgrim-

age to Sissinghurst, Great Dixter, and Barnsley House, returning
with lust in our hearts for things we cannot grow well, or at all, such
as *Meconopsis betonicifolia*.

Not long ago, I saw just such a putative English garden in Dallas. Delphiniums were perishing wherever I looked, but meanwhile
I couldn't find a single plant of the native southwestern and Mexican species of *Salvia* so well suited to local conditions. The odd
thing is that some British gardeners who have traveled extensively in
the United States also envy us. I have friends in England who tell
me they would give their eye teeth to see *Helianthus angustifolius*
blooming in its October magnificence, to have more tall ornamental grasses reach tassel and plume, and to have *Magnolia grandiflora*
as a huge, freestanding tree instead of a weakling clinging to the
south side of a wall. I haven't the heart to tell them about the large
scarlet fruits that spill out of the magnolia's hand-grenade seed cases
in midautumn, and how deliciously they smell of bay rum if
crushed ever so slightly.

❀ Dirt

A FRIEND OF MINE who writes often for a prestigious American gardening magazine tells me that he's increasingly angered over editorial highhandedness in changing his prose. Every time he writes the
word "dirt," an editor crosses it out and substitutes "soil." My friend
is deeply annoyed.

This delicate antipathy toward dirt is not universal among edi-
tors who deal with garden writing. I ran across the word just the
other day, in an article in *House and Garden*, a magazine that hardly
has a reputation for encouraging filthy language or plebian tastes. I
use the word daily. When I go out and dig in my garden, I dig in the
dirt, not the soil. When I come inside afterward, it's dirt, not soil,
that I scrub from under my fingernails. I also use the other word. I
have topsoil, not topdirt.

I come from a family of several generations of gardeners. Both
of my grandmothers and my mother called themselves plain dirt
gardeners, not plain soil gardeners. And gardeners of my vintage (I
remember Pearl Harbor) may recall the national radio show that

came over the air on Saturdays, right after *Let's Pretend*. There was a crusty fellow on the show, who talked about his garden. The name of the show was *The Old Dirt Dobber*, not *The Old Soil Dobber*.

We lived in deep country during World War II, and our nearest neighbor had a dirt yard, as was fairly common in the rural South then. Not a weed nor even a speck of grass grew in it. The path to her front door was neatly flanked by two rows of whitewashed stones. She swept it all almost every day with a broom, and she would never have dreamed of calling it her soil yard. (These dirt yards of the old South had their practical purpose, now almost lost to memory and consciousness: children could play in them without the danger of the copperheads that might lurk in grass.)

"Dirt" is part of some of the best American garden writing, by long tradition. In *My Summer in a Garden* (1870) Charles Dudley Warner, then the editor of *Harper's Magazine*, started out with these words: "The love of dirt is among the earliest of our passions, as it is the latest. Mud-pies gratify one of our first and best instincts. So long as we are dirty, we are pure."

Why, then, does my friend get blue-penciled every time he reaches for this word? Why is soil better, somehow, than dirt? I suspected the answer might lie in etymology, and in the development of the English language after the Norman invasion. One of the peculiarities of our tongue is its numerous pairings of words in which one is crude and the other polite, the first being Teutonic in origin and the second Latin, via French. It's a cow or a pig when it's walking around outside, but when it comes to the table it's beef or pork. There are no such animals as veals or muttons, either. I went to an unabridged dictionary in my town library. My suspicion was confirmed. "Dirt" comes from Old Norse. Its meaning is crude: excreta, basically. "Soil" comes from Old French, but its literal meaning isn't exactly highfalutin: it denotes a pig wallow.

But I wanted to take the pulse of some of my fellow gardeners on the burning issue of dirt versus soil, so I conducted a little informal poll for several weeks, asking friends who gardened which word they preferred and why did they think there was an animus against the Teutonic derivative in some editorial circles. Soil had its advocates, including a woman in Philadelphia who said that it was soil when it was where it was supposed to be (in her garden) but dirt when it was where it wasn't supposed to be (on her rug). Some people offered compromises, suggesting forgoing both words in favor of either "earth" or "ground," or else using the d-word and the s-word alternately, instead of judging the issue. But dirt won out hands down over soil among most of the friends I talked to. One of them even conducted his own supplementary informal poll, in the neighborhood bar he frequents on Monday nights when there's a football game on television. His fellow fans and drinking chums favored the d-word by a margin of two to one.

Another friend, a strong advocate of the d-word, suggested that the editorial policy of banning it needed to be placed in a broader cultural context. Ours is the day of the euphemism, he said, even in gardening. In some circles, mowing the yard has become "turf management" and planting has become "installation of plant materials."

My friend is right. Euphemisms are dangerous, because language becomes a means not of revealing but concealing the truth. Ruling out dirt as acceptable diction is a good example of the alienation in a modern society that protects us from the realities of our existence and our sustenance.

I saw what he was driving at. There are no pigs, nor pig wallows either, in our grocery stores — only pork. Chicken breasts seem to have come into being in trays of plastic foam covered with transparent film. Freshly washed and sometimes waxed fruits and vegetables betray no hint of what they grew in, except for the traces of composted manure on mushrooms (which may be why some people won't eat them).

I will leave alienation to social scientists to ponder. But I do know that gardening means to be connected to the larger world in its entirety, with our feet firmly on the dirt.

❧ Clover Is Okay — Really

I DON'T TEND MUCH LAWN, and what little there is out in the back garden looked awful late last August. A summer that felt at times like the surface of Venus had worked a lot of mischief on the greensward. Additional damage came from carpenters making repeated trips across the lawn, sometimes parking a truck there. Whole patches were sick or dying, and the turf looked tired even where it wasn't moribund. I could have called in the lawn-care specialists, who claim to be to grass what a hospital trauma team is to the seriously injured. They probably would have known what chemicals to use to get the green growing again, but I've never cottoned to these folks and their sprays.

Instead, I resorted to white clover, several pounds of seeds sown over the whole area and watered lightly twice a day until the little dark green leaves began to appear amid the exhausted fescue and bluegrass.

A lawn with clover in it is unpopular nowadays, heretical even. I had to visit several stores before I could find the seed. Clerks gave me funny looks. One of my neighbors, discovering what had been planted, warned, "Watch out. It will attract bees."

He was right, of course. There have always been some patches of clover in my lawn for I've planted it before. Once upon a time, from late spring to late fall, the lawn bloomed and the bumblebees and honeybees hummed. But in all the years we've lived here, no one in the family has been stung by a bee, even though we often go barefoot. We've been stung by wasps and hornets, but they are lured by prey, not nectar. As for the honeybees, they no longer hum much. Bumblebees do, but their former drinking companions have almost vanished here as in much of the country, now that the honeybee population has been decimated by varroa and tracheal mites.

Many Americans dislike clover in their lawns as much as they hate crabgrass. But a clover lawn is actually in the best national tradition. When Andrew Jackson Downing, the most influential agricultural and horticultural writer in our entire history, told people to plant lawns, he specified a mixture of white clover and Rhode Island bent grass, whatever that is. "Sow four bushels of it to the acre," he admonished, "and not a pint less as you plan to walk on velvet."

Downing admired clover hugely, for excellent reasons. It isn't subject to mildew and other blights that can affect lawn grasses. It greens up early, stays green late, and can take lean rations of water. Its flowers are pretty, starring the turf with pinkish white. Its fragrance, especially when newly mown, is proverbially sweet. Children with nothing else to do can amuse themselves for half an hour at least looking for sprigs with four leaves. Being a legume, it makes its own fertilizer by snatching nitrogen from the air. A clover lawn helps make honey in some remaining neighborhood hive, in a world that can use all the sweetness it can get.

Why doesn't everyone plant lawns with clover in them, then? The answer lies in the broad-leafed herbicides we've used prodigiously in this country since the end of World War II. They won't kill bluegrass or fescue or rye. They will kill dandelions and plantains—and clover. Since 1947 the advocates of these herbicides have campaigned successfully to give people the idea that white clover is a noxious weed, because if people valued it, as A. J. Downing did, they might be slower to reach for a chemical weedkiller.

I'd rather not spray. I like to walk on velvet.

🐾 Hiding Places

"ALLEN, where are you?" my mother calls.

I do not answer. No one can see me now, in this place that I have found.

"Allen, can you come in now? It's getting dark, and it's time to come inside."

I can see her, in the pale and fading light of this September dusk. But she cannot see me. I am alone, and only I know about this hiding place. But then a dog howls mournfully somewhere down the block. A barn swallow makes its final swooping flight against the fast-fading sky. "I'm here," I say, and make my way back to the safety of the house where I live, where my face and my name are known.

The child always remains in the grownup, and I have a little story to tell.

In the beautiful and historic Piedmont town of Hillsborough, the capital of North Carolina during part of its time as a colony, I walked up West Queen Street one sultry summer day with my friend Joanne Ferguson, and we discovered something so purely delightful that I would imitate it in my own garden if I could. I can't, because I have no ancient boxwoods, nor even juvenile ones.

Someone, perhaps a century ago, had planted four boxwoods, two on one side of the sidewalk leading from the street to the front door of a brick cottage, two on the other side. Over the decades, the boxes had billowed outward and upward, assuming the immense size that testified to their antiquity. They grew together, meeting overhead. I imagine, without being quite sure, that there was a time when they blocked the walkway altogether. Another path led along the front of the house from the gravel driveway. Perhaps the owners just went that way to their front door, allowing the boxwoods to grow unimpeded and the walk from the street to fall into disuse.

But the old front walk is usable now, and the evidence suggests that it has been for many years. Someone simply cut a tunnel through the shrubs. There's a small arch at the front, and another at the back.

Joanne walked through the front arch, disappeared from view for a moment, and then emerged on the other side, with a little laugh of delight. "Try it, Allen," she said.

I tried it, and it was wonderful. Once through the narrow arch, I was in a cozy little garden room, whose walls were the inner branches and limbs of the boxwood trees, barren of foliage because little light filtered in from above. It was cool and dark. I hunkered down for a few moments on the damp sidewalk. As my eyes grew accustomed to the dimness, I discovered a bird's nest hidden in a high branch. My senses sharpened. I could smell the pungent boxwood leaves, a scent that some people like, that others find faintly distasteful, and that no one can ever forget. I could hear an almost palpable quietness, since the foliage that enveloped this room inside a hedge dampened the sounds of automobile traffic on a busy thoroughfare nearby and of airplanes leveling off high in the sky above.

When I came out, back into the grown-up world, I had a big smile on my face.

❧ Garden Ornamentation

EVER SINCE REMOTE ANTIQUITY, the urge to make gardens has often been accompanied by the deep-seated desire to plant in them not only living green and flowering things but also artifacts. Especially common are those representing humans or other animals such as the statuary in the houses of Pompeii or the Boboli Gardens. Medieval gardens had their statuary of saints, and gardening supply companies like Smith & Hawken still offer statues of Saints Francis and Fiacre, who compete with one another as patrons of those who garden. Islamic culture forbids representation of the human form, but animals are acceptable, or at least they were in Moorish Spain. In Granada, the Alhambra offers many a pleasant sight, but none more pleasant than the Corte de los Leones, where a pride of wonderfully droll-faced stone lions face all points of the compass as they stand around a central fountain.

Historically, ornamentation has been used not only to depict living beings, as coinhabitants of a garden, but also to represent other times and cultures. The gardens of the Renaissance often made use of statuary modeled on classical ideals and mythology. Mock-medieval English gardens during the Romantic Period sometimes had mock-ruins (to encourage delectably mournful thoughts of decay and transitoriness) and imitation grottoes (to inspire meditation on the wild and the sublime).

The impulse to adorn gardens with a wide variety of material artifacts is alive today. On occasion, people express this impulse with great imagination, resulting in something purely individual and sui generis. The two best examples I can think of—although best described as being in front yards, not exactly in gardens—are found in private residences at opposite ends of my county. In one, the owner has erected well over fifty miniature electrical poles to display a collection of several thousand old insulators of green glass. In the other, the feature is row on row of plastic gallon milk jugs, painted brightly in many different colors. I can only admire the ingenuity that has gone into both of these productions, if not the aesthetic appeal of the result.

Ingenuity, however, is not necessary if someone has a garden and wants to spiff it up a bit with some statuary. Most garden centers offer a wide selection of ready-mades in materials that include concrete, plastic, and faux stone or lead. The animal kingdom, apart from humanity, is well represented here. The parking lots of local nurseries represent a kind of Peaceable Kingdom. Dogs and cats lie or sit side by side, in perfect amity. Bambi is omnipresent, also

212 • ALLEN LACY

Thumper—or perhaps Peter, Flopsy, Mopsy, and Cottontail, all
with price tags waving from their ears. There's an aquatic aviary too,
with its ducks, geese, and swans, also roosters and hens. Flamingos
congregate in huge flocks. Here be beasts of burden, especially bur-
ros, some of them pulling little carts. Raccoons and squirrels are
abundant. There's the occasional sheep, with or without Bo-Peep.
Turtles—or tortoises?—abide here. Some animals are conspicuously absent: snakes, opossums, and armadillos.

Human beings mingle with the other mammals, and with the
birds and reptiles. Few representatives of our own kind, however, are
grown up. There are little boys, sometimes peeing, and little girls,
never doing the same.

Not exactly human, but humanoid figures are part of the iconography of the garden center scene. There are more gnomes, lep-
rechauns, and elves to be found here than in anything by the
brothers Grimm. Theology also intrudes. Often Saints Fiacre and
Francis are near Madonnas of various sizes, some of them painted
white and Della Robbia blue. Let me not forget angels, mostly baby
ones, enough to form a huge celestial choir, except that many do
not look inclined to sing. Some lie down, awake or asleep. Some loll
and droop, with very poor posture. Occasionally one sits looking
grumpy, as if he has just had a bad-wing day.

The inanimate also is represented among all the other ready-
mades, in the form of birdbaths, gazing globes, benches and other
things to sit on, whirling plastic flowers, wishing wells, and bridges
arching toward nowhere.

By now, readers may possibly detect some slight snobbery on my
part. I confess it, but I must also add that bad taste can be fun. I have
friends who collect flamingos and flaunt that fact, as if they had borrowed the idea from Gertrude Jekyll herself. I have come to value
the impulse to adorn gardens, no matter how peculiar the result
may be—or how astonishingly wonderful.

My garden also has its artifacts. I think the antique Japanese
temple gong Hella gave me for Christmas one year is in perfect
taste. Some people may entertain doubts about the little angel
reclining by a small pool, but it amuses me; a dear friend gave it to
us, and I love it. As for the plywood Hereford peeking out from
behind our garden shed, I confess here: it was the result of tempo-

rary mental aberration when I bought it at a roadside stand in Maine some years ago.

Right next door there is an inspiring garden, tended lovingly by my often-mentioned neighbor, Ed. His late wife, Jean, was an avid collector of garden ornaments and much else. A devotee of garage sales and flea markets, she assembled a marvelous collection of folk-art or antique garden ornaments, from standing stags of painted concrete to witty wind vanes with propellers that make little people saw wood or fan themselves. I love to go next door as evening comes on and chat with Ed, meanwhile admiring the wagon wheel and the little rabbit of cast iron next to the old doghouse that's no longer inhabited. Jean was a person of enormous good humor and kindness who was passionate about rescuing objects from the past and giving them a home. She left behind a testimony of herself, obvious still in her garden. She gave meaning to *things*, and that is well worth treasuring.

❧ Jurassic Gardening

MOST GARDENERS like to know something about at least the most recent history of the plants they grow—when and from what source each came into their garden; when each began to be cultivated, whether it be a native North American plant or an exotic imported species; and who brought each into being in the case of deliberate hybrids. I like knowing that if a cultivar has 'Lambrook' in its name it almost surely originated in Margery Fish's garden in England; that if it's a daylily whose name has 'Siloam' as its first word the hybridizer Pauline Henry in Arkansas gets the credit; and that 'Eco' signifies nurseryman Don Jacobs in Georgia had something to do with getting a good plant into circulation.

I like, furthermore, to associate some of the favorite plants I grow with the friends who gave them to me. I look at this heuchera or that baptisia and think of someone else named Allen; at a particularly fine carex and think of Barry; at a truly splendid yellow daylily seedling that never got named or introduced and think of André, from whose hybridizing patch it came.

That said, most of the plants that gardeners grow have no history, in the strictest sense of the word, because they originated long before *Homo sapiens* appeared on the planet, and much longer before our species learned to write and to record events in historical records. The most highly developed plants, the flowering angiosperms that were the latest group to evolve, are themselves fairly new on the scene, having made their appearance in the plant kingdom during the Cretaceous Period about 125 million years ago, or 124.5 million years before *Homo sapiens*.

Some plants have an even greater antiquity than the angiosperms, and I love having them in my garden because they are a link with a span of life stretching so far back into the remoteness of time as to make our own species' presence on this earth a mere handbreadth, the Biblical twinkling of an eye. Mosses, liverworts, and lichens instill humility, for they are champions of endurance and survival. Liverworts are of dubious value in a garden. Mosses and lichens are debatable. They are despised by some, but to my mind stones or bricks encrusted with lichens have a venerable look that bespeaks dignity, and I love the emerald velour of moss, even when it has crept into a lawn. (To speak even more fondly of moss, I think that the most elegant of all lawns are those composed of moss alone.)

Moving up the evolutionary ladder a notch or two, the ancient races of ferns and equisetums are splendid in gardens, although the genera of ferns that have survived into historic times are mere shadows of the mighty plants they were when dinosaurs roamed the earth.

Equisetum hyemale

Likewise, equisetums, or horsetails: these primitive plants with a fascinating sculptural form and so loaded with silica that they once were used to scrub cooking pots (accounting for their other common name, scouring rushes) once included species as large as trees. (*Equisetum hyemale* and other species still extant today must be confined in pots; let loose to roam unfettered in garden soil they become invasive monsters). If forced to choose between horsetails and ferns, I would choose ferns hands down for their utter grace and enormous variety. Any shady garden is severely impoverished that does not have its lady ferns, its Christmas ferns, its hart's tongue ferns, its maidenhairs, and all the rest. Two ferns, both natives of eastern Asia, are indispensable. One is the Japanese painted fern (*Athyrium nipponicum* 'Pictum'), a deciduous plant whose fronds are beautifully washed with pewter, old rose, raspberry, and other hues from their first emergence in spring until the first frost of autumn cuts them down. The other is the autumn fern (*Dryopteris erythrospora*)—"autumn" for the coppery color of its fronds when they first unfurl. Among hardy evergreen ferns, this one is exceptional for remaining perky and upright and bright in color even when icy winter blasts get serious in January and February. Best in light to medium shade, it can withstand a fairly sunny location as well.

Two handsome woody plants in my garden qualify as living fossils in the strictest sense—species alive today that also are known from the fossil record imprinted by their direct ancestors in the mud that eventually hardened into sedimentary rocks.

The ginkgo or maidenhair tree (*Ginkgo biloba*) does not survive in the wild today, nor has it for some time. It resembles in this respect the American flowering tree *Franklinia alatamaha*, discovered by the Philadelphia Quaker botanists John and William Bartram in woodlands in Georgia in 1770 and never again found in its native habitat. Franklinia's discovery proved to be its rescue from imminent extinction, and somewhat the same thing is true of the ginkgo. The sole remaining species in its genus, it is also the sole representative now of the Ginkgophyta, a group of plants plentiful about 200 million years ago. It is unusual in that it has sperm that swim, a characteristic found otherwise only in cycads, another

Gingko

ancient group of plants, but not winter-hardy in gardens of the temperate zones. The ginkgo owes its survival to its commonly being planted in Asian temple gardens, from which it was imported to Europe and then North America some two centuries ago. One of the most handsome of all trees, it is lovely for its twin-lobed leaves from spring to summer, and when they turn in autumn, they fill the air with an unearthly but beautiful warm golden light.

Another living fossil on my home ground, and soon to be its largest plant, once it outstrips a fifty-foot Virginia juniper that seems, from old photographs, not to have grown an inch in seventy-five years, is a dawn redwood (*Metasequoia glyptostroboides*). I planted it as a four-foot sapling twenty-five years ago, soon after we bought our place and moved in. Now some forty-five feet tall, it is obviously a remarkably fast grower. A deciduous conifer closely kin to the larch and the bald cypress, as well as to the giant sequoia and the redwood, it is a fine plant for a garden. (I do wish I hadn't planted it so close to the power lines that run along our side street; representatives from our local electrical company dropped by the other day making me the resistible offer of chopping it down for free and planting in its place a dinky purple-leafed plum.) As conical as an ice-cream cone upside down, the dawn redwood has soft green foliage that turns to apricot-pink in the fall. Bare in winter, it allows light to penetrate to a colony of hellebores that ring it—and that welcome its shade in summer. My appreciation for this tree, as a well-behaved garden resident, stems not only from its year-round beauty, including its gorgeous exfoliating reddish-brown bark, but also from its deep-rooting habit. Unlike a nearby swamp maple that I love but still curse for its multitude of surface roots, the dawn redwood allows me to dig easily right up to its large bole, and it does not seem to rob moisture and nutrients from the upper layer of topsoil.

The dawn redwood was unknown even to botanists until the early 1940s, when it was discovered growing in Sichuan. At first it was thought to be a species of cypress (*Taxodium*) or possibly a true redwood (*Sequoia*), but eventually taxonomists gave it its own genus (*Metasequoia*). It owes its presence in American gardens to a shipment of seed in 1948 from China to the Arnold Arboretum, which publicized the plant and distributed it widely to other institutions.

Metasequoia glyptostroboides

Among other primitive plants I grow a couple of club mosses, but not, alas, the one I covet most. The peacock moss (*Selaginella uncinata*), which is also called rainbow fern although it's not a fern at all, is winter-hardy only to about Zone 8. A lover of dank, dark places, this low and creeping plant is astonishing for the rich blue and green iridescence of its needlelike foliage, a color one expects somehow in fabrics, metals, feathers, and the wings of butterflies, but not in one of the humbler members of the plant kingdom. To see this marvelous native of China is to long for it, and to lament any climate that rules out growing it close at hand.

❀ On Zones

I HAVE BEEN BROODING about climatic zones. Great Britain gets by with only two, unless you count some tiny altitudinous patches in Scotland. The United States has eleven, in the system used for the USDA Plant Hardiness Map. Our continent's climates range from virtual tundra where the growing season is barely long enough for gnats to breed, to tropical areas where the words "the changing seasons" are as meaningless as a campaign promise.

One of the givens of gardening is that you have to do it where you are, not someplace else. I've pointed this out already, but the principle is so often overlooked that it bears repeating. All gardening is local, even parochial. Place, and its attendant climate and latitude, impose limitations. We may resist these limitations pretending they don't exist and, say, live in Chicago but dream fondly of growing frangipani or oleanders outdoors.

But dreams, in combination with the perversity of desire, virtually define gardeners. In Freudian terms, the gardener's Id is constantly at work. The Pleasure Principle would rule our lives, if we let it. We want what we want when we want it—bearded irises in bloom half the year, docile red honeysuckles with the delicious fragrance of the horribly weedy Japanese kind, crabgrass that infests our neighbors' lawns and not ours. But the Pleasure Principle is a notoriously poor guide. It must be taken in hand and spoken to sternly by the Reality Principle. In the lingo of psychopop, our Inner Adult needs to sit on our Inner Child.

The various zonal systems—those of the Arnold Arboretum, of the United States Department of Agriculture (USDA), of *Sunset* magazine (for the West Coast, which meteorologically has almost nothing to do with the rest of the country)—represent the Inner Adult and the Reality Principle. They are based on the simple, rational idea that there's a natural correspondence between the weather in a particular spot on this earth and the requirements of particular kinds of plants. Some plants give up the ghost if the temperature hits 32°F. Some can take temperatures so far below zero that a polar bear would consider hibernating. Other plants range between these extremes, sorting themselves out along a continuum of winter-hardiness. It therefore makes sense to calculate the minimum winter temperature that is likely on average to occur in a particular location, to classify all plants in terms of the lowest winter temperature they can withstand, and then to select plants tailored to the conditions they will encounter.

Zonal systems are rational and akin to the common sense gardeners have always had, their almost instinctual recognition that people who live in Connecticut shouldn't waste their time and money on date palms. But I still have reservations about paying slavish attention to zonal labels when they are used to describe *plants*, not *places*.

First of all, zone designations for the same plants can differ by one zone, sometimes more, depending on which authority you consult. Most reference books tend to be conservative, sometimes saying that this plant or that is suitable for Zone 7, when it just might thrive in Zone 6. Some nursery catalogs, more sanguine or perhaps just more canny, err on the liberal side. I have seen one of the hottest new plants, *Loropetalum chinense* 'Rubrum', given as a Zone 7 plant, but I'm pretty sure it's not for my part of this zone. (I won't *know* that until I try—and fail.)

Second, in defining winter-hardiness these zones reflect only average minimum temperatures over a twenty-five-year period. An average figure in no way predicts how low the thermometer may drop in an untypical year. Furthermore, a zonal system in no way takes into account the problem of summer-hardiness—the ability of a plant to survive the prolonged high humidity and temperatures that prevail in much of the United States during the summer. A plant that can laugh at a Minneapolis winter may also perish in an Atlanta summer.

Third, there are many important variables besides temperature. My native Texas is divided into four zones (Z. 6–9) running east to west, according to the USDA. But it has eight different regions running north to south, with rainfall ranging from eight to fifty inches a year and the mean number of frost-free days from 180 to 340. I live in Linwood's Zone 7. I grew up in Dallas's Zone 7. They're not much alike. Experienced gardeners soon learn that climate is not absolute because of microclimates—the small variations of elevation, prevailing winds, air drainage, shelter, sun, and shade that combine to make it possible for a plant that would expire in one spot to thrive in another only a few feet away. A garden may technically be entirely in one zone, but parts of it may vary a notch or two on either side. Exposure and the presence of walls or other windbreaks are likewise important: on the north side of a stone wall winter may average 10°F colder than on the south side, although this difference may vanish if the south side is densely shaded by evergreen shrubbery or vines.

A good example from my own neighborhood of the difference a microclimate can make is *Passiflora edulis* or maypop. One of the reference books in my library describes it as marginally hardy into Zone 7 but reports that it will not produce here the edible fruit that it does farther south. One of my neighbors, however, has a luxuriant stand of it. It dies back to the ground in the autumn, but it always comes back in the spring, covering one side of the house with dense vines that produce a heavy crop of fruit as well as flowers. It grows on an embankment facing south, right next to the house's heated basement. Radiant heat from both the sun and the basement keep the soil temperature from falling much below freezing throughout the winter. Several years in a row I begged suckers of maypop from my neighbor in the spring, but they never bloomed, fruited, or made it through the next winter. Microclimate made all the difference.

My final reason for taking zonal recommendations with a pinch of sodium chloride is that believing them wholeheartedly takes away some of the adventure of gardening—the thrill of succeeding when there's been the warning of failure. A good example, again from my own neighborhood, concerns certain plants that grow well here that aren't supposed to. Local garden centers don't sell camellias, for the conventional wisdom is that these are "southern plants," and that New Jersey, even southern New Jersey, is not the South. Yet I find thriving, mature specimens of both *Camellia sasanqua* and *C. japonica* in gardens within a mile or so from my door. This evidence has led me to plant them, and my reward is the single or double, red, white, or pink flowers of *C. sasanqua* in the fall and *C. japonica* in very late winter.

Gardeners need to try some of the plants they dream about, undaunted by zonal pessimism, by unquestioned dedication to the Reality Principle. I have high hopes right now for a cultivar of *Gardenia fortunei* called 'Kleim's Hardy'. Like most southerners living up north, I miss gardenias a whole lot, miss the sensuousness of their haunting and heavy perfume. 'Kleim's Hardy' is reputedly able to take winter temperatures as low as −5°F. If I plant it, I may ultimately lose it, but that possibility doesn't mean I shouldn't give it a try anyway, for it just might prove to be even hardier than reported. The worst that can happen is failure, which is highly prevalent anyway.

❦ The Price of Convenience

IT'S TIME TO PUT IN A WORD for the high virtue of inconvenience in a gardener's life. Or maybe simply say a few grouchy things about convenience.

Over the past four decades, a great deal of effort has been expended to make things easier for gardeners. For example, it used to be that if we were to grow annuals we either had to plant them from seed or buy them as tiny plants in flats, with no idea what we were getting. Not anymore, however. By early January, wholesale growers are germinating the seeds of the annuals we will buy at our local nurseries in April or May. While still tiny plugs, the plants will be placed in plastic growing containers or market packs, each with four to six individual cells, in which we will purchase them. Clever hybridizers have been successful in breeding impatiens, salvias, petunias, marigolds, and other common annuals that will bloom in their market packs before the point of sale. We can see exactly what we are getting.

One result is that fewer and fewer Americans are planting seeds. My only evidence is anecdotal and impressionistic, but I trust it: every year at local hardware stores fewer and fewer seeds are for sale in the spring. There used to be three large racks from three different companies near the cash register. Fifteen years ago it was down to one, and every spring since then the number of packets and kinds of seeds have both declined. The presumption is that seed-planting is an endangered horticultural species, and that the market packs and the convenience they offer are responsible.

But convenience, like everything else, has its price, and the price in this case is the impoverishment of a gardener's life, particularly as regards annuals. For every annual that can be manipulated genetically to be blooming its fool head off when a customer sees it in a garden center, there are at least ten that don't like to be hurried. Some fine annuals, such as poppies, morning glories, larkspur, and viscaria, hate being transplanted at all. These insist on being sown in the same earth they will grow in. Otherwise, they may live, but with little vigor.

These reflections are occasioned by a pleasant hour or so with the spring catalogs of several seed companies whose computers haven't yet identified me as an inactive customer and purged me from their mailing lists. Early in this midwinter browsing, I was brought up short by annual candytuft. Candytuft! I haven't seen any in years, and I hate that absence, since the plant holds a keen place in my childhood memories. Partly it was the name, which I assumed to be a mysterious kind of candy that came in tufts. (It wasn't until I was grown that I learned the more pedestrian truth, that the name comes from *Candia*, another word for ancient Crete.)

But partly it was the fragrant clusters of little white, pink, lavender, or crimson blossoms that made this plant a childhood favorite.

I am vowing to go easy on market packs and try planting seeds instead, old-fashioned plants that I haven't seen in so long that they will seem new and unfamiliar. Besides candytuft, there will be four o'clocks, Mexican hat, calliopsis, California poppies, larkspurs, and moonflowers as well as morning glories. I will have lavateras, whose silken pink or white blossoms resemble those of the hollyhocks they are kin to. I will have love-in-a-mist, whose seedpods as well as flowers are such wonders of vegetative architecture.

And except for the moonflowers and morning glories, which to bloom well in the northeast need an early start, I do not mean to be in a great rush to plant. One of the most common questions gardeners ask about some plant or another is, when can I plant it? The question is generally taken to mean, how early can I plant it? A lesson I have learned is that annuals planted from seed in early summer or even as late as July 15 help enrich the garden in autumn and are more welcome then than in high summer, when so much else is in flower.

❧ *Gardening with the Left Hand*

AS CREATURES of bilateral symmetry, most human beings come into the world with two hands, each a mirror image of the other. A kindly providence might have arranged it so that we all could use either hand with equal facility, or that half of us would prefer the left hand, the other half the right. In this latter case, manufacturers of tools would have to accommodate us all, by making left-handed and right-handed implements, as Felco already does with its pocket pruners.

But providence has not been as kindly with humans as with other species, such as dogs and cats, who divide up equally between those that favor the left paw and the right paw. The two hemispheres of the human brain are not equal. In roughly 90 percent of us, the left side of the brain dominates, and a dominant left hemisphere decrees right-handedness, though not without exceptions.

The rest of us—and I am one—live left-handed in a right-handed world. Some recent thinking theorizes that we are not so much right-brained as mixed-brained, but whatever the case, we live constantly with inconvenience and with prejudice against us that is written in our very language, even as our preference for performing most tasks with our left hands is written in our genes. The English word "dexterity" comes from the Latin for right-handed, "sinister" from the Latin for left-handed. "Right" in English, as a term for what is fitting, just, and proper, is a metaphor derived from the hand of preference of the left-brained majority. So is "correct." In French, *droit* means to the right, and it comes into English as "adroit," meaning skillful. *Gauche*, meaning to the left, comes into English without modification and signifies awkward or clumsy. Things are no better in German, where *linkisch* has the double signification of left-handed and, as in French, awkward or clumsy. Even purely visual, nonverbal symbols betray such prejudice: the circle with the slash through it that means "no" (as in "no smoking" or "do not enter") derives from the bar sinister, the slash from upper left to lower right across a coat of arms to indicate an illegitimate branch of a family. We lefties, this message says, are just a bunch of bastards.

The disadvantages of being left-handed are many and obvious. We are forced to write from left to right, with the letters sloping rightward, when our genes would make it more natural to write from right to left, with the letters sloping leftward (as Leonardo da Vinci, a celebrated lefty, wrote). Right-handers complain unfairly about our handwriting.

There may even be some evidence that left-handedness correlates with average life spans shorter than those of right-handed people. A letter published in the *New England Journal of Medicine* in 1991 concludes that there is perhaps a difference of as much as nine years, maybe because left-handed people have a greater propensity for accidents. Our tendency, to avert an automobile collision, is to pull to the left, while right-handers pull right, placing them on the shoulder of a road instead of dead center. This theory, that we can expect fewer years of earthly existence than our right-handed brethren, has been disputed recently, but I wouldn't be surprised if it turned out to be true. I am used to accidentally smearing butter on my hand instead of on the muffin it holds.

Only in a mere handful of activities do lefties have advantages over the majority. In baseball, left-handed pitchers and batters perform better than right-handed ones, everything else being equal. The keyboards on typewriters and computers are easier for lefties to use, because they were originally designed to make right-handed people use their left hands as much as possible, in order to slow them down to a typing speed those early machines could manage.

Since gardening almost by definition involves the use of tools, we southpaws face problems unknown to our left-brained and right-handed brothers and sisters. Some tools present no difficulties. Hoes, shovels, and rakes are indifferent to a disposition to use one hand rather than the other. So are loppers used in pruning: they require both hands, as does an old-fashioned reel hand-mower to cut the lawn.

Anything with a curve in it is apt to be dangerous as well as awkward to use. I have a dandy little hand-weeding tool with an extremely sharp blade and a handle that curves sharply to the right. In the right hand, it chops weeds off just below the surface of the soil, sounding their death knell before they are big enough to be troublesome. It does its duties of execution safely to the right, away from the body of the person who weeds with it. Users holding it in the left hand, however, might end up performing inadvertent surgery on themselves.

Gasoline string-trimmers are another source of danger. Their exhaust pipes are on the right. A lefty could use one, but the danger of a painful burn is high. I once bought one, used it about five minutes, recognized that I might not get through the rest of the afternoon without an ambulance ride to the hospital for treatment of third-degree abdominal burns, and gave it to my right-handed neighbor next door.

The left-handed are also left-footed. To anchor a lawn mower in place while we start it, using the right foot on the little footpad on the left side of the housing is possible, but awkward. It feels more natural to use the left foot, but in this position we straddle the back of the mower, with the right foot on the ground, close enough to the rotating blade that a slip could mean the loss of some toes.

There is a theory that left-handed people are more creative than the majority. I would like to think that is true, but if it is I don't imagine that it is a matter of inheriting superior qualities. It is rather the product of realizing early in life that one is different from most other people, and of learning to make do with tools that aren't suitable for the hand of preference.

❦ Sit to Weed?

IT IS WELL-NIGH AXIOMATIC, one of the eternal verities if there ever was one, that all gardeners weed. I do not, incidentally, count as true weeding the kind of warfare that employs chemicals that turn water white and smell funny, or that extirpates the foe with flame throwers. Nongardeners, it must be added, do not understand the act of weeding. They believe that it is work, when the truth is that it is something joyous, or so some of my friends testify.

My friend Samantha tells me that her weeding time is often like an act of meditation. Pulling one weed after another almost becomes a mantra. She speaks of how Gandhi used the repetitive, rhythmic motions of spinning in this way. Occasionally, she says, a group of birds joins her at arm's length in their search for seeds and she is entranced. She goes on to tell me that weeding is in general therapeutic. It eliminates headaches, calms stress, and puts the world to rights. She even complains that when she mulched her garden one year she disliked the successful outcome. "I hated it," she explained. "There weren't enough weeds to pull, and I need a few weeds. Weeds give purpose to a gardener's life, and justify the desire to putter endlessly."

But all weeding and all weeders are not the same. The element of style enters into weeding as surely as it does in playing tennis, deciding what to wear to a party, or playing a musical instrument. Weeders fall into two basic stylistic categories: the all-out sort, who wait until there are sufficient weeds to be worth a concentrated pitched battle; and the constant vigilantes, who get rid of weeds one by one, giving each a mortal yank as soon as they spot it.

All-out weeders may note that crabgrass is sprouting in their lawns or borders and that sidewalk spurge and purslane have made their annual appearance as the weather turns warm, but they take no immediate action. They allow the weeds to grow for a while, awaiting the little mental click that admonishes them: "You must do something about those weeds." And then they launch their attack, often at dawn, in an assault that goes on till dark. At nightfall, piles of wilting mugwort, plantain weed, and ragweed lie everywhere, the body count of the day's campaign against the vegetative enemy.

The constant vigilantes never have to devote an entire hour to weeding, much less an entire day (or week, for the dedicated procrastinators among those who wait to weed). For these assiduous souls, to spot a weed is to remove it immediately. A weed no sooner sprouts and shows a tiny leaf or two before it is pulled up by the roots and left to perish in the sun. The vigilantes know their enemy, and they dispatch it before it becomes lusty of life, an affront to their sense of tidy good order.

The relations between the practitioners of these two contrary styles are uneasy at best. The vigilantes are contemptuous of their all-out brethren, and the all-out weeders feel sorry for those in the opposing camp. The vigilantes hold those of the other persuasion in contempt for much the same reason that those who watch television in an upright position scorn those who lie down to catch the evening news. Those who wait to weed almost universally sit to weed, a position that smacks of congenital laziness. Weeding may be a lot of work when these people get round to it, but it's their own fault. They deserve to recite the words of the General Confession in *The Book of Common Prayer:* "We have left undone those things which we ought to have done. . . . And there is no health in us."

For their part, those who wait to weed and then sit to weed feel sorry for the vigilantes, whose schedules are ruled by their weeds. They don't know the joys of being sloppy, of letting things go and then wading into a sudden frenzy of action deferred, but action nonetheless. Vigilantes pay a heavy price for their constant wariness.

My friend Anna speaks for those firmly in the sitting camp.

"Why kneel, bend, or stoop, when you can sit?" she asks. She is a devout sitter of the truest kind, those who sit on the ground when they weed. She believes that this substyle of the art overcomes alienation and puts her in touch with the throbbing pulse of life. "When I sit on the ground to weed," she explains, "I really feel in the thick of the garden, a part of it. I can examine a flower in detail, or watch a bee just a few inches away collecting pollen."

Sitters, I have noted, don't like to wear gloves when they garden. Gloves get in the way of direct experience, of feeling. The practitioners of the all-out, sedentary style want to feel those roots being teased out of the ground. They want to feel the dirt in their hands, have it all over them when they're done. And if they are among the truly fortunate of this earth, when day is done and the garden is littered with the corpses of their victims, they will sit some more, relaxing in the soothing water of a hot tub on a deck.

I pretend to no objectivity in this analysis of the two rival styles. Hella, my gardening companion, may have vigilante tendencies, but I do not. Thanks to her, there are never as many weeds in our garden as there would otherwise be, but there are always still enough, in some corner or other that she hasn't visited lately.

I go there to weed. But unlike Anna, I am not a ground-sitter. When I sit to weed, I use a sturdy little Roughneck stool, a Rubbermaid product that has been my joy and comfort for two decades at least. It is scratched and scarred, spattered with paint and discolored from ground-in dirt, but it serves my needs very well indeed. And when I move about the garden, I turn the stool upside down as a handy means of carrying a trowel, pocket pruners, and market packs of bedding plants from one spot to another.

Sometimes I catch Hella watching me. She doesn't say a word, but I sense her disapproval. She wishes that I would mend my ways, going after every weed the moment I see it, bending over or stooping down from the upright position that is the sign and sacrament of righteousness. But she knows that her hope is unfounded, that I am too set in my ways to change the habits of a lifetime.

I wonder: Was it thus in the Garden of Eden? Did Eve weed standing up, and Adam sitting down? On this question, the Book of Genesis has nothing to report.

✿ *Double-Digging*

"TO OWN A BIT OF LAND, to scratch it with a hoe, to plant seeds, and watch their renewal of life—this is the commonest delight of the race, the most satisfactory thing a man can do." That's Charles Dudley Warner's *My Summer in a Garden*, once again. The book is almost endlessly quotable. But Warner was no sentimental fool about work for work's sake. Essential in any gardener's life, he said, was "the love of digging in the ground (or of looking on while he pays another to dig)."

He had it dead right. While gardeners may extol the virtues of raising our tomatoes and our dahlias by the sweat of our brows, we also keep a crafty eye out for ways to make our perspiration only metaphorical. "Labor-saving device"—no words are sweeter or more seductive to the ears of gardeners, a fact attested by the rapid accumulation of portable electric pruners, and gasoline-powered tillers in our sheds or garages.

The growing of perennials in herbaceous borders, the kind of gardening I practice most, traditionally calls for quite a bit more work than scratching the earth with a hoe. To establish a proper perennial border, the conventional wisdom holds, the soil must first be double-dug and then amended. Translated into ordinary English, this means that the top foot and a half of dirt must be spaded out and placed to one side of the border-to-be. Then the next eighteen inches of soil are removed and placed on the other side. Next, standing hip deep in the resulting trench, the gardener (or someone she or he has sensibly paid to do the real work) is ready to amend the soil. Generous amounts of peat moss, thoroughly moistened, are mixed with the former topsoil, which goes to the bottom of the trench. Then the old subsoil is shoveled back into its new location nearer the light of day and amended with even more peat. The bed is ready for planting.

Such British horticultural theorists and practitioners as Margery Fish and Vita Sackville-West were staunchly in favor of double-digging and soil-amending as the necessary preconditions of any perennial border worth the name. For years I followed their advice, but with a nagging awareness of the difference between their lives and mine. They looked on while others did the work. I did my own double-digging and amending. Over the years I moved tons and tons of dirt and turned them topsy-turvy. I also bought enough bales of Canadian peat moss to help strengthen our neighboring country's economy.

But I will dig no more and never moisten a speck of peat again. A few summers ago I prepared a new border measuring ten by forty feet. That fall another new border went in adding, in all, 800 square feet of flower bed to the garden, with no digging and no peat. And the work took just two afternoons.

I take no credit for this accomplishment, just for knowing a good idea when I hear it. A gardening friend in North Carolina buttonholed me one day to discourse on peat moss and on the ancient wisdom that holds it essential to put twenty-five-cent plants (are there any?) in fifty-cent holes. Where he lives and gardens, summer heat and humidity make peat decompose in such short order that it doesn't much improve the soil. He also carried out some radical research, placing identical plants in two-bit holes and also in adjacent four-bit holes. After observing the results for several years, he concluded that there wasn't a penny's worth of difference. He now evangelizes for a simpler method of planting than Vita Sackville-West ever dreamed of. Just stick plants in holes a little bigger than the containers they grew in, water them deeply, and then mulch them with three or four inches of wood chips. A slow-release fertilizer should be added generously, since the chips absorb nitrogen from the soil as they decompose. New chips are added each year.

This scheme is the lazy gardener's dream—a low-maintenance garden, albeit not a no-maintenance one, something that hasn't existed since our first parents got kicked out of Paradise. But I have modified it somewhat. First, I cover the earth with a wide swath of the spun polyester horticultural fabric that has recently come on the market. Unlike a sheet of black plastic, this fabric allows moisture to reach the soil easily.

Second, I use salt or marsh hay, a covering six inches deep, instead of wood chips. I also tried straw in one section of the border, but brought this experiment to a quick conclusion. It is less expensive than marsh hay, but it breaks down more quickly, and as it decays it produces an unwanted crop of some of the most loathsome-looking fungi I have ever seen.

The plants in the beds prepared in this easy way look just as healthy and happy as those in the beds that were double-dug and heavily amended with peat. There is virtually no weeding to do, and as a result of this happy discovery the old flower beds also have their deep cover of salt hay.

Salt hay has been getting scarcer and scarcer in this area, but the gods have now smiled on every gardener in Atlantic County. Our Utilities Authority has instituted a sophisticated recycling program with an impressive plant that turns glass, paper, and plastic into usable raw materials for new products. It also gathers grass clippings, tree limbs, and other vegetative waste into its vast fermenting chambers, allowing them to burn in a slow microbial fire. When the process is finished, the result is beautiful compost, of a dark chocolate color that promises health and vigor for any plant growing in it. I can buy bags of the stuff (called Eco-soil) at $3 for forty pounds, but if I rent a truck I can get it for only $20 a ton.

I'm going to rent a truck. For once in my life, there will be enough compost in the garden—three tons, enough to mulch all the borders deeply with pure gardening gold the color of a Hershey bar.

❦ Sprinkling

No ONE HAS EVER WRITTEN more tellingly about it than James Agee, in "Knoxville: Summer, 1915," the prologue to his classic novel A Death in the Family. "It is habitual to summer nights," Mr. Agee wrote, "and is of the great order of noises, like the noises of the sea and of the blood, her precocious grandchild." The noise he remembered from his childhood was that of the fathers in his neighborhood performing the evening rite of sprinkling their lawns, filling the air in a great nocturnal chorus, never to be forgotten, once heard.

Sound horticultural practice in general rules out sprinkling lawns, or anything else that grows. Sprinkling, the experts tell us, is superficial. It encourages mildew and other diseases. It results in roots that stay shallow rather than plunging deeply into the earth. Plants with deep roots are healthy plants, well supplied with nutrients and able to resist summer heat and drought. It is better to water a lawn or a garden thoroughly once or twice a week, depending on natural rainfall and on the kind of soil you have, than to haul out the hose every night and give everything a light dowsing.

Some ancient wisdom, however, points out that we often know the good but do something else. I make here my confession. Although I water deeply my garden and what little lawn I have, moving hoses and oscillating sprayers and rubber soakers in their weekly circuit about my property, I also sprinkle when I can't resist the temptation.

Some evenings I detach a hose from the sprayer, replace it with a brass nozzle exactly like the one I remember from my childhood and surely like the one James Agee's father used eighty-five years ago, and spend half an hour sprinkling the grass and lightly watering the flower beds until the entire garden gleams, as with a heavy dew. Then, oddly comforted, I turn off the water and go inside feeling a sense of accomplishment.

I leave it to psychologists to explain the satisfaction that comes with sprinkling. Perhaps it is an expression of territoriality, an animal instinct that predates reason and science. Perhaps it is something more beneficent, a desire to get in touch with all the plants in the garden, including the weeds, in the quiet of the evening. Perhaps it is inexplicable. The fact of that odd comfort, however, remains.

But in the fall, those of us who are still in the grip of the deep-seated love of sprinkling get a kind of King's X in the matter, the permission of all the experts to sprinkle our lawns (but not our flower borders). It's more than permission, in fact. It has become the right and proper thing to do.

This King's X—the term meant time-out in a game of tag, back when I was growing up—comes when it's necessary to remake an old lawn. Accumulated neglect has taken its toll. Chickweed and dandelions in the spring, crabgrass and purslane in the summer

have together choked the more desirable fescue, bluegrass, and white clover almost to death. The stress of summer drought has given the turf a look of dusty exhaustion. It is time to go over the entire lawn with a rake and to buy good grass seed, broadcasting it generously along with the seeds of annual rye, a quick-germinating nurse grass that protects the tinier seeds of the fescue and bluegrass and raises the humidity to help them sprout.

When the seed is sown, sometime in September in most places, it is then time to bring out the hose and the sprinkler nozzle, and then to sprinkle—not just once, but three times a day, morning, noon, and night.

Within a week the rye will germinate, its rather coarse but sparkling green blades appearing and bursting into lusty growth, thanks to the ideal conditions of warm days and cool nights combined with regular, soul-satisfying sprinkling. The other grasses, more delicate, will begin to sprout about a week later, at first a mere green fuzz insinuating itself among the scuttling colonies of crabgrass, then becoming more substantial, as the hot days vanish and the crabgrass slows its growth. Meanwhile, I keep right on sprinkling.

But once all the grass has germinated, the sprinkling nozzle is put away. It is now time to water less often but more thoroughly, so that roots can grow deep into the soil before the last flame of autumn and the coming of winter.

✿ Raking

AT NO TIME are my neighbors more in evidence than on autumn weekends, when the weather is clear and cool, the oaks and the maples are a blaze of gold and crimson, and the leaves have started to fall. There are a few holdouts, people who wait until mid-November to do their raking just once and for all, but they are exceptions to the general rule that fifty leaves on the ground are reason enough to lure most home gardeners outside to tend to the prime chore of the season—the leaf-harvesting that takes place repeatedly until the trees finally stand bare and denuded and winter has arrived in earnest.

A sturdy bamboo rake and an old sheet or painter's drop cloth to haul the leaves to the curb or the compost heap used to be sufficient tools for this autumnal task, but now the leaf-raking chore has a host of technological handmaidens. As my neighborhood performs the rites of autumn, the street hums with the noise of machinery. Electrically powered shredders buzz and roar as they digest the bundles of leaves fed into their hoppers and spew out uniform tidbits of organic matter. Leaf blowers, which move the air and the fallen leaves at speeds of 125 miles per hour or more, are increasingly in evidence, something like personal hurricanes.

I admit it. I have a chipper/shredder, a dandy German machine that efficiently reduces maple leaves and moribund zinnias and petunias to easy fodder for the bacteria inhabiting the compost heap. Bought originally to ease the leaf chores of autumn, it has turned out to be a year-round tool. Capable of grinding any limb smaller than a half inch in diameter, it justifies its existence by cutting way back on the organic waste from our household that county workers have to haul off to our local composting facility. (Enough virtuous-sounding words: it's Hella who has the self-discipline to rev it up regularly and do the chopping and the grinding.)

I also have a personal hurricane. I'm not so proud of that toy. It blows leaves from here to Kingdom Come like a wind god, but it gets used only about three times a year. A bamboo rake and an old sheet are still sufficient to the rites of autumn. I can justify this equipment with a little effort: Wouldn't it be a trifle unfriendly, even solipsistic, to gather my leaves so silently, producing only the scratching sound of the rake against the earth and a dry rustle, instead of adding to the chorus of machinery at work that unites an entire neighborhood in late October?

Another confession: I miss the autumnal bonfires of my childhood. They polluted the air. They wasted organic matter more properly composted. But at one time in my life, on bracing, cool evenings in autumn, the scent that hung in my nostrils and clung to my clothes brought with it a powerful sense of well-being.

VI Peeves, Complaints, and Observations

❧ Birddogging Finger Blight

GARDENERS ARE, on the whole, a generous lot. We all have had the experience of visiting someone else's garden, admiring this plant or that out loud, and then discovering as we are ready to depart that the garden's owner has a gift for us—seeds, cuttings, even an entire plant of the object of our admiration. Occasionally, however, a visitor may take things (literally) into his or her own hands instead of gambling on a host's generosity. The British writer Christopher Lloyd once described this practice as "finger blight."

I have no idea how many gardeners' souls are touched with larceny, but I do know this: if a great many people visit a garden at the same time, the incidence of theft increases exponentially, not arithmetically. Many centuries ago St. Augustine enunciated this principle in his *Confessions*, where he wrote of his youthful sin of stealing pears, in the company of some friends. The pears were not especially desirable, he later recalled. He would not, he said, have stolen them on his own. Going to the perverse heart of this matter, he said that it wasn't that he wanted the pears and in getting them thus became a thief. No, he wanted to steal, to be a thief: the pears were merely the means to that end.

Late this past summer, our friend George, whose garden in Delaware is filled with choice plants, many of them rare, asked a favor of Hella and me. Two busloads of visitors—members of a group on a three-day horticultural pilgrimage to gardens starting with Wave Hill in the Bronx and ending with Brookside Gardens in Wheaton, Maryland—were coming to see his garden that weekend, right after their stop at Longwood Gardens. Fearing larcenous souls among them, he was taking precautions. Certain plants had been covered from view with shredded leaves or whisked out of sight entirely. Some plant labels had been removed. And there would be a team of "birddoggers"—people assigned to keep an eye on the crowd and help prevent or at least discourage horticultural larceny. George asked us to join the birddoggers. We said we'd be delighted, and we could even swell the team by two since our friends Martha and Garry Blake-Adams were visiting us that week.

There were two other birddoggers: Frank, another friend of the garden's owner, and Megan, Frank's fourteen-year-old niece. Frank brought walkie-talkies, one for himself, one to pass among the rest of the crew.

The six of us stationed ourselves throughout the garden just as the buses arrived, disgorging the passengers, all presumed guilty until proven innocent. Martha found a sunny spot on some terrace steps with a view of the perennial borders and the gazebo, pulled out a sketchpad, and began making pencil drawings. The rest of us slowly ambled, occasionally signaling one another with a nod of the head in the direction of a particularly likely-looking plant larcenist. The visitors were aware of our presence we were sure. One woman said to another in a loud stage whisper, "We're being watched!"

The purpose of birddogging is more the prevention of crime than the detection or punishment of it. In his *Republic*, Plato observed that if perfectly law-abiding citizens could somehow manage to become invisible they might commit incredible atrocities. The possibility of being seen doing something wrong keeps us on the straight and narrow path of virtue. (That's why there are TV cameras in stores and at automatic teller machines.)

Megan was the best birddogger. She was everywhere. I don't know how she did it, but one moment I would see her walking down the path leading to the camellia garden, and the next she'd be standing by the fountain halfway across the grounds. Her body language was eloquent. At only fourteen she had managed the skills teachers must finally perfect to proctor exams. She never looked as if she were singling anyone out, but she gave every impression of being able to spot anyone about to do something the least bit out of line.

Megan was also the only one of us who actually apprehended a thief. Just as the buses were ready for boarding, she confronted a portly, dignified gentleman, pointed at his midsection, and said, "I'll take that."

He just laughed.

"I mean it," she said. "Hand over the stuff inside your shirt. Otherwise I'll have to call security."

He stopped laughing, reached down his shirt, and pulled out a plastic bag full of cuttings and a small pot of *Zephyranthes candida* in full bloom. "But some are really mine," he complained. "I swiped them at Longwood."

✿ Why Do They Keep Changing Those Names?

I NEVER OVERLOOK an opportunity to stress that scientific names are essential although I always try to do so with nondogmatic good humor and a dash of sympathy.

Common names are by no means to be despised. They are often charming. *Sedum acre*—meaning a plant that sits somewhere and has a bitter taste—may be precise, but welcome-home-husband-though-never-so-drunk, for the same plant, inspires both puzzlement and admiration. Like bleeding petunia, crybaby, and heart-bursting-with-love, it is one of what Elizabeth Lawrence in *Gardening for Love: The Market Bulletins* (1987) described as "sweet country names, many of them belonging to Shakespeare and the Bible."

Despite their poetry, common names have obvious drawbacks. Different plants may have the same common name. The same plant may have several common names in any given vernacular. Common names, furthermore, seldom translate easily from one language to another. Instances of these liabilities are easy to come by. Almost anything can be called a "buttercup" (including, in some parts of Tennessee, a daffodil); and, as has come up already, "marigold" (one of many names honoring the Virgin Mary) sometimes denotes a *Tagetes*, sometimes a *Calendula*. One of the common English names for some species of *Impatiens*, "busy Lizzie," translates neatly into German as *fleissige Lieschen*, but what is an Alpine violet in German is called sow's bread in English. However, no matter what vernacular people speak, the plant in question is some kind of *Cyclamen*. Common names can be so misleading as to be dangerous. The flowers of some jasmines make delicious teas, but anyone who puts Carolina "jasmine" to such a use may die quickly and painfully. Ambiguity is sometimes fatal, but there's no ambiguity for someone who knows that *Gelsemium* and *Jasminum* are different beasts altogether.

While the old maxim that every rule has its exception is a huge untruth, some rules do have exceptions. Botanical or scientific plant names generally are more reliable than common names, so much so that they seem to be fixed and unchanging, as seemingly eternal as the stars in the heavens, but the unfortunate truth is that names do change. The evidence is plain in the recent reprinting of all three volumes of E. A. Bowles's 1915 trilogy about his garden in spring, summer, and autumn and winter. An eight-page glossary by Peter Barnes at the back of each volume brings Bowles's terminology up to date. His *Aegle pennsylvanicum* is now *Acer pennsylvanicum*. He wrote *Berberis Aquifolium*, but if he were writing now it would be *Mahonia aquifolium*. More shockingly, considering that Bowles was a great authority on the genus *Crocus*, sixteen of his species names for these bulbs have been overhauled. (*C. zonatus*, for example, underwent a great metamorphosis from which it emerged as *C. kotschyanus* ssp. *kotschyanus*.)

Mr. Bowles's crocuses didn't switch genera, but certain bulbs have been highly subject to nervous nomenclatural wanderings. The wood hyacinth used to be *Scilla hispanica*, linked by name and supposedly by blood to *S. autumnalis* and *S. siberica*, but now (along with *S. indica* and *S. non-scripta*) it's been yanked from the company of all its former squill relations and dumped into another genus altogether, *Hyacinthoides*.

I don't know when this happened exactly. Taxonomists, the scientists who preside over the naming (and name-changing) of living things, have a way of working behind the backs of gardeners. We use a certain botanical name for years and years and then discover that we're wrong, that the plant in question is now something else. Take sweet autumn clematis, for example. It happens to be one of my favorite plants. Until 1980 or so, like everyone else I knew, I called it *Clematis paniculata*. I loved those two euphonious words, those eight syllables that tripped so melodiously from the lips. Then, suddenly, this fragrant vine from Japan that fills the early autumn air with its vanilla perfume was no longer *C. paniculata*. Instead, *C. paniculata* was an obscure plant from New Zealand that almost no one has ever grown or even seen. And sweet autumn clematis? We had to learn a new name for it, *C. maximowicziana*—three syllables longer than its former name and not euphonious at all. Reluctantly and grudgingly, I went along with the name-changers. Then, some years later, there was more news. *C. maximowicziana* was out. Sweet autumn clematis had another new name, *C. terniflora*.

There have been other changes during my lifetime in the names of some of my favorite plants. Among the leadworts or plumbagos there were two I admired especially. One, *Plumbago larpentiae*, a fall-blooming groundcover from western China with cobalt flowers and green leaves that veer toward crimson in October, was at some point wrenched from its former genus and renamed *Ceratostigma plumbaginoides*. The other, a tender, clambering South African subshrub with phlox-like clusters of pale blue, deep sky-blue, or white flowers, was *P. capensis* when I first made its acquaintance in Dallas in the late 1940s. Now it's *P. auriculata*. As for quite another plumbago, the one from Australia that used to bear the name *P. auriculata*, the high priests of taxonomy now decree that we call it *P. zeylanica*.

How many different scientific names can one plant accumulate? I don't know for sure what the prizewinner is, but it's probably the engaging little South American spring bulb commonly called blue starflower. There has been unanimity on the species name: the flowers come in ones, and thus it's either *uniflorum* or *uniflora*, depending on the gender of the genus name, but the genus name has been unstable, to put it gently. Since the early nineteenth century when blue starflower entered cultivation, it has been placed successively in the following genera: *Triteleia, Milla, Ipheion, Brodiaea, Leucocoryne, Hookera,* and *Tristagama.* (In bulb catalogs it can turn up under any of the first three names. *The New RHS Dictionary of Gardening* opts for *Ipheion uniflorum*, which is odd, for a reason I'll get around to shortly.)

Even though these name changes are vexatious to gardeners, we are not to think that they are made with the deliberate intent to vex,

244 • ALLEN LACY

nor that the changes are wrought without good and sufficient reason. There are rules. Whatever name a plant is given when it is first
described in published botanical literature is its valid name, even if
it later comes to be called something else entirely by the entire
world. If the name *Zinnia* was first applied to the genus we all know
now as *Hemerocallis*, then we're going to have to start calling
daylilies zinnias and then find some other name for zinnias (probably not *Hemerocallis*, though). That's the rule, but this turns out to
be one of those rules that has exceptions, in the form of so-called
conserved names. An international botanical congress can decide
that even though a particular name is invalid in the strict sense it
can be kept anyway. (I suspect that such a congress would let
things stand in my hypothetical case about zinnias and daylilies.)
Incidentally, back to blue starflowers, I don't understand why
the RHS dictionary has settled on *Ipheion*. A botanist named
Rafinesque published that name in 1834, but another botanist
named Lindley had beat him to the punch in 1830 with *Triteleia*.
Go figure!

Names get changed for other reasons. A botanist may argue successfully that two different plants once thought to be in the same
genus (or the same species) are really distinct enough to be in two
genera (or two species). Conversely, it may be decided that two
plants once thought to be in different genera (or species) may really
be in one genus (or species). The former taxonomical procedure is
called "splitting," and the latter "lumping." A recent example of
lumping that I have heard rumored concerns the genus *Cimicifuga*.
If the gossip is correct, the British botanist James Compton has managed to dissolve that genus, lumping all of its species with everything
already in the genus *Actaea*. This is not especially happy news for
people who may be partial to cimicifugas but lukewarm toward
actaeas.

No name changes, however, go as far as those that have over-
taken the erstwhile genus *Chrysanthemum*. A comparison of two
standard reference works separated by less than two decades tells the
story. *Hortus Third* (1976) asserts that the genus embraces somwhere
between 100 and 200 species and then goes on to describe 39
of them. *The New Royal Horticultural Society Dictionary of Garden-*

ing (1992) reduces the number of species to a mere five. Former species of *Chrysanthemum* are banished to a gaggle of other genera. The most familiar garden plants long resident in the old genus, the "mums" of autumn and roadside stands, are now housed in *Dendranthema*. (Should we now call them "mas" for short?) Nippon or Montauk daisies, formerly *C. nipponicum*, now must trip across the tongue as *Nipponanthemum nipponicum*. Shasta daisies, formerly *C.* × *maximum*, are now *Leucanthemum* × *maximum*. For marguerites, which used to be *C. frutescens*, we now must say or write *Argyranthemum frutescens*. Other species have been relegated to strange and unfamiliar-sounding genera, such as *Coleostephus, Leucanthemopsis, Plagius,* and *Pyrethopsis.*

There's another change in botanical nomenclature favored by some, but not all. This one concerns not species names nor genus names, but the next class above the genus, the plant family. Many such families have names that end in *-aceae* and are derived from the names of one of the genera they include: thus Solanaceae, from *Solanum* (potato, eggplant); Ranunculaceae, from *Ranunculus*; and Primulaceae, from *Primula*. Eight families, however, and these include some of the most important ones to the human race, were named before rules were established in this matter. These do not end in *-aceae*, and their names don't echo any actual genus name. Another system has been proposed (and is used by some authorities) in which some names are abandoned and other names substituted for them. Here are the eight families, with the proposed substitutions in parentheses: Compositae (Asteraceae), Cruciferae (Brassicaceae), Graminae (Poaceae), Guttiferae (Clusiaceae), Labiatae (Laminaceae), Leguminosae (Fabiaceae), Palmae (Arecaceae), and Umbelliferae (Apiaceae).

The need for these changes is hard to fathom. Do they arise from the sheer restless desire to do something, change something, where no harm has come from doing nothing, just following a long tradition? I don't know, really.

But it's good to report that although *The New RHS Dictionary* caved in on the genus *Chrysanthemum* (and may just do the same with *Cimicifuga* in a later edition) it holds the line on the Compositae and the Leguminosae.

And here's some late-breaking news. This piece was originally published in 1997. Now, 1999 brings word that in response to an impassioned plea from an English botanist back in 1995, an international botanical congress turned the question of the name of those garden chrysanthemums over to its Committee on Spermatophyta. By a vote of nine to three, the committee changed *Dendranthema* back to *Chrysanthemum*—just when some of us were getting used to the new name. So it's still "mums," not "mas."

❧ *Catalog English*

AT THE START of a new year, like most gardeners, I suffer from the cabin fever whose sole remedy is to plunge knee-deep in seed and nursery catalogs. Is there any gardener who doesn't know that these catalogs, particularly those filled with color photographs, are sometimes less than forthright? Most of them deal in illusions, the staple substance of the genre. In a catalog, everything blooms at once. Peonies consort with chrysanthemums, cannas with daffodils, and apple trees in bloom with apple trees in fruit. These combinations occur only within the covers of a gardening wish-book designed to tempt the winter-weary to look toward spring by making out an order and mailing a check. The procession of bloom in a garden is a long parade, not a sudden invasion, and the real joy of seeing daffodils in the spring is knowing that the garden will slowly unfold, each new plant blooming at its ordained time.

Catalogs also speak a peculiar language, a dialect ruled by evasiveness, not plain talk.

At my left hand one of these winter wish-books lies open to a page with a fetching photograph of a vine called *Akebia quinata*, a closeup of the plant's soft-purple flowers. The picture is so lovely that it's tempting to forget some things I know about akebias, starting, but not ending with the fact that the flowers appear quite briefly and are often concealed beneath the foliage. The accompanying text doesn't mention these things—nor some others that anyone contemplating acquiring an akebia should know. It speaks of the delicately textured foliage of this vine, but it tells of no bad habits it might have. There is a slight hint in the offhand remark that it grows to forty feet, but the reader is lulled by the reassuring follow-up: it can easily be controlled by pruning.

Other catalogs that sell akebia describe it with additional adjectives. It is "easily grown." It is "vigorous." It is "trouble-free." These terms are all euphemisms, nice-sounding code words for a nasty reality: *Akebia quinata* is a highly invasive vine. So is *Akebia trifoliata*. So are the hybrids between them, which have the added muscle of hybrid vigor. Akebias are steamroller plants. A friend has described them as the next kudzu, except that kudzu is the plant that ate the South; akebias pay no attention to the Mason-Dixon line.

Another catalog waxes eloquent about the beauty, the vigor, and the appealingly twisted growth of another vine, Asian bittersweet (*Celastrus orbiculatus*). Despite the eloquent testimonial, the truth is that this bittersweet is a belligerent woody weed, and a pestilence that is almost impossible to control once it has gotten a toehold. It not only grows as a tidal wave that will strangle and choke other vegetation, but also comes easily from seed. Rip every last shred of it out of the garden, but those seeds will still sprout.

Inspired by my winter reading, I have decided to try my hand at catalog-description writing, to see if I have any knack for it.

Here goes:

Toxicodendron radicans. This relative of sumac is a vigorous, easily grown vine or shrub native to North America. The British envy us because it grows better here, and will not fruit in their climate. The handsome, deep green, trifoliate leaves are so glossy that they seem almost varnished. In a breeze the whole plant shimmers, as if in pleasure and joy. This plant has no insect foes or other enemies to mar its beauty. It is highly drought resistant, requires no fertilizer, and will grow in full sun or partial shade. The brilliant foliage in autumn is followed by stunning gray-white fruits. Hardy from Zone 3 to Zone 10. Sturdy plants in one-gallon containers, $29.95 plus shipping.

Here's another effort:

Stellaria media. Here is a fine, seed-grown annual for added interest in the winter garden. Untemperamental and easy from seed, it germinates in late summer, but does not reveal its beauty until most autumn leaves have fallen from the trees. Then *Stellaria media* begins to expand into low rosettes of fresh green leaves tipped with a multitude of tiny but lovely star-shaped greenish white flowers. The best news of all about this superb plant, which has never quite received the praise it deserves, is that it reseeds itself generously to return the following year. A lifetime investment in beauty costs just $.95 per packet.

I think I'm getting the hang of it, but let me try my powers of persuasion just one more time:

Digitaria Grass. Homeowners plagued by recent droughts that burned up their lawns by midsummer several years in a row will be delighted by this vigorous annual grass that requires no extensive watering. No fertilizer needed. Low-growing, this substitute for bluegrass and fescue requires less mowing than its rivals. It spreads laterally in a vigorous way, rather than growing upright. It will remain bright green when other grasses burn to brown, but it assumes a pleasant hue of pinkish-mauve in the fall. To seed 5,000 square feet requires only a one-ounce packet. $7.95.

I did leave out some common names. *Toxicodendron radicans* is poison ivy. *Stellaria media* is chickweed. *Digitaria* is the genus name of several species known collectively as crabgrass.

Most gardeners don't need to order any of these. They have probably grown them for years.

✿ *Please, Mr./Ms. Weatherperson*

I DON'T TRUST ALL those polls that keep coming out telling us that gardening is America's number one leisure activity. For one thing, there are many, many more good gardening magazines in England than in the United States. Perhaps that's only to be expected, as the British have a head start on us, going back to at least 1066 and maybe to the time they found it chic to paint their bodies blue. It's much more telling that Germany has more good gardening magazines than we do—like *Mein Schöener Garten,* to name one I read with huge pleasure, albeit haltingly. (It took me a while to figure out that *Stauden* meant perennials—but please allow me to digress just a bit. Germany has much more relevance for American gardeners than England does, and I know this observation is heresy. Most American climates are more like the continental climate of Germany than the maritime climate of England. End of digression . . .)

For another thing, people who quote these statistics about this supposedly widespread American passion for gardening never see any need to define what gardening is, exactly. My suspicion is that revving up the lawn mower once a week when the fescue is on the muscle qualifies as gardening. By that definition, but none that makes any real sense, every guy on my block is a Henry Mitchell, except those who hire lawn services.

I strongly suspect and fervently hope that in the twenty-first century America will become a real nation of gardeners, not just tenders of lawns. But we aren't there yet. If we were, there would be a much greater awareness of the needs, desires, and true interests of American gardeners by the people who report the weather on television.

One millennial day these persons who greet us each morning over a cup of coffee and each evening over a martini (if that's our wont) will just *stick to the facts:* it's going to be very hot and humid, or it's going to be very cold; it's going to rain, or it's not going to rain, or it may or may not rain, depending.

At present, these people editorialize, discussing the weather in moral terms, assessing each day as good or bad. Their criterion of judgment is simple. A good day is balmy and sunny. On a bad day it never stops raining. If it rains only part of the day, that day is morally ambiguous.

A rainy day is not always welcome. Rain five days in a row is depressing, and our spirits lift when the clouds part and the sun comes out. Rain that soaks the earth beyond its capacity to absorb any more moisture, so that creeks and rivers rise and levees give way, can become a natural disaster, entirely too much of a good thing.

But these weatherpersons do not discriminate. Raging floods in North Carolina are on a par, as they see it, with a fresh summer shower that washes away dust and makes all growing things clean and healthy. And a rainy weekend is tantamount to a terrible hurricane or an earthquake that measures 7.5 on the Richter scale. Their moralistic attitude shines forth unmistakably, even if for six months there's been a drought so severe that fields of corn stand only as high as a rabbit's eye.

These announcers occasionally appear in fertilizer ads. However, they don't know weather as gardeners know it. They don't know that sunshine and rainfall are balanced and harmonious goods—yin and yang, meat and salad. They don't realize that in an ideal world it would rain gently but steadily every day from one to two in the afternoon, then turn bright and clear, with a rainless day only when there's going to be a garden party. Why don't our weather prophets get it? The answer is simple. They're not gardeners. They're golfers.

❦ Which Came First—the Chicken or the Potato?

FOR PEOPLE WHO enjoy worrying, now there's something else to worry about—transgenic plants are already on the horizon in major food crops.

A transgenic plant is a plant that carries certain genes that are borrowed from another kind of organism altogether: consider, as examples, corn with genes from wheat, sunflowers with Brazil nuts in their family tree, lettuce and cucumbers that are kissing cousins to petunias and tobacco. Far more startling examples involve plants with genes derived not from other plants but from much more distant sorts of organisms—potatoes with snippets of DNA from silk moths and chickens, tomatoes with flounder genes, tobacco with genetic connections to hamsters, corn with genes from fireflies. These are not mere possibilities and not the product of the over-

heated imagination of a writer of science fiction. As of 1993 the United States Department of Agriculture had applications from bio-engineering firms to field-test each.

But why? The answer is simple. The end, in each case, is entirely practical. Tomatoes with flounder genes may be more resistant to damage from freezing than tomatoes with the more conventional ancestry. Lettuce and cucumbers with genes from tobacco and petunias may have immunity to certain diseases. I'm not quite sure about the contribution fireflies make to corn, except that it probably won't give us ears of table corn that glow in the dark. The bottom line turns out to be the bottom line, as it generally is. A transgenic plant can be patented and becomes a money machine for the owner of the patent.

There has been some concentrated effort—and already some payoff—in two areas: food crop plants that are immune to nonselective herbicides like Roundup (glyphosphate) and those that manufacture their own insecticide. Each has obvious advantages, at least in the short run. A field of corn immune to a herbicide that kills all other vegetation can be weeded easily and economically by spraying. Plants that manufacture their own insecticides are nothing new, for plants are the most sophisticated chemists on earth and many have evolved to make any insect that tries to devour them very sick and sorry very soon. What's new is that transgenic plants plagiarize from other organisms to get what they need. Such is the relation between a transgenic tomato and *Bacillus thuringiensis* (*Bt*), a commonly used biological control for caterpillars like the horned tomato caterpillar or the cutworm.

Some people—and I am one—are worried about this brave new world of transgenic plants. Newspapers have reported demonstrations in Germany and the Netherlands against shipments from the United States and Canada of soybeans with alien genes. Apart from the aesthetic issues (many of us would prefer to eat our flounder alongside, not inside, our ripe tomatoes), there are some genuine environmental concerns, two in particular.

First, alien genes conferring immunity to herbicides like glyphosphate might spread by hybridization from cultivated or domesticated crops to their wild relatives. We might thus be creating superweeds to plague us in the future. Imagine crabgrass—which after all is a species of millet—on the march with no impediment whatsoever. Imagine poison ivy with far more resistance to us than we have ever managed to have to it. Imagine a brave new little shop of horrors . . .

Second, if the insecticidal properties of *Bt* were to be *in* food crop plants, rather than *applied to them* only when needed, the result would in effect multiply the presence of such insecticides in the environment in an exponential way. Insects evolve fairly rapidly to deal with threats to their existence. Since the introduction of antibiotics and their widespread use in medicine since the 1940s, we have seen bacteria evolve that are immune to these drugs—and thus we need newer and ever stronger antibiotics. By analogy, we cannot rule out supercaterpillars of the not-so-distant future that may munch with impunity on plants that have been custom designed to kill them.

Proponents of genetic engineering tell us that there's nothing to worry about. I'm not convinced, however. One of the most ancient pieces of wisdom I know is that some things that seem like good ideas when they are first dreamed up turn out to be something else entirely.

✤ Saying It Right

SOME YEARS AGO Allen Paterson, the well-known English horticul-turist, lecturing to about nine hundred members of the Perennial Plant Association, spoke about daylilies and called them by their Latin name, Hemerocallis, which he pronounced hem-err-ROC-uh-lis. There were nine hundred sharp intakes of breath. It was pretty clear what was going through his listeners' minds: *He must be right: he's English. That means I'm wrong. I've said hem-err-oh-CAL-iss all my life. Everyone must know I'm an ignoramus.* Paterson kept right on speaking, seemingly oblivious to the mental distress he had just caused. I say "seemingly," because Paterson's sense of humor is legendary. He might have been playing a joke on his listeners.

The resistance of some American gardeners to Latin botanical names is notable. We use them all the time, whenever we speak of a lobelia, zinnia, petunia, or anything else that doesn't really have a common name, but we flinch at the prospect of saying *Cornus florida* instead of eastern dogwood, although these two Latin words aren't at all difficult. Why do some people balk at using them? At least part of the answer must surely be fear of mispronouncing Latin rather than getting it right.

Let's cut to specifics, say, to diascias—in Latin, the genus *Dias-cia.* I read an article about these plants that insisted that the name of this genus had to be pronounced "dye-ash-KEE-uh." I don't say it that way. I say "dye-ASS-ih-uh." So does everyone else I know. If other people want to turn "ass" into "ash" and not to emphasize that syllable but the next one instead, that's okay. The world is large enough for both linguistic persuasions. As Cole Porter taught us, some say toe-MAY-to, and some say . . .

Some clematis fanciers insist that the name of their favorite plant may under no circumstances rhyme with "lattice," but their disfavor doesn't seem to have had much effect on the general pub-lic. As for cyclamen, there is strong agreement that neither the sec-ond nor the third syllable must be accented, but the first. There is disagreement, however, about how this syllable is pronounced.

Some say "sigh," others "sick." (How do I pronounce it? Sometimes one way, sometimes the other.)

What about *Asarum?* I accent the second syllable and rhyme it with "pear." I have friends who accent the first syllable and pronounce it like "ace." One of the books in my library offers a third opinion: "ASS-a-rum." *Deutzia?* I say "DOOT-si-ah," but some say "DOYT-si-ah" because, so they claim, the genus was named for Johann van der Deutz, a German. (Actually he was a Swede, and I have no idea whether *eu* in Swedish is pronounced like "oy" in "boy" or "oyster.")

Horticultural Latin, ever since Linnaeus straightened out biological nomenclature in the eighteenth century, is indeed universal. The spring bulbs that to speakers of English are "daffodils" may be *"Osterglocken"*—which translates as "Easter bells"—to speakers of German, but for both, these plants are *Narcissus.* But the pronunciation of botanical Latin varies noticeably among people with differing mother tongues. Spanish speakers tend to trill their *r*s in Latin words. I do not know whether all Germans say it, but on several occasions I have been nonplussed on hearing very proper Germans speak of the genus *Pinus.*

There is, furthermore, sometimes divergence between American English speakers and British English speakers in pronunciation of plant names. "Dahlia," one of those words that is both a common name and a Latin botanical name, is pronounced by most Americans—not all, however—so that the vowel in the first syllable sounds like the vowel in "bad." The Brits rhyme it with "day." Who is correct? Both, I suppose, although it could also be argued that both are wrong. Dahlias are named for the Swedish botanist Andreas Dahl (1751–1789), so we probably should pronounce *dahl* as "doll."

I am not saying, I should emphasize, that there is no such thing as mispronunciation of Latin plant names. I was once embarrassed to discover that rudbeckia had only four syllables, not five, for like a few other Texans I had been saying "rudibeckia," inserting an extraneous *i* after the first syllable.

No one ever corrected me. I wouldn't have minded if someone had, but then letting me make my mistake was nicely polite.

But I have been corrected recently, by a dear friend, in not only the pronunciation but also the spelling of the scientific name of the Swan River daisy. I told my friend that of late some interesting improvements had been going on with the genus *Brachycome*, which I pronounced with the accent on the first syllable, thus— BRACK-ih-comb. "You're missing an s," she said. "It's *Brachyscome*, and it's pronounced bra-KISS-co-may."

My friend is almost always right, but this time I was sure she was wrong. I checked in Liberty Hyde Bailey's three-volume *Standard Cyclopedia of Horticulture*, in T. H. Everett's *Encyclopedia of Gardening*, in *Hortus Third*, and in *The New RHS Dictionary of Gardening*. All had *Brachycome*, not *Brachyscome*. I then went to the Internet, and typed in *Brachycome* on a search. Forty references appeared, from the United States, the United Kingdom, and Israel. *Quod erat demonstrandum*, but just to nail down my correctness, I also went ahead and typed in *Brachyscome*. Oops—106 references popped up on my computer screen, mostly from Australia, but one from Monterrey Bay Nursery in California, a wholesale outfit that specializes, in part, in plants from Australia and New Zealand.

The weight of printed authority in both England and the United States spanning over half a century notwithstanding, I'm switching to *Brachyscome*. The Swan River, after all, is in Australia. Furthermore, the genus is native entirely to Australia and New Zealand, except for a few tropical sorts from New Guinea. I figure that if it's spelled with an s where it originated I'll spell it that way, too.

❦ *The Invasion of the Garden-Snatchers*

ALL GARDENERS, wherever they may live on this planet, struggle with unwanted plants. Many were never wanted in the first place, for no one in sound mental health would deliberately invite them onto the premises—or so it seems at first. I shall shortly have more to say about the reality that lies behind this appearance, but first I want to address one of gardening's dirtiest little secrets. We create some of our worst problems by introducing into our gardens plants that have no manners whatsoever and try to take over the entire place, shoving everything else aside. We find this plant or that to our liking, acquire it for our own, and then discover that it roams and frolics, spreads and colonizes, making itself too much at home, like Sheridan Whiteside in *The Man Who Came to Dinner*.

Among my own instances of regret, I admit it was a grave error to think that the plume poppy (*Macleaya cordata*) would behave itself under my supervision. It has its merits, to be sure. It is commanding, handsome, and stately in height. Its feathery racemes of pinkish-tan flowers are lovely and so are its scalloped leaves, downy white on their undersides when they move in the breeze. But the vices of plume poppy far outweigh its virtues, for it is relentless in its rapid spread both by stolons and by seeding itself around. It is not by any means my only attractive malefactor. Double bouncing bet (*Saponaria officinalis* 'Rosea Plena') blooms over a long season in midsummer, its fluffy pale pink flowers imparting to the air a delicious scent of cloves, but it also spreads voraciously in a colony that grows wider and wider with every passing year, despite my efforts to keep it within bounds.

The shorthand term for plants that get out of hand is "invasive," a word that has already turned up at several junctures in these pages. I have barely gotten started with my inventory of the invasive vegetation flourishing in my garden because I set plants loose without knowing their potential for mischief. All of the lysimachias I have grown, with the possible exception of *Lysimachia congestiflora* (which I have not grown long enough for a sure judgment), are invasive, some highly so. The worst offenders are *L. ciliata* 'Purpurea' and *L. clethroides*, although the former has handsome purple foliage in the spring and the latter, commonly called gooseneck lysimachia, bears oddly bent spikes of white flowers that do, regrettably, give the appearance of geese in tight formation marching mercilessly through the herbaceous border. The green form of creeping jenny or moneywort (*L. nummularia*) is an aggressive low spreader that makes a tough and handsome groundcover if sited properly (where nothing else is desired to grow). The golden-to-chartreuse variant, 'Aurea', is much more tractable, perhaps because its leaves are smaller and carry on less photosynthesis than the type. I must also add yellow archangel (*Lamium galeobdolon*), for despite its celestial name, it is the dickens to eradicate once planted. It has its uses. Its silvery leaves persist in winter, and it is a serviceable groundcover for places where little else will grow, as in dry shade, but it's a perfect nightmare in a mixed border. I know this from prolonged experience in being unable to get rid of it; the least little piece left in the ground will bounce back into rampant growth almost overnight. (The cultivar *L. g.* 'Hermann's Pride' is, however, docile and unaggressive, and has highly attractive narrow, notched leaves stippled with silver; in fifteen years in my garden it has spread only about a foot. Also, the cultivars of *Lamium maculatum* — 'Beacon Silver', 'Pink Pewter', and 'White Nancy', to name a few of many — are all good garden citizens, offering no grounds for complaint.)

I am almost unreasonably fond of ornamental grasses and grasslike plants, but some have given me trouble. *Pennisetum alopecuroides* 'Moudry' has striking dark purple-black flower heads, but virtually every seed formed will germinate wherever it lands. Gardener's garters (*Phalaris arundinacea*) may be fetching for its leaves striped green and white (with pink tinges in the early foliage of the unfortunately named cultivar 'Mervyn Feesey's Form'), but it has galloped through my garden in the mere five years since I gave it foothold. I am fond of our native northern sea oats (*Chasmanthium latifolium*) for its graceful, nodding stalks of seeds, lovely in late summer and wonderful dried for winter arrangements, but I must take great care to remove every stalk before the seeds ripen, because otherwise our garden would soon look like a savannah.

I severely regret having ordered one each of several hybrid tradescantias or spiderworts from a well-known mail-order nursery almost thirty years ago, in the earliest days of making our garden in New Jersey. They turned out to be prodigious self-seeders whose descendants I have not been able to oust in many years of earnest effort. No other plant in my experience is able to wrestle with a hemerocallis and win.

Some herbs self-seed themselves in troublesome ways. I would never single out bronze fennel for condemnation for its lavish self-seeding, as I love its anise scent and feathery foliage that in certain conditions of light looks like woolly bear caterpillars climbing a pillar of smoke, but it was a bad day when I introduced lemon balm (*Melissa officinalis*) into the garden. Its leaves smell most agreeably of lemon, but it seeds abundantly everywhere, in both sun and shade. *Perilla frutescens*, an annual herb used in Japanese cooking as *shiso*, can also get out of hand if volunteer seedlings are not quickly and ruthlessly exterminated wherever they are not wanted. In the shady spots it prefers, sweet woodruff (*Galium odoratum*) also takes over. I enjoy the fresh hay scent of its leaves—and the taste they impart to German May wine—but it is best grown in pots, where it can be kept under control.

I once planted lily-of-the-valley in a far corner of my garden, for what garden should be without its graceful nodding bells in late spring? But I now have a sheet of it fifteen feet in every direction that must be confined by ripping out great numbers of plants each year. I should have known better. Southern New Jersey has many abandoned farmhouses whose fields have returned to scrub forest. The lilies-of-the-valley that once grew against house foundations now cover acres of woodland floor—together with another great colonizer and escapee, *Vinca minor*.

I have said nothing so far about another major category of unwanted plants that I must struggle with in my garden, my weeds. Many of these are so-called aliens or exotics, plants that originated elsewhere and then made themselves too much at home in my part of North America, and often many other parts as well. Some of our imported weeds came more or less by accident, in ships' ballast or as seeds hidden away in shoe leather or in the folds of clothing. Plantain weed—which Native Americans called "white man's foot"—would seem to have arrived in this way. Spotted spurge, I imagine, did also. Humans brought other plants here deliberately, with no realization that they would ever become troublesome weeds. Dandelions were imported by English, Dutch, German, and French settlers alike as a pot herb. Purslane, which came here the same way, still has virtues despite its pushy ways. Charles Dudley Warner may not have minced words in condemning purslane in *My Summer in a Garden* (1870) as "a fat, ground-clinging, spreading, greasy thing,"

260 • ALLEN LACY

in 1862 from Yokohama to the Parsons nursery in Flushing, New
York, by Dr. George Rogers Hall, who in a major piece of misjudg-
ment doubted that it could survive outside a conservatory. Japanese
honeysuckle offers undeniable delights in its sweet nectar and sublime fragrance but is, by any reckoning, a menace wherever it grows,
especially in the eastern United States southward from New York to
Georgia and westward to Texas.

Honeysuckle was by no means the last disastrous import. In the
Deep South, water hyacinths clog streams, canals, and rivers, cost-
ing millions of dollars annually to attempt to control. The list
of takeover plants that afflict Florida, such as Australian "pine"
(Casuarina equisetifolia), is daunting. Other malefactors there include the Brazilian pepper tree, Schinus terebrinthifolius, introduced in the 1890s, and the Australian cajeput, Melaleuca quin-
quenervia. Floridians today have good reason to resent John C.
Gifford, a professor at the University of Miami, for introducing this
plant. Both the cajeput and the Brazilian pepper tree compete too
successfully with native shrubs and trees, and also cause painful skin
rashes in susceptible persons.

Our northern and northwestern wetlands are plagued by purple loosestrife (Lythrum salicaria, L. virgatum), whose undeniable
beauty (particularly when seen from an airplane) is matched by its
viciousness in eradicating more desirable native vegetation, such
as cattails. By the time it is five years old, one loosestrife plant will
have produced 2,700,000 seeds, and in a one-acre stand of it there
will be 80,000 plants or more. It has been claimed that certain cultivars of loosestrife are not ecologically destructive because they
are self-sterile. This safety, however, is a delusion, for self-sterile
forms such as L. salicaria 'Robert' and L. virgatum 'Morden Pink'
may cross with unselected, seed-grown plants of their species and
also hybridize with one another. We generally utter the words
"hybrid vigor" approvingly, but applied to loosestrife, they signal a
nightmare.

New such nightmares keep turning up. The danger signs are
already up for Ampelopsis brevipedunculata or porcelain vine, an
East Asian plant that is currently in vogue for its striking blue
berries—and in some forms for its variegated foliage. Like honey-

but its leaves are delightfully crisp in salads, have a lemony tartness, and are full of vitamin E and certain fatty acids that protect against coronary disease. As for crabgrass, the U.S. Patent Office brought it in from Europe as a forage crop in 1849, but it owes its true toehold in North America to late nineteenth-century immigrants from central Europe who used it as a cereal grain.

Then, turning from my garden and its invaders to those that romp and rampage in the larger landscape, there's kudzu (*Pueraria lobata*), which thus far is only established in New Jersey, down around Cape May, although it likely will eventually thrive at least in all coastal areas. It first appeared here in a Japanese garden in Fairmount Park, Philadelphia, at an exposition in 1876. People loved its tropical-looking deep-green leaves and blue-purple flowers that had an intoxicating odor like ripe grapes. In the South it was widely planted for shade as a porch vine. Nurseries that sold plants by mail order in the 1920s touted its merits as forage for cattle, and between 1935 and 1942 the United States Conservation Service paid farmers $8 an acre to plant some eighty-five million kudzu plants on fallow land. The idea was to control erosion, but no one seemed to notice that the foliage was so sensitive to cold weather that the vines were leafless four months out of the year. It wasn't until 1972 that our federal government recognized that kudzu was a bane, not a boon, and had become one of our most noxious perennial weeds. By that time, kudzu had eaten much of the South, all the way from North Carolina to Mississippi.

Rosa multiflora is another chastening example of a seemingly good idea gone wrong. As recently as 1980 it was touted officially as an ideal quick-growing hedge or screen and recommended by state authorities as a barricade between opposing highway lanes, as were several species of *Elaeagnus*. Both shrubs were also praised as sources of food for birds and other wildlife; they ate the fruits eagerly and then spread the seeds widely to become extremely rank and pestiferous woody weeds.

Certain purely ornamental exotic plants have escaped from gardens to become pernicious weeds in the larger landscape. One of the first and most notorious examples of such a vegetative Trojan horse was Japanese honeysuckle (*Lonicera japonica*), first brought suckle and multiflora rose, birds relish its fruits and then excrete the seeds everywhere they fly, which is of course anywhere they please. The same thing is true of some other pestilential alien plants deliberately introduced here, like Asian bittersweet (*Celastrus orbiculatus*) and autumn olive (one of the aforementioned species of *Elaeagnus*), both major problems in my county in southern New Jersey. Another particularly nasty invader is mile-a-minute vine (*Polygonum perfoliatum*), a hideously thorny plant accidentally imported to Pennsylvania in a fairly recent shipment of rhododendrons from Japan. Now beginning to spread insidiously by birds far from its point of arrival, it bids fair to outdo another species in its genus, *P. japonicum*, Japanese knotweed, as a champion weed.

This catalog of alien villains could go on at great length. Enough is almost enough, but I must not omit the Chinese tree-of-heaven (*Ailanthus altissima*), brought here as an ornamental, although it is entirely vicious. It is a perfect prodigy of reproduction, with an enormous crop of seeds that float down like little helicopters far from the trees that bore them. It also produces a herbicide that poisons the ground and weakens other plants. If that were not enough, some people have extreme allergic reactions to its great quantities of wind-borne pollen.

It is easy to point a finger of blame at Dr. Hall and others (some of whom are unknown) who have unwittingly introduced exotic plants that have found parts of North America entirely too much to their liking, except that all gardeners with even minimal powers of observation must admit that we have committed such sins in our own private Edens.

In retrospect, the lives of gardeners and the general population alike would be much more comfortable today if the advocates who introduced dandelions, tree-of-heaven, autumn olive, water hyacinths, multiflora rose, and other pestilential plants could have foreseen and stayed their hands. I should acknowledge that some pests are in the animal not the plant kingdom. If you hate gypsy moths, you can thank Leopold Trouvelot, who immigrated here from France after the Civil War and imported these insects, thinking to start a silk industry in Massachusetts. Do you dislike starlings? Every last one in America today, and they number in the many millions, descends from sixty birds released in Central Park in 1890 by someone who thought it ought to be home to every bird Shakespeare mentioned. Starlings thrived, but nightingales didn't make it. In various parts of the country, there are other worrisome exotic animal species—fire ants in Texas and the Deep South, zebra mussels in the Great Lakes and Mississippi Basin, European green crabs in the coastal waters of California, New York, and New England.

There are two conceivable ways to avoid the undeniable damage caused by exotic or alien invasive species. One, a positive approach, is to encourage the planting of native species (North Ameica is an enormous territory, so that in a sense what is native to southern New Jersey may be alien in Delaware and most certainly in Texas). The other, more negative approach is the exclusion of exotic species. By law, such exclusion already is in place, but only for certain, definitely identified species. The possibility is at least thinkable of excluding not just some but all exotics.

As to our native flora, there is little question but that North Americans have often overlooked its merits, meanwhile lusting after beauties native to shores other than our own. I must defer here to Bernard M'Mahon, who immigrated to Philadelphia from Ireland in 1796 at the age of twenty-one, and who wrote and published in 1806 the first truly American gardening book, *The American Gardener's Calendar*. In his *Calendar*, which I have referred to earlier and which went through many editions, M'Mahon spoke eloquently on behalf of native American plants:

> I cannot avoid remarking that many flower gardens, &c., are almost destitute of bloom during a great part of the season; which could be easily avoided, and a blaze of flowers kept up . . . from March to November, by introducing from our woods and fields the various beautiful ornaments with which nature has so profusely decorated them. Is it because they are indigenous that we reject them? Ought we not rather to cultivate and improve them? What can be more beautiful than our Lobelias, Orchices, Asclepiases, and Asters; Gerardias, Monardas, and Ipomoeas; Liliums, Podalyrias, Rhexias, Solidagos,

and Hibiscuses; Phloxes, Gentianas, Spigelias, Chironias, and Sisy-rinchiums; Cassias, Ophryses, Coreopsises, and Cypripediums; Fum-arias, Violas, Rudbeckias, and Liatrises; with our charming Limodo-rum, fragrant Arethusa, and a thousand other lovely plants which, if introduced, would grace our plantations and delight our senses? In Europe, plants are not rejected because they are indigenous; on the contrary, they are cultivated with due care; and yet here we cultivate many foreign trifles, and neglect the profusion of beauties so bounti-fully bestowed upon us by the hand of nature.

M'Mahon's appreciation of native American plants was con-crete and real, not abstract and sentimental. Thomas Jefferson des-ignated the nursery M'Mahon owned in Philadelphia as a recipient of many of the plant treasures brought back from the Lewis and Clark expedition—and it is for him that the genus *Mahonia* is named. He was, moreover, perfectly correct in his apprehension that Americans tended to overlook many fine native plants. He may not have seen, however, that we have had to learn to appreciate them from other gardeners, for whom they were exotics, not natives. English and German gardeners understood quickly the high merits of our native species of asters, and Gertrude Jekyll's affection for our yuccas were not matched on our side of the Atlantic until compara-tively recently.

The exclusion of plants from elsewhere can seem unfair, I know. One of my earliest and most bitter memories is of a day trip with my father and mother from San Antonio into Mexico in 1939, when I was four. My father bought my mother a bouquet of deliciously fragrant gardenias, but when we recrossed the border, a guard confiscated the flowers and threw them into the RioGrande. My mother wept, and so did I, but with tears of anger. Later, how-ever, I came to understand. It is more than the fear of the beagles our customs officials use to sniff out smuggled plants that causes me to go through all the trouble to import plants legally, washing every speck of soil from their roots and obtaining all the necessary phy-tosanitary certificates. I would hate to go down in history as a mod-ern equivalent of Leopold Trouvelot, who gave us gypsy moths.

Likewise, wariness of exotic species is entirely sensible. Who wants to be the next person who blesses us with something like kudzu or worse?

But the issues that involve pitting native plants against exotic ones are far from simple and easily decided.

✿ A Horticultural Declaration of Independence?

Williamsburg, Virginia
July 4, 1999

TODAY AT NOON I heard a man in late eighteenth-century garb read the Declaration of Independence from the steps of the courthouse to a large audience of mostly tourists. I had never read the entire document that Thomas Jefferson drafted. On this occasion, by common if incorrect reckoning the last Fourth of July in the twentieth century, I found his words deeply moving, but my thoughts kept drifting back to a recent conversation with an acquaintance—not a friend, by any means—who had proposed what he called a Horticultural Declaration of Independence. "Down with foreign plants!" he had told me and everyone else within earshot. "We are already overrun with exotic species, and they are nothing but trouble. I say let's have American plants in American gardens. There's one thing I'm absolutely sure of—our native plants are good enough for me and they ought to be good enough for everybody else."

The strength of this utterance was unusual, but not its underlying sentiment. Lately I've been increasingly aware of an attitude of disapprobation of any plant that's exotic and of enthusiastic approval of any plant that is native (whether native to a small and parochial ecosystem in America, or to a much larger territory). Friends have told me about the rudeness of some visitors to their gardens who have upbraided them for growing exotic plants. One such friend reports that a visitor trampled Asian arisaemas in her woodland garden and then observed, "Your place is simply lousy with foreign plants." A visitor to my own garden expressed his negative feelings in milder, somewhat more palatable terms: "I see you are still growing exotic plants instead of sticking to natives."

Today, here at Colonial Williamsburg, I have tried to sympathize with the sentiments at work in these comments. Colonial Williamsburg tries in every way possible to give visitors the impression that they have stepped back across two centuries of American history, but the realities of the present day keep intruding. Automobiles are generally off limits, but every ten minutes or so new tourists arrive, disgorged by motor buses. The sound of airplanes overhead is hard to miss. The gardens in this place try to be authentic to the eighteenth century or earlier, but they really aren't, because their weeds are modern. Japanese honeysuckle has the entire town (as well as the whole Eastern Seaboard) in its sweet-smelling stranglehold. Plantain weed and crabgrass are underfoot everywhere. You don't have to go far to find kudzu. Much of the battlefield at nearby Yorktown has now returned to cool, quiet forest, but in every slightly moist and shady spot Japanese stilt grass (*Microstegium vimineum*) has shoved any scrap of native understory vegetation aside.

There is no doubt whatsoever in anyone's mind but that bringing some exotic species to our shores was a bad mistake. There is also no conceivable doubt that some native American species of plants are sadly neglected by many gardeners. But I shudder to think of the implications of a Horticultural Declaration of Independence, for this notion rests on a pair of unsupportable equations. The first is that exotic equals invasive and is therefore evil. The second is that native equals well-behaved and is therefore righteous.

How, logically, does anyone get to either of these equations? It is simple, really, and here I must speak as a professional philosopher, not an amateur gardener. The record is plain. The introduction into North America of one exotic species after another has been harmful, not because these plants are exotic but because some of them are invasive. Similarly, many of our native species are surpassingly fine. To a certain extent, their value may relate to their being native, if, say, they have evolved under the particular conditions of soil and climate that prevail in a given location. But ultimately they are valuable because they are valuable, not because they are native. To leap from evidence about the invasiveness of some exotic plants to a conclusion that all are invasive, and from evidence about the high merits of some native plants to a conclusion that all are meritorious is an ancient and pernicious logical fallacy of syllogistic reasoning. Only by a severe logical misfire is it possible to argue that all exotic species are bad and all native species good.

Neither proposition happens to be true. To begin with, many exotic species are utterly lovely and also perfectly well mannered. I would not want to be in Williamsburg on a blazing hot July day and have to forgo its crape myrtles, with their fine, glossy foliage, their beautiful exfoliating bark, and their luscious, long-lasting flower clusters in watermelon red, radiant pink, and cool white. Nor would I wish to do without daylilies, irises either bearded or Siberian, arisaemas, epimediums, and hundreds of other plants I could list if there were room enough here. As for the other equation, from the fact that some plants are native to some parts of North America, it doesn't follow at all that they aren't invasive. Consider ragweed. Poison ivy. Pokeweed. Several of our native grapes. Trumpet creeper. The showy evening primrose that is so lovely in March along roadsides in the Texas Hill Country.

One of the worst weeds in my own garden is rudbeckia 'Goldsturm', meaning a storm of gold. Despite its German name, this plant is really a selected strain of *Rudbeckia fulgida* var. *sullivantii* and is widespread. It has been popularized by landscape architects, especially James van Sweden and Wolfgang Oehme. It blooms over a long period and remains attractive after flowering, with dark brown seed heads that provide food for songbirds. It is immune to insect damage. It has no known diseases. It is highly tolerant of severe drought. The Perennial Plant Association named it Perennial of the Year in 1999. I grew it for years without the faintest hint of trouble, but recently it has revealed itself as by far my most invasive weed, spreading like a malicious rumor everywhere, by both seed and underground runners. Rudbeckia 'Goldsturm' just happens to be native to Virginia and the Carolinas.

Invasiveness is not always absolute. I have friends who have grown 'Goldsturm' for almost two decades, without a lick of trouble. They give me a quizzical look when I complain about gardener's garters and spiderwort and assure me that they find in them no demerit. It turns out that they garden on heavy clay, I on sandy loam, which seems to make a great difference—and even in sandy soils, gardener's garters can be tamed somewhat by being sited in medium shade. Clay, however, has no effect whatsoever on certain malefactors. A friend who gardens on heavy, gummy soil curses the day her sister gave her a small start of *Liriope spicata*. Although *L. muscari* and its cultivars are manageable clump-formers, *L. spicata* is as noxious as the dread weed nut-grass sedge, which it strongly resembles. (I grow the variegated cultivar *L. s.* 'Silver Dragon' without distress so far, but I am still keeping an anxious eye on it for misbehavior.)

The idea of a Horticultural Declaration of Independence has considerable support nowadays. I have read comments about Japanese stilt grass in the literature of one of our native plant societies that it makes "another case for leaving native plants where they are native." I have seen suggestions in one of our most successful recent books on gardening that tax incentives be given to gardeners in proportion to the number of native species they grow, and the index of the same book includes the heading "Alien (invasive) species." On February 3, 1999, President Clinton signed Executive Order 13112, which was headed simply "Invasive Species." This extraordinary document sets up at the very highest level of government an Invasive Species Council, consisting of, inter alia, the Secretaries of State, Treasury, Defense, Interior, Agriculture, Commerce, and Transportation. The council is charged with making preliminary recommendations within eighteen months leading to controlling "alien species within particular ecosystems."

This executive order does not equate invasive species with exotic species, but it tends strongly in that direction. Taken literally, it worries me. It worries me as a gardener because if the tendencies it embodies were turned into legislation and then enforced, it would criminalize gardeners. It worries me as a human being who has to eat and enjoys doing so, for I would have to rely for sustenance on persimmons, pawpaws, blueberries and huckleberries and cranberries, pecans, hickory nuts, the roots of a perennial sunflower that goes around under the name Jerusalem artichoke, and very little else. For meat, I could have some native rodents and ruminants.

Most everything that we rely on in America for nutrition, whether meat or vegetable, is alien or exotic, not native. Moreover, all Americans descend from ancestors who originated elsewhere. Only the timetable and circumstance of arrival differ.

We must sort out plants, dividing them into good guys and bad, but place of origin is not a suitable criterion. The very idea, in fact, reeks of prejudice, xenophobia, and isolationism. We should instead do things the hard but proper way, making judgments on a case-by-case basis. And in this task, we have a fine guide to follow.

Thomas Jefferson may have given us our Declaration of Independence from England in 1776, but ten years later he was touring Chiswick, Stowe, Kew, and other fine English gardens, always with an appreciative eye. He was constantly arranging shipments of native American plants—*Itea virginica, Liquidambar styraciflua, Magnolia grandiflora*, and many others, including Venus flytrap—to gardening friends in England and France. It was a two-way trade, for he imported to Monticello many exotic plants, including some that would not survive there, like oranges and olives.

But, turning to *Thomas Jefferson's Garden Book*, I will let Mr. Jefferson speak for himself, as he did so eloquently in a letter written to Dr. John P. Emmet on April 26, 1826, only a couple of months before Jefferson and his fellow patriot John Adams both died, on the Fourth of July:

> For three-and-twenty years of the last twenty-five, my good old friend Thouin, superintendent of the garden of plants at Paris, has regularly sent me a box of seeds, of such exotics, as to us, as would suit our climate, and containing nothing indigenous to our country. These I regularly sent to the public and private gardens of the other States, having as yet no employment for them here. But during the last two years this envoi has been intermitted, I know not why. I will immediately write and request a re-commencement of that kind office, on the ground that we can now employ them ourselves. They can be here in early spring.

Among the seeds that Jefferson coveted were those of the cork oak, the cedar of Lebanon, and the "Indian rubber tree of Napul

(30°), Teak tree, or Indian oak of Burman (23°)" and "the various woods of Brazil."

As it happened, Jefferson's friend André Thouin had died, and his successor had been sending the seeds desired to Jefferson's neighbor, James Madison, as president of the Albemarle Agricultural Society. Jefferson didn't have long to live. But one thing was clear. Had anyone ever proposed a Horticultural Declaration of Independence, he would have roundly opposed it, for in much that counts he was a man of solidly cosmopolitan instincts and convictions.

Resources
Bibliography
Index

❦ Resources

EVEN IF 90 PERCENT of the lives of gardeners is taken up with caring for the plants already in their custody, most of the fun and excitement lies in the other 10 percent—acquiring plants in the first place. Gardeners come by their plants in many ways. Some are passalong plants that arrive as gifts from friends or neighbors. Some turn up in garden centers, although these places cater to the general run of customers and thus seldom offer anything that's truly unusual. Roadside nurseries with greenhouses attached may provide some delightful surprises, which is why many gardeners shun interstate highways in favor of backcountry byways. On a recent trip to the Carolinas, I came back with a back seat full of goodies, mostly from a nursery called Big Bloomers in Sanford, North Carolina, and from Thomas's Nursery, near Chincoteague, Virginia. Here's a partial list of the plants I bought: *Allium senescens* var. *glaucum*, *Anthriscus sylvestris* 'Ravenswing', *Brunnera macrophylla* 'Langtrees', *Cimicifuga ramosa* 'Hillside Black Beauty', *Cryptotaenia japonica* 'Atropurpurea', *Dicentra formosa* 'Boothman's Variety'—and I'll just stop at this point in the alphabet.

The major source of plants for committed gardeners, however, is mail-order nurseries. America is blessed with many of these, as is attested by Barbara J. Barton's indispensable guide, *Gardening by Mail: A Source Book* (5th ed., Boston: Houghton Mifflin, 1997). Fearful gardeners may resist the idea of ordering plants by mail (which nowadays includes e-mail), and indeed it is possible to have discouraging experiences, but these are rare. A good rule is to avoid ordering anything from a mail-order nursery catalog that comes unsolicited and supposedly free. Bulk mailing is such an expensive proposition that any nursery resorting to it almost certainly needs to scrimp on the quality of its plants.

As a new century and a new millennium begin, gardeners and nurseries alike have a fine new resource at their command, the Internet and the World Wide Web. These make it possible for small nurseries to offer pictures and expansive descriptions of their plants at a tiny fraction of what it would cost to print them in a paper catalog. Many, if not all, of the nurseries I recommend have Web sites, but the sites even of wholesale nurseries that do not sell to the general public may provide valuable information. Monterey Bay Nursery, whose mailing address is P.O. Box 1296, Watsonville, CA 95077, is the best example at present. Its Web site is a fine reference for many plants (http://montereybaynsy.com), especially subtropicals, including those of Australian origin. Its description of the Australian bottlebrush, *Callistemon* and its species and cultivars, for example, takes up several pages, with thirty detailed photographs.

Since I began writing about gardening in the early 1980s, I have avoided at all costs writing about plants I have not had experience with, whether it be growing them myself or observing them closely in gardens other than my own. (I would not, say, undertake a disquisition on species and cultivars of *Callistemon*.) Similarly, I must distinguish between the mail-order nurseries with which I have had direct and ongoing experience over several years and those of which I have a good opinion based on what other gardeners have said. The following annotated list includes mail-order nurseries I have used with good results, plus a few that are highly recommended by people I trust.

Alannah's African Violets, P.O. Box 2, Danville, WA 99121. Alannah's offers collections of both scented and fancy-leaf pelargoniums. Cat. $2; no Web site.

Asiatica, P.O. Box 270, Lewisberry, PA 17339. Barry Yinger, a noted authority on East Asian plants, describes his company as a micronursery. It sells astonishing numbers of rare species of *Arisaema* and *Arum*, as well as CITES-certified species of *Calanthe* and other hardy terrestrial orchids. Ships only in the spring. Cat. $2; www.asiatica-pa.com.

Avant Gardens, 710 High Hill Road, North Dartmouth, MA 02747. This nursery puts out an excellent list of tender tropical and subtropical plants especially suited for container gardens. Offers many diascias. Cat. $2; no Web site.

Canyon Creek Nursery, 3527 Dry Creek Road, Oroville, CA 95965. Canyon Creek's co-owner, John Whittlesey, writes a delightful, charmingly personal catalog that always seems to offer several dozen herbaceous perennials not to be found elsewhere. Specialties are dianthus, diascias, euphorbias, geraniums, scented pelargoniums, and violas. Especially good for both tender and hardy species of *Salvia*. Cat. $2; no Web site.

Paul Christian Rare Plants, P.O. Box 478, Wrexham LL13 9XR, U.K. I have not bought from this company yet, but it sells an extraordinary number of extremely rare and exquisitely expensive species of *Crocus*, *Fritillaria*, *Galanthus*, and other primarily bulbous genera. I have spent many hours looking at photographs of these treasures on the Christian Web site. Cat. $3; www.rareplants.co.uk.

Deerwood Geraniums, Route 4, Box 525A, Buchanan, WV 26201. Faye Brawner, a well-known expert on pelargoniums, who has a collection of almost 400 fancy-leaf cultivars, will propagate them to order, but imposes a limit of only one plant per kind per customer. The process takes six weeks or more before delivery. Cat. $3; no Web site.

Digging Dog Nursery, P.O. Box 471, Albion, CA 95410. I haven't ordered from Digging Dog—just haven't gotten around to it yet. The attractive, stylish catalog always tempts me by offering things I haven't seen sold elsewhere. Cat. $3; no Web site.

Fairweather Gardens, P.O. Box 330, Greenwich, NJ 08323, was founded in 1989. In its early years it dealt almost exclusively in woody plants, but it has gradually added a limited but choice selection of herbaceous perennials. Its offerings are particularly rich in several genera—*Cornus*, *Ilex*, *Magnolia*, and *Viburnum*. The plants it ships are notably larger than is common in mail order, and the packing is exemplary. Cat. $3; no Web site.

ForestFarm, 990 Tetherow Road, Williams, OR 97544. ForestFarm's thick catalog on newsprint offers great variety of both woody and herbaceous plants, native and exotic. Many of its plants are inexpensive, as they are small and grown in tubes that double as shipping containers. Gardeners can grow them on to size, in effect starting their own little nursery. Cat. $4; www.forestfarm.com.

Glasshouse Works, P.O. Box 97, Stewart, OH 44041. Both the catalog and the greenhouses of this nursery founded in 1973 are as teeming with plant life as any tropical rain forest. Those who are as smitten with coleus as I have been for the past decade will discover that Glasshouse is the perfect place to begin their own collection. Cat. $2; www.glasshouseworks.com.

Heaths & Heathers, E. 502 Haskell Hill Road, Shelton, WA 98584. Its name describes what it sells—heaths and heathers by the hundreds. Cat. long SASE; no Web site.

Heronswood Nursery, 7530 N.E. 288th Street, Kingston, WA 98346. In existence only since 1987, Dan Hinkley's Heronswood Nursery is easily the most remarkable in the country, with a catalog that runs to over 300 pages and describes some 2,500 woody and herbaceous plants, many grown from seed collected in China, Nepal, Vietnam, Chile, and other places on the planet. I rely more on this nursery than any other for new plants—and so do a great many other American gardeners. Heronswood offers an enormous number of species of *Arisaema*. Cat. $8 for two years; Web site consists of entire catalog text with no pictures: www.heronswood.com.

Klehm Nursery, 4210 N. Duncan Road, Champaign, IL 61822. This family-run nursery, in business since 1852, specializes in daylilies, hostas, and peonies, many of them its own introductions, but it also offers a wide range of other herbaceous perennials. Cat. $4; www.klehm.com.

Mountain Crest Gardens, P.O. Box 724, Etna, CA 96027. This nursery specializes in sedums and sempervivums, offering many species and cultivars of each at very reasonable prices. Cat. $2; no Web site.

Mt. Tahoma Nursery, 28111–112th Avenue E., Graham, WA 98338. I haven't ordered from this nursery that specializes in alpines, but friends speak highly of it as a good source for seed-raised hardy cyclamen species. Cat. $1; no Web site.

Munchkin Nursery, 323 Woodside Drive N.W., Muncie, IN 47115. Owner Gene Bush specializes in plants for shade. He sells a fine assortment of *Trillium* that come either from his own garden or with CITES-certificates assuring that they have not been wild-collected. Cat. $3; www.munchkinnursery.com.

Plant Delights Nursery, 9241 Sauls Road, Raleigh, NC 27603. Owner Tony Avent has a wry sense of humor and allows it to show in his catalog. Hostas are the specialty here, but a wide assortment of unusual herbaceous perennials are also offered. This is another nursery I rely on heavily. Plant Delights is a good source for pitcher plants—and the only source I know of for the soapwort gentian. Cat. 10 first-class stamps or a box of chocolates; www.plantdel.com.

Porterhowse Farms, 41370 S. E. Thomas Road, Sandy, OR 97005. Dwarf conifers are one specialty here, but so are sempervivums and jovibarbas—over 400 cultivars! I have bought generously. Cat. $6; no Web site.

The Primrose Path 921 Scottdale/Dawson, Scottdale, PA 15683. This nursery specializes in shade-tolerant plants, including co-owner Charles Oliver's hybrids of American heucheras and tiarellas. Cat. $2; www.theprimrosepath.com.

Seneca Hill, 3712 Court Route 57, Oswego, NY 13126. Moderate-sized list of choice perennials, including *Arisaema* and other East Asian species. Cat. $1; www.senecahill.com.

Shepherd's Garden Seeds, 30 Irene Street, Torrington, CT 06790. Besides vegetable seeds particularly appropriate for home gardeners, Shepherd's is a good source for nasturtiums. Cat. free; www.shepherdseeds.com.

Southern Perennials and Herbs, 98 Bridges Road, Tylertown, MS 39667. I haven't yet ordered from this company, but it has a good reputation and its Web site is generously illustrated with photographs of both hardy and tender herbaceous plants. Cat. free; www.s-p-h.com.

Andre Viette Farm and Nursery, State Route 608, Fishersville, VA 22939. Open to the public on beautiful rolling land outside Waynesboro, with a spectacular view of the Blue Ridge Mountains, Viette has one of the largest assortments of herbaceous perennials in the country. It sells on-site as well as by mail order. Cat. $5; no Web site.

Woodlanders, 1128 Colleton Avenue, Aiken, SC 29801. Specializes in native southeastern species of both woody and herbaceous plants. Cat. $3; no Web site.

Woodside Nursery, 327 Beebe Run Road, Bridgeton, NJ 08302. Daylilies and more daylilies here, mostly those bred by owner Dr. Darrell Apps. Cat. $2.50; no Web site.

One more address may be in order here. Some readers may wish to subscribe to the newsletter from which the pieces in this book were taken. Its address is *Homeground,* P.O. Box 271, Linwood, NJ 08221.

❧ Bibliography

Armitage, Allan M. *Herbaceous Perennial Plants: A Treatise on Their Identification, Culture, and Garden Attributes.* Athens, Ga.: Varsity Press, 1989.

Avery, Amos G., Sophie Satima, and Jacob Rietsoma. *Blakeslee: The Genus Datura.* New York: Ronald Press, 1959.

Bailey, Liberty Hyde. *The Standard Cyclopedia of Horticulture.* Three volumes. New York: Macmillan, 1935.

Bartram, William. *Travels through North and South Carolina, Georgia, and East and West Florida.* London: 1792. Facsimile edition. Charlottesville, Va.: University of Virginia Press, 1980.

Bender, Steve, and Felder Rushing. *Passalong Plants.* Chapel Hill: University of North Carolina Press, 1993.

Betts, Edwin Morris. *Thomas Jefferson's Garden Book.* Philadelphia: The American Philosophical Society, 1944.

Bowles, E. A. *My Garden in Autumn and Winter.* London: T. C. and E. C. Jack, 1915. Facsimile edition. Portland, Or.: Timber Press, 1998.

——. *My Garden in Spring.* London: T. C. and E. C. Jack, 1914. Facsimile edition. Portland, Or.: Timber Press, 1997.

—— *My Garden in Summer.* London: T. C. and E. C. Jack, 1914. Facsimile edition. Portland, Or.: Timber Press, 1997.

Clausen, Ruth Rogers, and Nicolas H. Ekstrom. *Perennials for American Gardens.* New York: Random House, 1989.

Druse, Kenneth. *The Collector's Garden: Designing with Extraordinary Plants.* New York: Clarkson Potter, 1996.

Earle, Alice Morse. *Old-Time Gardens.* New York: Macmillan, 1901. Reprint. Detroit: Singing Tree Press, 1968.

Everett, Thomas H. *The New York Botanical Garden Illustrated Encyclopedia of Horticulture.* Ten volumes. New York: Garland, 1981.

Farrer, Reginald. *The English Rock-Garden.* London: Edward Arnold, 1919.

——. *The Rainbow Bridge.* London: Edward Arnold, 1926. Reprint. Little Compton, R.I.: Theophrastus, 1977.

Foster, H. Lincoln, and Laura Louise Foster. *Cuttings from a Rock Garden and Other Essays.* New York: Atlantic Monthly Press, 1990.

Gerard, John. *The Herball, or Generall Historie of Plants.* Second edition. London: 1633. Facsimile edition. New York: Dover Books, 1975.

Grieve, Mrs. M. *A Modern Herbal: The Medicinal, Culinary, Cosmetic and Economic Properties, Cultivation and Folk-Lore of Herbs, Grasses,*

Fungi, Shrubs & Trees, with Their Modern Scientific Uses. New York: Harcourt Brace, 1931. Reprint. New York: Dover Books, 1971.

Haughton, Claire Shaver. *Green Immigrants: The Plants That Transformed America.* New York: Harcourt Brace Jovanovich, 1978.

Hinkley, Daniel J. *The Explorer's Garden: Rare and Unusual Perennials.* Portland, Or.: Timber Press, 1999.

Hortus Third: A Concise Dictionary of Plants Cultivated in the United States and Canada. New York: Macmillan, 1976.

Jelitto, Leo, and Wilhelm Schacht. *Hardy Herbaceous Perennials.* Portland, Or.: Timber Press, 1990. Translation by Michael E. Epp of 3d ed. of *Die Freiland-Schmuckstauden.* Stuttgart: Eugen Ulmer, 1985.

Lawrence, Elizabeth. *Gardening for Love: The Market Bulletins.* Edited by Allen Lacy. Durham, N.C.: Duke University Press, 1988.

Mitchell, Henry. *The Essential Earthman.* Bloomington: Indiana University Press, 1981. Paperback reprint. Boston: Mariner Books/Houghton Mifflin, 1999.

M'Mahon, Bernard. *The American Gardener's Calendar.* Eleventh edition. Philadelphia: Lippincott, 1837.

The New Royal Horticultural Society Dictionary of Gardening. Four volumes. New York: Stockton Press, 1992.

Oudolf, Piet. *Designing with Plants.* Portland, Or.: Timber Press, 1999.

Parkinson, John. *Paradisi in Sole: Paradisus Terrestris.* 1629. Facsimile edition. London: Methuen, 1904.

Robinson, William. *The English Flower Garden.* Fifteenth edition. London: John Murray, 1933. Reprint. New York: Amaryllis, 1984.

Scott, Frank J. *The Art of Beautifying Suburban Home Grounds of Small Extent.* New York: D. Appleton, 1870.

Spondberg, Stephen A. *A Reunion of Trees: The Discovery of Exotic Plants and Their Introduction into North American and European Landscapes.* Cambridge: Harvard University Press, 1990.

Stearns, W. T. *Botanical Latin.* London: David & Charles, 1983.

Thaxter, Celia. *An Island Garden.* Boston: Houghton Mifflin, 1894. Facsimile edition. Boston: Houghton Mifflin, 1988.

Thomas, Graham Stuart. *Perennial Garden Plants: Or the Modern Florilegium.* 3rd ed. Portland, Or.: Saga Press/Timber Press, 1990.

Ward, F. Kingdon. *Plant Hunting at the Edge of the World.* London: 1930. Reprint. London: Methuen, 1974.

Warner, Charles Dudley. *My Summer in a Garden.* Boston: Field, Osgood, 1870.

Waugh, Frank A. Preface to Leonard H. Johnson, *Foundation Planting*. New York: A. T. DeLaMare, 1927.

Whittle, Tyler. *The Plant Hunters*. Philadelphia: Chilton, 1970.

Wilder, Louise Beebe. *Colour in My Garden*. New York: Doubleday, Page, 1918.

——. *The Fragrant Path*. New York: Macmillan, 1932.

Wilson, Ernest H. *A Naturalist in Western China, with Vasculum, Gun, and Camera*. London: Methuen, 1913.

Index